D0445057

# The Millennium Bug

# The Millennium Bug

## How to Survive the Coming Chaos

Michael S. Hyatt

REGNERY PUBLISHING, INC.
*Washington, D.C.*

Library of Congress Cataloging-in-Publication Data
Hyatt, Michael S.
The millennium bug: how to survive the coming chaos / Michael S. Hyatt.
p. cm.
Includes bibliographical references and index.
ISBN 0-89526-373-4 (alk. paper)
1. Year 2000 date conversion (Computer systems) I. Title.
QA76.76.S64H93 1998
005.1'6—DC21 98-11505

Published in the United States by
Regnery Publishing, Inc.
An Eagle Publishing Company
One Massachusetts Avenue, NW
Washington, DC 20001

Published in association with the Literary Agency of Wolgemuth & Hyatt, Inc.,
330 Franklin Road, Suite 135A-106
Brentwood, TN 37027

Grateful acknowledgment is given to Mike Phillips for permission to reprint "Y2K and Banks," A Message to Susan Heller on CompuServe's Year2000 Forum, 24 September 1997.

Distributed to the trade by
National Book Network
4720-A Boston Way
Lanham, MD 20706

Printed on acid-free paper
Manufactured in the United States of America

10 9

Books are available in quantity for promotional or premium use. Write to Director of Special Sales, Regnery Publishing, Inc., One Massachusetts Avenue, NW, Washington, DC 20001, for information on discounts and terms or call (202) 216-0600.

*To my dad, who always taught*
*me that I could accomplish*
*anything I set my mind to.*

If you are interested in having Michael Hyatt speak to your group, please contact:

Tim Grable
Ambassador Speakers Bureau
P.O. Box 50358
Nashville, TN 37205

Phone: (615) 377-9100
Fax: (615) 661-4344

E-mail: Tim@AmbassadorAgency.com
Web site: www.AmbassadorAgency.com

# Contents

# Introduction

## Moving Beyond Denial

### *Ignoring the Year 2000 Computer Crisis Will Not Make It Go Away*

**Nothing is easier than self-deceit. For what each man wishes, that he also believes to be true.**

—Demosthenes

"Don't worry," I assured him, "You can bet that someone a lot smarter than either one of us will come up with a solution for this. If we can put a man on the moon, we can certainly fix the Y2K problem." Sound familiar? This was my response the first time I heard about the Millennium Bug.

For nearly six months, my good friend and colleague David Dunham forwarded me articles from the Internet about "the Year 2000 Computer Problem," or "Y2K" for short. As you probably know, this problem causes many computers to interpret the date "01/01/00" as January 1, 1900. I don't know why he thought I was interested. At the time, I didn't think it was that big a deal. I tried to be polite, but I usually deleted the articles without reading them. I was confident that Bill Gates or some other cyber genius would come up with a solution. After all, how much trouble could two measly digits cause?

As it turns out, plenty. At first I didn't believe it. I didn't *want* to believe it. Life has enough problems without having to deal with a crisis that is so global, so enormous, and, well... so stupid. I didn't have time to worry about it, and I was sure someone else was doing the worrying for me. I continued in this state until I saw the June 2, 1997, *Newsweek* article entitled, "The Day the World Shuts Down." It wasn't just any old article, mind you; it was the *cover story*, complete with flashy photos, quotable quips, and commentary from a dozen experts. With an article like that you would expect the stock market to crash, the bank runs to begin, and panic to sweep the nation. But you know what happened? Absolutely nothing. Business as usual. In fact, the week after the article broke, the stock market achieved its highest level in history. Clearly, no one took this stuff seriously.

**In my extensive research, I have encountered *no one* who has told me that the Y2K problem is under control.**

But I did. I wasn't totally convinced by the article, but I was unsettled. And I began to worry. So, I rolled up my sleeves and set out to do some research. I was confident that I could debunk the whole thing and set my mind to rest once and for all. I surfed the Web (including little-known government and military sites), downloaded articles, reviewed thousands of newsgroup and forum messages, talked with scores of other programmers, and researched the subject at length at a major university library near my home. I read everything on the subject I could find.

Contrary to what I had hoped, the more I read, the more convinced I became that there was, in fact, something to worry about. Something serious.

## My Background

Perhaps you are wondering, *So what makes you qualified to evaluate this problem, anyway?* That's a fair question. Let me admit at the outset: I don't have a degree in computer science. And, for what it's worth, neither does Bill Gates or Steve Jobs; they don't have degrees at all. I have never claimed to be a computer expert, and, quite frankly, I'm proud of that for three reasons.

*1. It was the* **experts** *who got us into this mess.* I'm not trying to be a "Monday morning quarterback," but the Year 2000 Problem is a potential disaster that was completely avoidable.

*2. It is not just the* **experts** *who will suffer from the Year 2000 Problem.* It will affect *every* person in *every* civilized country on earth—including you and me.

*3. It is not a technical problem requiring* **experts** *to fix it.* Actually, it's an amazingly simple problem. The real issue is a *management* one. How do we organize the resources at our disposal to repair the billions of lines of code infected with the Millennium Bug? Programmers can't tell you, and very few managers have a handle on it either. Bottom line: When it comes to the Millennium Bug, *there really are no experts.*

I am a businessman with a good deal of experience in management. I have been involved in the publishing and entertainment industries for most of my twenty-one–year career. I have been an executive for two large publishing companies, working in both product development and marketing. In addition, I have owned my own company since 1986. My business partner and I specialize in selling intellectual property rights and organizing large-scale conferences. Like many people in business, my day-to-day life is made up of doing research, evaluating options, and making informed decisions—sometimes with good results and sometimes with bad. In either case, I feel the full weight of my responsibility, and I've learned to live with the consequences of my choices. Sometimes it's not much fun, but it's definitely a great way to learn.

While I wouldn't call myself a computer expert, over the past sixteen years, I've taught myself the art of writing computer software and am fluent in Pascal (Delphi, to be exact) and three dialects of BASIC, including WordBasic, Visual Basic, and Visual Basic for Applications. Programming languages are similar to human languages: the more you understand one, the easier it is to learn another.

As a part-time programming enthusiast, I have written numerous custom applications for my own firm as well as other companies around the world. (I have customers as far away as Iran and New Zealand, for example, and all of my work for them is conducted over the Internet.) Some of these programs are fairly simple; some of them are quite elaborate, involving entire software systems. I am the author of two software packages that are commercially available as "shareware." I am also an active beta-tester for Microsoft, Corel, and several other major software companies.

So, although I'm not a computer *expert*, I do have significant computer *expertise.*

But my biggest responsibility is to my family. I have a wife to whom I have been happily married for almost twenty years, and five daughters (no, I'm not kidding)—all of whom I want to protect from the potentially disastrous fallout of Y2K.

## Why None of Us Is Safe

They're everywhere. Over the past thirty-five years, computers have quietly infiltrated nearly every aspect of our existence. Except for the PC that sits innocuously on your desk, you probably never notice them. But they are there. Millions of them. They all make possible the quality of life you and I take for granted every day, and almost all are dependent upon other computer systems.

Consider, for moment, a day in the life of "Gary Anderson" (a fictional character).

Gary is vice president of marketing for a large office supply wholesaler in the Midwest. He has worked there for three years. He and his wife, Nancy, live in a suburb outside the city. They have three children: fifteen, eleven, and seven.

Almost all of Gary's work is done on a state-of-the-art notebook computer. He never goes anywhere without it and often uses it at home to finish work he couldn't get done at the office. Nancy, a freelance writer, also has a desktop computer that she uses to run her small, home-based business and manage the family finances.

Gary and Nancy are completely dependent upon their computers. Neither of them realizes, however, that they are dependent upon *millions of computers* in ways they are unaware of or simply don't think about. These computers run quietly in the background of their existence, invisible to their field of vision, but making possible their twentieth-century creature comforts and amusements.

**Think about it: Computers affect virtually *every* aspect of our lives—what happens if some or all of them crash?**

Picture this. It's Tuesday morning at the Andersons'. Everyone is still asleep. The lights are out, but the Andersons' electronic alarm system, a computerized, high-tech sentry, is standing guard. Although the system was not expensive, it is comprised of a sophisticated array of embedded computer chips that monitor every door and window in the house. (As you may know, embedded chip systems are computer chips that have the actual program "burned into" the hardware.) If the system detects a break-in, the alarm sounds, waits two minutes, and then automatically dials the local police station. The alarm has not gone off in over a year, which was the last time the Andersons had it tested.

At 6 AM the alarm clock goes off. Gary reaches over, turns off the alarm, and then reluctantly throws his feet over the side of the bed. His alarm clock is built into his digital clock radio. It is run by a computer—albeit a simple one—that allows it to keep the current time, and store the wake-up time and the presets for his favorite radio stations.

While Gary heads for the bathroom, Nancy turns on the light next to her bed. The electrical power for the Andersons' neighborhood is generated by a large hydroelectric power plant. The processes inside the power plant and the distribution system outside the power plant are monitored and maintained by mainframe computers and thousands of embedded chip systems. Transformers, using embedded chips to regulate voltage levels, raise the generated power to the high voltages that are used on the transmission lines. The electricity is sent from the plant to substations, where, once again, computer chips embedded in transformers step down the voltage to the voltage on the subtransmission lines. A final set of transformers steps the voltage down even further, to the level used by consumers to power electronic devices. To protect all the elements of a power system from short circuits and overloads, and for normal switching operations, automated circuit breakers are used. These, too, use computer chips.

As Nancy wakes up the children, Gary gets in the shower. He's never given much thought to how the water is delivered to his home. All he knows is that, as he turns the shower knob, out comes the water. But this, too, is a convenience made possible by the use of a highly computerized system. The Andersons' water comes from a large river that flows through the center of the city. This water must be treated before it can be used. The entire treatment process is monitored by mainframe computers and controlled by embedded chip systems linked to those computers. The water moves through the aeration, filtration, and chemical treatment processes at the command of these automated systems.

From the shower, Gary heads to the kitchen to eat breakfast. The Andersons' food comes from farmers who use computers to control irrigation levels, from truckers who use computers to schedule and route shipments, and from grocers who use computers to monitor inventory levels and perform automatic re-orders. The modern food chain is completely dependent on computers.

Gary heads for the garage. As he turns the ignition of his late-model sedan, more than fifty microprocessors, embedded chip systems, and microcontrollers are activated. These computers regulate and monitor everything from the oil pressure to the temperature.

When Gary arrives at the office, he encounters even more computers:

- He plans his day's activities using a personal information manager, checks his corporate e-mail and his CompuServe account, and asks his secretary to hold his calls. He launches Microsoft *PowerPoint* and begins working on a proposal.

- He finishes it at 11:15. He has thirty minutes before lunch, so he returns phone calls—oblivious to the complex tapestry of computers, switches, and embedded chip systems that transfer his voice from one area of the country to another.

- He has lunch with the company's vice president of sales. Gary pays for lunch with his corporate Visa card. The card is read by a magnetic reader on the cash register. A modem transmits the account number to a bank for authorization. The computer at the bank looks up the account, verifies that he has credit available, and sends the restaurant's computer an authorization code. The whole process takes less than two minutes.

- Gary drives home to pack for a business trip. Turning into the driveway, he stops and collects the day's mail from the mailbox. Nothing but bills and a few pieces of junk mail. Gary doesn't stop to think about the computers—mostly mainframes—that collect the transactions for those bills, sorting them by customer, and then generating the necessary invoices. Nor does Gary stop to think that this simple system of invoices and payments is the lifeblood of our economy.

- He quickly packs, throws his things in the car, and drives to the airport—just a little too fast. He gets pulled over by a policeman for speeding. The officer uses his built-in computer system to run Gary's plates and driver's license through the state highway patrol's computer database. He wants to make sure that the driver has no outstanding warrants. Finding Gary clean, the policeman issues him a ticket and sends him on his way.

- Gary parks his car at the airport, taking a date-stamped parking ticket from the dispenser. He hurries through security (which is, of course, all computerized) and dashes onto the plane. After take-off, the captain puts the plane on auto-pilot, content to let the on-board computers fly the 737 to its destination. These computers navigate by determining their exact location using the Global Positioning Satellite system maintained by the U.S. Navy.

I could go on, but I think you get the point. Almost every aspect of our lives is regulated, controlled, monitored, enhanced, or made more convenient or efficient by computers. Whether they are large mainframe computers running in the sterile environment of a corporate Information Systems Department, a combination of client-server systems and personal computers, or embedded chip systems soldered into virtually every appliance and electronic device, computers run the show. And we are dependent upon them in ways that we have difficulty comprehending. What happens if some—or all!—of them crash?

## Overview

I'm not sure where you are in your exposure to and evaluation of the Millennium Bug. You may be confident that someone else will solve the problem (as I was initially), skeptical about what you've heard reported in the media, or already convinced that it is a *very* big problem. Regardless, this book is written for you. My primary goal in writing this book is to lay the facts before you, help you understand how they will affect you, and then help you decide what you must do—*personally*.

The book is divided into three parts:

- *Part I, "The Eleventh Hour,"* will give you an overview of the Year 2000 Computer Crisis. The focus is on the facts *in general.*

- *Part II, "Against the Clock,"* discusses the implications and impact of the Year 2000 Problem on various segments of our high-tech civilization. The focus is on the facts *in particular.*

- *Part III, "The Day After,"* is designed to help you prepare for life after the Year 2000 Computer Crisis. The focus is on what the facts *mean* and what you can *do* about them.

In short, I am convinced that the Y2K problem presents us with, potentially, the most significant, extensive, and disruptive crisis we have ever faced. I am not alone in my assessment, as you will see. But unlike every other crisis you and I have either experienced or read about, not only do we know about it before it strikes, but we can actually predict when it will begin, down to the precise *second.* The only question that remains is this: Will you and I be ready for it?

# Part One

## The Eleventh Hour

*An Overview of the Year 2000 Computer Crisis*

# Chapter One

## Penny Wise and Pound Foolish

### *The Critical Importance of Two Little Digits*

**To err is human, but to really foul things up requires a computer.**

—BBC Radio

It's probably safe to say that everyone who has ever owned a personal computer has, at one time or another, experienced a computer crash. And most of us, unfortunately, are not prepared for it. As a result, we must reinstall programs and piece together the data we have lost. But none of us has experienced the kind of worldwide computer crash that might happen as a result of the Millennium Bug.

The Millennium Bug is a sort of "digital time bomb." *When the clock strikes midnight on January 1, 2000, computer systems all over the world will begin spewing out bad data—or stop working altogether!*

When this happens, it will be similar to a giant hard-disk failure: It's inevitable, and it's going to be terribly ugly when it happens. The only difference is that it is going to be *a billion times worse* than the worst microcomputer crash you have ever experienced—or could ever imagine. It will affect almost every mainframe computer on earth, many microcomputers, and even embedded computer chips in various appliances, instruments, and other devices. When it happens, you will pine for the good ol' days when the worst you could expect was a personal computer malfunction.

*Newsweek*'s June 2, 1997, cover story, entitled "The Day the World Shuts Down: Can We Fix the Year 2000 Computer Bug Before It's Too Late?", opened with this scenario:

> Drink deep from your champagne glasses as the ball drops in Times Square to usher in the year 2000. Whether you imbibe or not, the hangover may begin immediately. The power may go out. Or the credit card you pull out to pay for dinner may no longer be valid. If you try an ATM to get cash, that may not work, either. Or the elevator that took you up to the party ballroom may be stuck on the ground floor. Or the parking garage you drove into earlier in the evening may charge you more than your yearly salary. Or your car might not start. Or the traffic lights might be on the blink. Or, when you get home, the phones may not work. The mail may show up, but your magazine subscriptions will have stopped, your government check may not arrive, your insurance policies may have expired.
>
> Or you may be out of a job. When you show up for work after the holiday, the factory or office building might be locked up, with a handwritten sign taped to the wall: OUT OF BUSINESS DUE TO COMPUTER ERROR.
>
> Could it really happen? Could the most anticipated New Year's Eve party in our lifetimes really usher in a digital nightmare when our wired-up-the-wazoo civilization grinds to a halt? Incredibly, according to computer experts, corporate information officers, congressional leaders, and basically anyone who's given the matter a fair hearing, the answer is yes, yes, 2,000 times yes! Yes—unless we successfully complete the most ambitious and costly technology project in history, one where the

> payoff comes not in amassing riches or extending Web access, but securing raw survival.[1]

Unless the Millennium Bug is tracked down and squashed, you, your family, your friends, and your friends' friends are at risk. Many of the things you have learned to depend on and take for granted could suddenly disappear, leaving you, for all practical purposes, in the year 1900. The difference, of course, is that if you were suddenly transported back to the beginning of the twentieth century, people would know how to cope with life *without* the aid of computers. In our high-tech, computer-permeated society, few do.

**The Millennium Bug will affect everyone—you, your family, your friends, and your friends' friends.**

## "A Fine Mess You've Gotten Us Into"

So how in the world did we end up in this mess, anyway?

In the early days of computers, data storage was limited and expensive. The first computers used punch cards, and it took a handful of cards to store the amount of information we can store today in a space smaller than a speck of dust. "Computer storage cost ten thousand times (that's 1 million percent) more than it does today."[2] Any method that could save storage space was readily seized. One such method was to shorten years to two digits by deleting the century. For example, 1967 became "67"; 1984 became "84."

When these programs were written, no one considered what would happen when you got to the year 1999. What happens when you add 99 + 1? Obviously, the answer is 100, but remember you only have two digits to work with. Consequently, most computers will represent the date as "00" and think this means "1900."

Contrary to the PC market, where raw computing power doubles every eighteen months and new software upgrades are made available on an almost annual basis, mainframes

> ...have turned out to have very long lives, much longer than anyone expected when they were first installed. Programs written in the 1960s, developed in an era when using a two-digit date reference was standard practice, are still in use today. These programs have developed like onions over the years, with more and more layers being added, unlike a word processing package which might be replaced in total every year or two as upgrades become available.[3]

## Blind Dates

The Millennium Bug creates enormous problems in all kinds of date-based calculations. Noncompliant computers have *four* specific problems with January 1, 2000.[4]

***1. It starts with a "2."*** Some programs, especially data validation routines, will only recognize years beginning with a "1."

***2. It ends with zeros.*** Some random-number generators, which create account numbers, for example, use the computer's system date and divide by the last two numbers. These programs either lock up or crash when they try to divide by "00."[5]

***3. It starts on a Saturday.*** Many programs use a "day-of-week" function to perform certain tasks. These can be as simple as an automated back-up procedure to opening a bank vault if it is Monday but locking it if it is Saturday or Sunday. The problem is that January 1, 1900, was a Monday; January 1, 2000, is a Saturday. If the computer thinks the year is 1900 (as noncompliant systems will), the vault will swing open on Saturday and lock shut on Thursday. This will affect all other routines that use day-of-week calculations to perform certain actions.

*4. It is a leap year.* Most people assume that every fourth year is a leap year. Well, only every fourth turn-of-the-century is a leap year. 1900 was *not* a leap year; the year 2000 is. Therefore, if the computer doesn't account for the fact that 2000 will have a February 29, then all kinds of calculations will be off, including billing cycles.

To see what effect this might have, think about the following. The Social Security Administration (SSA) uses date calculations to determine eligibility for benefits. Consider a person who was born in 1932. Subtract that year from 1997 and you get 65, the age at which most Americans begin receiving a monthly Social Security check. But in 2000, the SSA's computer system will subtract 32 from 00, leaving the person at minus thirty-two years old, and will cut off his monthly benefits.

**When Honolulu's electric utility system ran a test to see what would happen on January 1, 2000, the power system simply stopped working.**

Long-distance carriers use a computerized timer to track the duration of phone calls. Suppose you place a phone call to your brother at 11:59 on 12/31/99 and finish at 12:04 on 01/01/00. The telephone company will interpret the second date as 1900. The computer will calculate your billing not at five minutes but at one hundred years and five minutes![6] Your bill could be more than $5 million.

Some billing cycles run from the first day of the month to the last. Most do not. For example, my electric bill runs from the fifteenth of the month to the fourteenth of the next. Generally, this is no problem. But what happens when I get my electric bill in January of 2000? If the electric company's computers are not "Year 2000–compliant,"[7] I'll be in for a surprise. Either my bill will not include the dates that fall into the next century (the computer will think they belong to the year 1900) or it might include every date for the last one hundred years! Either way, I will likely refuse to pay my bill until it is corrected. The electric company won't be able to correct the billing until its computers are repaired. In the meantime, how does the electric company generate a positive cash flow, so that it can continue to pay its employees and suppliers?

These are merely *representative* problems. There are hundreds—if not thousands—of others that could be cited. In addition to generating erroneous results, computers may also simply refuse to accept legitimate dates. If the operator enters into a data-entry screen a date such as "03/01/00," the computer may reject it as an illegal entry, thinking that the date falls outside the acceptable range.[8] Or worse, many computers may refuse to run altogether.[9] If that happens, then the scenario depicted by *Newsweek* becomes reality. "It represents the ultimate indignity: the world laid low by two lousy digits."[10]

**We know exactly what the problem is and how to fix it; we just don't have enough time.**

But we really don't have to wait until the year 2000 to see some of these kinds of anomalies. Already, we can see the warning signs of things to come:

- Honolulu's electric utility system recently ran a series of computing tests on the city power grid to see what would happen on January 1, 2000. The power system simply stopped working.[11]

- "Visa had to recall some credit cards with expiration dates three years hence—the machines reading them thought they had expired in the McKinley administration."[12]

- "In Britain, computers at Marks & Anderson company have already mistakenly ordered the destruction of tons of corned beef, believing they were more than 100 years old."[13]

- "At a state prison, a computer glitch misread the release date of prisoners and freed them prematurely."[14]

- "In Kansas, a 104-year-old woman was given a notice to enter kindergarten."[15]

## A Bird's-eye View

Is this a big problem? You bet. Representative Constance Morella (R–Maryland) says, "We are all right now competing in a race against time to avert an impending computer catastrophe... just about every human on the planet may be affected."[16]

To be fair, no one writing software in the 1960s, 1970s, or even 1980s thought his software would still be functioning at the turn of the millennium. Most thought it would be retired, replaced, or rewritten. Therefore, there was no reason to ensure that it would run into the next century. But these systems have survived *much* longer than anyone anticipated. They are in use *everywhere*. As the June 2, 1997, issue of *Newsweek* made clear, "Virtually every government, state and municipality, as well as every large, midsize and small business in the world, is going to have to deal with this—in fact, if they haven't started already it's just about too late."[17]

Any software package that uses dates or calendar routines will be affected. This is also true of embedded date routines in hardware (sometimes called "firmware"). The Millennium Bug will affect mainframe computers, personal computers, and microcontrollers, which are embedded in all kinds of machines and appliances. Some common applications that will have to be modified include:[18]

- Software with long-range calculations such as mortgages, life insurance premiums, interest compounding, pension payments, and social security benefit calculations.

- Software calendar utility functions in commercial spreadsheets such as Lotus 1-2-3, Excel, Quattro, and many others.

- Calendar functions and features embedded in personal information managers (PIM) and hand-held devices as well as those in personal computers.

- Software on aircraft, weapons systems, and satellites.

- Computer operating systems that utilize calendar and clock routines.

- Software that controls telephone switching systems.

This list outlines how the Year 2000 Problem will likely affect computers in general, but how will it affect *you* in particular? Every time your personal life intersects with a computer, you face the potential for chaos. For example:

- Your local bank is controlled by a powerful mainframe computer. So is the ATM machine.

- Your local city water supply system is controlled by a powerful mainframe computer.

- Your local and regional electric power grid is controlled by a powerful mainframe computer.

- Your local natural gas supply is controlled by a powerful mainframe computer.

- Your favorite commercial airline is controlled by a high-tech satellite guidance system which is in turn controlled by a powerful mainframe computer.

- Your brokerage firm (or the one that administers your retirement plan) is controlled by a powerful mainframe computer that keeps track of all your stock, mutual fund, and other investment accounts.

- Your local hospital's intensive care unit, neonatal unit, X-ray equipment, CT scanners, patient-record databases, blood bank dating systems, and prescription dispensing systems are all controlled by embedded computer chips that are not Y2K-ready.

- Your local police department's emergency system ("911" in the United States) is controlled by a powerful mainframe computer.

- Your local telephone company is controlled by a powerful mainframe computer.

- Every major retail store in your town (your local Wal-Mart, your local Sears, your local Home Depot, and even your local grocery store) stocks goods that are brought in by railroad. Today, old-fashioned manual switching yards no longer exist. Instead, the world's railways are controlled by powerful mainframe computers.

As it turns out, government agencies and large corporations all have *millions* of lines of code to review and repair. The U.S. Defense Department (DoD) has as many as one billion lines. AT&T has five hundred million lines. The IRS has over one hundred million lines. The SSA has over thirty million lines. The nation's two largest banks—Chase Manhattan and Citicorp—together have more than six hundred million lines.

To put this into perspective the SSA started correcting its Y2K problem relatively early. In 1991 the SSA assigned four hundred full-time programmers to the project. By mid-1996, after five years of steady work, they had reviewed and repaired six million lines of code—only 20 percent of the total! The Gartner Group, which is arguably the most respected and highly quoted Y2K research company in the world, estimates that half of all businesses are going to fall short.[19] They also estimate that half of all government agencies are not going to make it.[20]

## The Quest for the Silver Bullet

If you are like most people, you are probably thinking, *Surely, someone, somewhere will write a program that will fix the problem.* Right? Wrong. It's not quite as simple as that. "It seems that in most mainframe programs, the date appears... about once every fifty lines of code."[21] Finding and repairing all this code will take an enormous effort—even with automated software tools. According to Jeff Jinnett, a Year 2000 expert, in his testimony before Congress:

> There is no technological silver bullet for the Year 2000 computer problem. The reason for this is that although "silver bullet" technologies may be developed to automate and speed up corrective work on certain software languages, there may be as many as *five hundred different software languages in current use* and automated corrective tools will not be developed for all of these languages [emphasis added].[22]

Worse, although these five hundred different software languages may currently be in use, many of them are no longer understood. The programmers are either retired or dead.

But there's an even more serious problem. The source code for many programs no longer exists. Without the source code—the language that humans read and write as opposed to the *compiled* code that machines read and write—programmers can't make any changes to the program. Their only options are to rewrite the program completely from scratch or try to "de-compile" it, which is messy and often inaccurate.

Even if the code can be repaired in time, it still must be thoroughly tested.

> Testing is particularly laborious because the modified software must be tested in conjunction with all possible combinations of other software programs it interacts with to ensure functioning has not changed.[23]

In other words, the software can't be fully tested until every program in the system is compliant.

This is the missing element in many of the Y2K considerations. Some experts estimate that for every hour spent finding and repairing the computer code, *four* hours will be needed for testing.

## All Hands on Deck?

You would assume that a problem of this magnitude has *everyone* mobilized. Right? Wrong.

In a recent survey of Fortune 500 Information Technology Officers, "under 13 percent said their firms had implemented plans to correct the Year 2000 Problem. Another 18 percent said they had developed a plan of action. Of the 18 percent, 87 percent said they planned to hire outside firms to do the work."[24] In July 1997 Larry Martin, president of Data Dimensions, testified before the U.S. Senate:

> Little action has been taken to address the Year 2000 problem. Although much has been written about it, somehow few think that the problem really applies to them.... Current estimates by reliable industry groups suggest that only one-third of U.S. companies and government agencies have seriously started work on a Year 2000 fix. And the rest of the world has been even slower to take action. A recent British study says that fewer than one in five businesses have taken action. Those figures

> only represent companies that have started work on the millennium. We would roughly estimate that only 5 percent of the total work to complete Year 2000 compliance has been accomplished. That means 95 percent of the work remains to be done. This is not a problem about money. It is about time and resources.[25]

Unfortunately, many companies—even very large ones—are still in a state of denial. Writing for *InformationWeek*, William Ulrich observed:

> Two years ago, analysts observed that as organizations came to terms with the year 2000 crisis, they would move through stages of denial, anger, and panic. Today, a more dangerous stage has emerged—delusion. If we are to believe private- and public-sector surveys, organizations will have all year 2000 problems corrected by the end of 1998. This time frame would provide a comfortable cushion to perform integration testing and let managers shift resources back to other initiatives near the end of the decade. In my experience, nothing could be farther from the truth. The executives answering these surveys are in a serious state of delusion. They're either lying to customers, financial analysts, and constituents—or worse, lying to themselves.[26]

When I first began researching the Year 2000 Problem, I became increasingly alarmed. I kept thinking that I would run into someone who would tell me I was overreacting, that the problem was well under control, and that I had nothing to worry about. Unfortunately, I have not encountered such a person—not one. In fact, *I have had exactly the opposite experience.*

The chief information officer for a multibillion dollar Fortune 500 company told me he had just met with his company's board of directors the week before our dinner to brief them on the Year 2000 Problem and its potential impact on their business. "I asked for the money to create a small Y2K department," he said. "They told me no. They didn't see how we could afford it."

"Is it really that big a problem?" I asked.

"Absolutely," he replied. "Most of our company's growth has come through acquisitions. We are adding more than twenty new companies to our portfolio each year. Each of these separate companies has its own mainframe computer system, and each of these systems is running scores of custom-written applications, none of which is Y2K compliant. If we stopped the acquisition of new companies immediately, I could focus on what we have. Even then, I seriously doubt that we could finish on time. But given the fact that we are continuing to acquire new companies at a record pace, and given the fact that my CEO and board of directors are still in denial, I don't think we have a chance!"

"So, what are you going to do?" I asked.

"Look for a new job," he shot back. "I'm definitely *not* going to hang around and go down with the ship."[27]

## An Unmovable Deadline

When you get right down to it, the Year 2000 Problem is *not* a technological problem. We know exactly what the problem is, and we know how to fix it. We just don't have enough time. The job is too big, and we are starting too late.

Capers Jones, a leading Y2K consultant, says, "Unfortunately, the year 1996 is the last year in which 'average' programmers working without sophisticated automation could have had a reasonable chance of fixing the year 2000 problem in a typical midsized corporate [environment]."[28]

The problem is probably worse than that because software developers are notoriously bad at estimating how long their projects will take. Standish Group International reported that "only 16.2 percent of all corporate software-development projects are completed on time. Those completed on time are rarely under budget."[29]

The Year 2000 is not a deadline that can be extended. President

Clinton can't sign an executive order delaying January 1, 2000, for another year or more. David Copperfield can't conjure up some grand illusion to make the deadline disappear. And, unlike Joshua, who made the sun stand still so the Israelites could finish their battle against the Amorites, it is unlikely that some religious leader will be able to extend December 31, 1999, until the task can be completed.

Peter G.W. Keen recently wrote in *ComputerWorld:*

> The problem is far worse than even the pessimists believe. Gartner Group's much-cited figure of $600 billion to fix it is misleading. If God or Bill Gates wrote out a check for the full amount, nothing much would change. The year 2000 problem is a people- and time-resource issue, not just a financial one. You can't buy the time at any price.[30]

## Conclusion

Have you ever tried to call a large company's customer service department when the computers are down? I have, many times. It is no fun being told by the bank clerk or the telephone company representative, "I'm sorry, sir, our computers are down. Please try back later."

Recently, the computers operated by my Internet service provider (the company that provides my personal access to the Internet) were down for almost a day. Like most computer problems, at first you are not sure if the problem is *theirs* or *yours*. So, I decided to call the Help Desk (the more user-friendly term for Tech Support). It was busy. I called again. Same result. I kept trying all day, to no avail. I was surprised that I wasn't at least rolled over to voice mail. Evidently, thousands of other users were banging away at their phone system and simply overloaded it. Callers all over the country experienced a continuous busy signal.

What do you think will happen in the year 2000 when you try to call some government agency because you didn't get your monthly check? Or when you try to call your bank to straighten out some errors on your checking account statement? Or when you call your credit card company to find out why you were billed for hundreds of thousands of dollars in interest charges?

Of course, even getting a busy signal assumes that the phones themselves are still working.

# Chapter Two

## Bigger Than Big

### *The Scope and Magnitude of the Year 2000 Computer Crisis*

> **Everyone confesses in the abstract that exertion which brings out all the powers of body and mind is the best thing for us all; but practically most people do all they can to get rid of it, and as a general rule nobody does much more than circumstances drive them to do.**
>
> —Harriet Beecher Stowe

There's nothing worse than starting a job, then realizing you are not going to finish on time. That is what people working on the Year 2000 Problem are experiencing. But unfortunately there will be no one to bail the programmers out if they can't finish in time. There is no Plan B.

The Year 2000 Problem is an unbelievably massive project. *Newsweek* called it "the most ambitious and costly technology project in history"[1] and *ComputerWorld* said "the problem is far worse than even the pessimists believe."[2]

## Mainframe Computers

Because mainframe computers are largely invisible to most ordinary citizens and because nearly all of the attention in the past few years has been on microcomputers, many people hold false beliefs about them. Here are a few of the more popular myths:

*Myth #1: Mainframe computers are no longer widely used.* And because of this (so the myth goes), the Y2K Problem will have little effect upon most organizations. But this is not the case. As Bruce H. Hall, an acknowledged Year 2000 expert, reminded Congress in their Year 2000 hearings:

> The fact is that large, mainframe systems remain at the heart of information technology processing for organizations both public and private worldwide. A small minority of these larger systems have been "downsized" to client/server [systems] or otherwise modernized. However, the total amount of large mainframe processing power actually *increased* in 1996 by 20 percent, and is projected to increase again in 1997 by another 20 percent. And, for those that think that investment in mainframe technology has been slowed or suspended, consider that 55 percent of large scale systems running today are less than two years old.[3]

Mainframe computers are the backbone of government agencies, banking, telecommunications, public utilities, and nearly every system that forms the elaborate and complex infrastructure we too easily take for granted. Where there is a large volume of transactions to process, there you will find mainframe computers.

*Myth #2: Mainframe hardware can easily be replaced with PCs.* Maybe you've heard someone say, "You know, today's desktop computers have more processing power than a room full of yesterday's big mainframes." The problem with this statement is that it assumes that mainframe technology has remained static. It hasn't. It is true that some systems have been replaced with client/server networks involving microcomputers. But some mainframe-driven systems *can't* be replaced. The processing power contained in this hardware cannot be duplicated by microcomputers, regardless of how many of them you string together.

More important, perhaps, mainframe computers have *enormous storage* capabilities that simply can't be replaced with microcomputers. A six-gigabyte hard drive, which is standard on many new desktop systems, sounds like an almost unfathomable amount of storage capacity. Compared to a basic mainframe system, this is nothing. Mainframe systems typically have thousands of times more storage than this.

**Amazingly, some computer manufacturers are *still* shipping machines that are not Y2K-ready.**

*Myth #3: Mainframe software can simply be upgraded.* It's not that simple. In the PC world, most users buy off-the-shelf software packages and run them "as is." As a result, they can easily secure upgrades that fix bugs and add new functions. If an accounting program doesn't work as advertised, they can complain to the vendor and usually receive a "patch" or fix in a few weeks or months. If the vendor doesn't supply such "fixes" in a timely fashion, then users abandon the product and move on to competing ones. As a result, the original vendor is soon out of business. Not so in the mainframe world.

While some mainframe software is of the off-the-shelf variety, most of it is the result of *custom programming*. Even off-the-shelf programs are often customized to meet the unique needs of individual organizations. Once these programs are installed and debugged, they are maintained by the company's Information Systems staff. But if something needs to be fixed, the original programmers are often long gone. Sometimes they can be hired to come back and repair or enhance the program they wrote. But in the case of "legacy systems" that were written in the 1960s or 1970s, the programmers are either retired—or dead!

If the original programmers are not available, then the current computer staffers have to:

- *locate* the source code (which is often missing or virtually useless because so many piecemeal patches have been applied since the source code was first written);

- *familiarize* themselves with a program they didn't write (and which may also lack adequate documentation or contain confusing documentation);

- *modify* it, hoping in the process that they don't introduce too many *new* bugs; and

- *test* the program to make sure it still works.

That's why this task is such a monumental one. It can involve thousands of programmer-hours of work and require "looping" back through the above development cycle numerous times.

## Microcomputers

Contrary to what a lot of people believe, microcomputers are *not* immune to the Millennium Bug. There are approximately 250 million PCs in use throughout the world. These systems are used in large corporate offices, small businesses, and homes. And they must be compliant at three different levels: (1) the hardware level, (2) the operating system level, and (3) the applications software level.

*1. Many PCs will experience problems at the hardware level.* Every PC has what is called a "BIOS chip" ("BIOS" stands for Basic Input Output System). This chip handles all the low-level interaction of the hardware itself, including maintaining the computer's system clock. This is why, for example, you can turn your computer on and off, and it still knows what day and time it is. The problem is that some of these BIOS chips are *not* Y2K–compliant. As a result, when the date rolls over from December 31, 1999, to January 1,

2000, the PC will think it is either 1980 or 1984, the first years in which the IBM PCs were made.

Seventy-nine percent of pre-1997 BIOS chips cannot roll over from 1999 to 2000, and 14 percent do not know that the year 2000 is a leap year.[4] Amazingly, at this writing, there are some computer manufacturers who are *still* shipping machines that are not Y2K–ready. *ComputerWeekly* recently reported that you have only a fifty-fifty chance of buying a new computer that will run correctly in the next century.[5]

**Even if all programmers did nothing except work on Y2K projects, they could not fix the problem in time.**

The easiest way to check to see if your PC is compliant is to download a copy of TEST2000.ZIP. You can download this from the Internet at <http://www.rightime.com>. This program will determine if your machine is compliant and whether it can be made compliant. You can also ask your computer vendor for a "Y2K flash BIOS patch," which will upgrade your hardware.

*2. Many PCs will experience problems at the operating system level.* The standard PC computer maintains two system dates: One is the CMOS Real Time Clock chip that gets its date from the BIOS; the other is in the computer's operating system.

Remember DOS, the nongraphical "disk operating system" that predated Windows? Guess what—it's not Y2K–compliant. And, yes, there are millions of computers still running this seemingly ancient software. This is particularly true where companies are running vertical market applications, like real estate and doctors' offices.

Windows 3.0 or 3.1 (also known as 16-bit Windows) can also be a problem. An estimated four out of five computers running this operating system will reboot to the year 1980 or 1984.[6] Again, you can download a copy of TEST2000.ZIP to test your system. One bit of good news: Windows 95 and 97 are fully Y2K–compliant, as are all Macintosh operating systems.

*3. Many PCs will experience problems at the applications level.* Since most applications get the current date from the operating system, and since the operating system generally gets its date from the BIOS, the Year 2000 Problem can cascade into your applications. This is probably the biggest problem of all. However, *even if* the BIOS and the operating system are compatible, you can still experience problems. Greenwich Mean Time, a Year 2000 consulting firm, reported that 2,568 out of a total of 4,000 software packages tested in mid-1997 were infected with the Millennium Bug.[7]

If you are running major applications from major vendors, you can likely make your system compliant by simply ordering an upgrade from the vendor. Be forewarned, however: If you do not upgrade, it is likely that your applications will not be compliant. To make sure:

- See if your applications can sort dates in the correct sequence. For example, December 31, 1999, should appear before January 1, 2000, if you are sorting dates in ascending order. You can try sorting dates in your spreadsheet or word processor. Most have a "sort" feature. You can also look at any database applications you are running and enter a few records with dates into the next century.

- See if your applications allow for the entry of February 29, 2000. You might want to try this in your contact management or calendar program. Also test your spreadsheet and database program by attempting to enter this date into a field or spreadsheet cell.

- See if your applications can correctly handle "date math." For example, in a spreadsheet subtract today's date (whatever that may be when you are reading this) from any date in the next millennium. See if it gives you the expected result. For example, subtracting 12/01/99 from 01/01/00 should give you 31.

Your company's custom applications may be the hardest of all to deal with. Similar to the problems with mainframe software, your company will have to test *all* its software for compliance. If it is not compliant—and most will not be—it will have to be revised or replaced.

## The Embedded Chip Problem

Embedded chips are often called "firmware" because the programming is contained within the chip itself. In other words, the programming is not stored on external media; it is written onto the physical chip. All embedded systems are computers, and some of them are date-sensitive.

These devices are used by a wide variety of electrical appliances and automated devices. The average car, for example, contains some fourteen microcontrollers, and some contain more than forty-five.[8] But almost *all* of the technology we take for granted today relies to some extent on embedded chips or microcontrollers. *ComputerWeekly* recently referred to them as "the unseen guardians of our lives." Just to give you a sense of their pervasiveness, Table 2.1 contains a partial list of embedded systems.[9]

**Table 2.1:**
**Partial List of Embedded Computer Systems**

*Office systems and mobile equipment:*

Answering machines
Cellular telephones
Desktop computers[10]
Fax machines
Laptop and notebook computers
Personal digital assistants and organizers
Photocopiers
Still and video cameras
Telephone systems
Time recording systems
Voice mail

*Building systems:*

- Air conditioning
- Backup lighting and generators
- Building management systems
- Burglar and fire alarms
- CCTV systems
- Door locks and keypad access systems
- Elevators, escalators, and lifts
- Fire control systems
- Heating and ventilating systems
- Lighting systems
- Safes and vaults
- Security access control systems
- Security cameras
- Sprinkler systems
- Surveillance and security systems
- Switching systems

*Manufacturing and process control:*

- Automated factories
- Bottling plants
- CAD systems
- Energy control systems
- Manufacturing systems
- Nuclear power stations
- Oil refineries and related storage facilities
- Power grid systems (transformers, etc.)
- Robots
- Switching systems
- Time/clock stamps
- Water and sewage systems (pumps, flow regulators)

*Transportation:*

- Air traffic control systems
- Airplanes (avionics, flight, and cabin systems)
- Automated check-in systems
- Automobiles
- Baggage handling
- Buses
- Car parking and other meters
- Command and control systems
- Emergency equipment
- Marine craft
- Passenger information systems

*Transportation (con't.):*

Photo surveillance systems
Radar systems
Signaling systems
Speed cameras, radar detectors
Ticketing systems/machines
Traffic lights
Trains

*Communications:*

Cable systems
Global Positioning System (GPS) receivers
Satellites
Telephone exchanges and PBXs
Telephone switches

*Banking and finance:*

Automated tellers
Credit card authorization systems
Credit card systems
Safes and vaults

*Medical:*

Automated intravenous drip machines
CT scan machines
Monitoring systems (heart, ECG)
Pacemakers
Sonogram machines
X-ray equipment

*Domestic equipment:*

Automated sprinkler systems
Central heating and cooling
Microwaves
VCRs and entertainment equipment

Many in the press have tried to dismiss the embedded chip problem as trivial. They cite, as an example, the embedded system that controls the clock on your VCR or microwave oven. "Who cares," they argue, "if the clock is blinking '12:00' continuously." But these systems are used in millions and millions of nontrivial devices as well, as you can readily see from the table above.

The number of embedded chip systems in use far exceeds the number of mainframe and microcomputers.[11] In 1995 more than three billion programmable microcontroller chips were shipped. And in 1996 *more than seven billion* were shipped.[12] The Gartner Group has estimated that "more than fifty million embedded-system devices worldwide will exhibit Year 2000 date anomalies in 1999."[13] Although this number is small in comparison to the number of systems shipped and in use, they still must *all* be checked to ensure Year 2000 compliance. Anthony Parish, director-general of Great Britain's Federation of Electronic Industries, said, "For every thousand embedded chips you look at, you'll find two or three that need correction. But those two or three are the ones that can close a blast furnace... or stop power distribution. The problem is finding those two or three that are not compliant."[14] But that figure of two or three per thousand refers to *all* systems. According to a report published in the United Kingdom, of those systems responsible for running *critical processes* (e.g., oil and petrochemical production, electrical power, and aviation), *one in five* will fail in the year 2000.[15]

According to one report:[16]

- A petrochemical firm tested 150,000 embedded chips and found 100 that were not compliant.

- Another firm has 10,000 embedded systems buried in the North Sea. It will cost approximately $75,000 to check *each* chip under the seabed.

- A major British 500–megawatt power plant failed because of a date and time malfunction in an embedded system.

There are at least *ten reasons* why we should be worried about embedded systems as they relate to the Year 2000 Problem:

***1. Embedded chip systems are pervasive.*** There are billions of them in use, and they control a vast array of systems that we take for granted. Many of them are old.

***2. Accessing embedded chip systems is often difficult.*** Some systems are on satellites. Some are under the ocean floor. Some are inside buried pipelines. Some are deep inside concrete bank vaults, and still others are in pacemakers in patients' hearts.

***3. Replacement chips are generally not available for systems that are more than three years old.*** The embedded chip system industry is highly competitive. And like all computer companies, manufacturers are constantly introducing newer, more enhanced systems. When they do, they generally stop producing the older chips.

***4. Embedded chip systems are difficult to program.*** The code is often written in a proprietary language. As a result, compilers (the programs that turn computer code into machine language) may not be readily available. For some systems, they may no longer be available at all.

***5. It is difficult to find programmers to work on these systems.*** Because the systems are sometimes old and the language used to program them is often proprietary, the original programmers have either retired or died. Even when programmers can be found, they are often unwilling to do the work, because it is tedious and boring, regardless of how much they are offered.

***6. Once these embedded systems are found, they are difficult to test.*** The device has to be taken off-line, meaning that a process has to stop. Sometimes when a device is taken off-line and tested with no errors found, it is put back on-line and fails immediately. This is because the tester inadvertently introduced an error into the programmable code during the test.

*7. Most embedded chips are not socketed for easy removal.* In other words, you can't simply unplug a noncompliant chip and plug in a compliant one. Often chips have to be removed and replaced with a soldering gun. When this can't be done, the entire device has to be replaced.

*8. The process of making embedded chip systems compliant cannot be automated.* At least with mainframe systems, there are automated software tools that assist programmers in revising code and making it Y2K–compliant. None of these tools is available for working with embedded chips. The chips themselves must be physically inspected.

*9. There are thousands—if not tens of thousands—of embedded chip manufacturers.* Once a noncompliant chip has been identified, the manufacturer must be contacted. Sometimes these companies have changed their names, their locations, or are no longer in business. And often, as I mentioned earlier, even when they can be located, they may no longer be manufacturing that particular system.

*10. The small number of systems that are destined to fail will likely all do so at once.* When the century rolls over, noncompliant chips will fail or begin to make a mess of the processes they are designed to control. As a result, engineers will have to deal with simultaneously occurring problems, and they could easily be overwhelmed.

As you can see, the potential for an embedded chip-related disaster is frightening. As *ComputerWeekly* noted: "Even without the prospect of multiple Chernobyls, there is already a report of a microcontroller governing the sewage outlets on a beach which cannot interpret the tide timetable after the end of the century."[17] This is only one example of the kind of thing we can expect.

## Between the Lines

Embedded chips are not the only problem. There are enormous obstacles at the software level as well. Perhaps you are thinking, *Why can't they use computers to fix the computers?* In other words, *Why can't someone write a simple search-and-replace program that will track down the errant code and replace it with compliant code?*

The truth is that many automated tools have been developed to aid programmers in tracking down the Millennium Bug. These tools, however, do not provide anything close to a cure-all. Consider, for example, just how many computer languages are involved.

### *A Multitude of Software Languages*

In 1996 the Software Productivity Research catalog of programming languages identified almost five hundred different languages in current use. These include languages such as BASIC, COBOL, FORTRAN, ADA, PASCAL, MODULA, and a host of others. COBOL is by far the most prevalent, accounting for nearly 70 percent of all current software running on mainframe computers today.[18] It has the most plentiful supply of Year 2000 tools and services available. It may have more support than all the other languages combined.[19] But this still leaves approximately 499 languages *without* adequate support.

Finding and repairing Year 2000–related problems will be much more difficult in some languages than others. "Assembly language applications will probably be the toughest because many date calculations are hard to find since they are performed using register manipulation."[20] (In other words, bits have to be turned on or off, one at a time.) There are a number of other languages with Y2K problems that have a shortage of either available tools or programmers.[21] In addition, there are a host of proprietary languages that companies have developed for their own use.[22] And "although 'silver bullet' technologies may be developed to automate and speed up corrective work on certain software languages... automated corrective tools will not be developed for all of these languages."[23]

The problem is further compounded because many applications are written in *multiple languages*. Some have estimated that this may involve almost 30 percent of all programs.[24] As Capers Jones noted, "It is hard enough to find and fix year 2000 problems for applications containing only one language, and those containing multiple languages will be even harder."[25]

### *Difficulty of Identifying Dates*

Regardless of the language used, programmers must track down each piece of date-related code. These are not as easy to identify as you might think. In the past, programmers have employed a variety of date-manipulation routines and subroutines. They vary from language to language and from application to application. Sometimes the way in which they are written depends on the skill of the programmer. And attempting to correct them depends on the availability and quality of the program's documentation. Sometimes this documentation is nonexistent.

### *No Agreed-Upon Standards*

Once the date-related code has been identified, the battle is not over. The programmer must decide how he is going to fix it. The real problem is that there is no agreed-upon standard for storing or displaying dates. For example, should January 1, 2000, be stored as "20000101," "01012000," or some other format? Right now every organization does what is right in its own eyes, which could, ironically, be planting further time bombs for the future.

### *Not Enough Programmers*

Perhaps the biggest obstacle of all in dealing with the Year 2000 Problem is that there simply aren't enough programmers to review and repair all the code that needs to be fixed. There are only about

1.9 million professional software personnel in the United States. While this may seem like a lot, it is woefully inadequate to deal with the mountain of programs that need attention. "It is estimated that the shortfall of programmers to get this job done by the year 2000... is 30 percent worldwide for COBOL alone."[26]

**The deadline comes even *before* January 1, 2000; we need at least a year for testing corrected systems.**

According to the National Institute of Standards and Technology, an experienced programmer working with automated tools can review and repair approximately 100,000 lines of code per year.[27] This means, for example, that if the 550,000 COBOL programmers we currently have in the United States did nothing except work on Y2K projects, they could fix fifty-five billion lines of code per year. But there is probably many times that amount of code to repair. As a result, "the Gartner group predicts that more than half of all organizations worldwide will not fully complete the year 2000 effort."[28]

Amazingly, COBOL is no longer taught in most colleges and universities. When my brother-in-law, a COBOL programmer and systems analyst, called one of his old professors at Baylor University to ask about the Year 2000 Problem, he was told, "We don't even teach COBOL here anymore." As a result, a variety of "Learn COBOL in Six Weeks" courses are springing up to fill the need. Evidently, many people are reading the handwriting on the wall and hoping to cash in on the Y2K consulting bonanza. The question, however, remains: What kind of quality programming can you expect from someone who has had only six weeks of training?

### *The Problem Abroad*

Computers in the United States are not the only ones infected with the Millennium Bug; the problem is worldwide. Harris N. Miller, president of the Information Technology Association of America, says, "I can tell you from first-hand experience that as far behind the curve as we may think we are, America is out in front of the curve when compared to our international counterparts."[29] By late 1997 only 10 percent of U.K. companies had begun the assessment phase as the first step in addressing the Y2K Crisis.[30] Part of the problem in the United Kingdom and Europe is that these countries are frantically trying to modify their systems to accommodate the introduction of the Euro dollar, which is scheduled for—coincidentally—January 1, 2000. This project *all by itself* has seriously overloaded the available programming resources. Add to this the Year 2000 Problem, and you have a recipe for disaster.

**In mid-1997, only 302 of over 7,000 federal government systems—4 percent—were compliant.**

Japan is not in much better shape, and the rest of the world lags even farther behind. The real problem is that because our economy has become so global and because the computer systems are so interdependent, noncompliant computers in one area of the world will affect computers in other areas.

## It's Later Than You Think

January 1, 2000, will come right on schedule—whether we are ready or not.

Many people falsely believe that Y2K problems won't surface until January 1, 2000. They could not be more wrong. The Gartner Group warns that companies that don't deal with the Year 2000 Problem could see up to 60 percent of their applications fail or deliver bad numbers *before* the year 2000.[31] This is particularly true of any software that makes projections into the future. As we move closer to "D-Day," these failures will increase.

Many programs don't just "look back" to perform their calculations; they "look forward." As a result, noncompliant systems will fail as soon as they encounter the year 2000.[32] Some systems stumbled across this problem in the 1970s when they attempted to calculate thirty-year mortgages. Other systems experienced failures when they projected depreciation and amortization schedules as well as actuary tables.

In addition, in the 1970s mainframe programmers used "000000" for the first file in a series and "999999" as the software version of a full stop. According to *CNN Financial Times*, systems that used this convention will shut down on September 9, 1999, crashing almost five months ahead of schedule.[33] Some may come to an abrupt stop on January 1, 1999, a full year ahead of schedule, and for these systems, it is already too late, because it requires a full year to test a revised Y2K program.

### *Project Management*

It should be clear by now that the Year 2000 Problem is not primarily a technical one. It is fundamentally a *project management* problem. Unfortunately, it is a gargantuan problem that is daunting for even the best project managers. And most Information System managers are programmers first and project managers second. Many of them have had little or no formal project management training. What they know, they have learned on the job—and on much smaller, less-ambitious projects.

> Most CIOs [Chief Information Officers] don't have the training and/or experience to manage such large and complex jobs. For example, they may be outstanding with a $3 million per year budget, but now find themselves responsible for a Year 2000 Project that runs $30 million with ten to twenty times the staff—most of whom are newly hired or outsourced.[34]

More important, how are CIOs going to manage such large and complex projects while still trying to maintain their existing systems and processes? Business can't come to a standstill while the computers are repaired.

### *Testing*

Experts agree that 60 percent of a Y2K project's expenses, both in time and money, will be consumed in testing.[35] This includes not only testing applications to make sure that they perform as expected, but also *regression testing* to make sure that any newly introduced bugs are squashed. In the opinion of most experts, many companies are not allocating an adequate amount of money or time to the testing phase of the project. As a result, a number of these systems will fail or produce unexpected results when they are put into full production.

One of the biggest challenges all companies and agencies face is the difficulty of finding comparable hardware to test their rewritten software on. "The tests will require access to comparable hardware platforms, but few companies are in a position to duplicate their tests that can take days to complete."[36] They cannot simply suspend their normal data processing activities in order to load a new system onto their hardware and test it. The business enterprise must continue to function while the existing software is being tested. As a result, some companies are renting out their excess computer capacity to companies that need a system for testing. Such capacity is in short supply, however, and it is evaporating quickly.

### *History*

Perhaps the scariest part of the whole Y2K repair effort is the miserable record that corporate software developers have in completing projects on time. As *Newsweek* asked, "When did you last see a huge software project that met its deadline and worked perfectly?"[37]

The Gartner Group summarized it this way:

> Unfortunately, we believe that a number of factors make full compliance somewhat improbable at this point. Top on this list is the inability of IT [Information Technology] managers to execute highly complex management tasks on time. The complexity of project management is com-

pletely underestimated, and project management skills are among the most difficult to find. A litany of other detrimental factors, including technical factors (heterogeneous operating environments, missing source code, new bugs, etc.) and management issues (competing priorities and lack of business focus), all compound our concerns.[38]

## So What's It Going to Cost?

According to the prestigious British news magazine *The Economist*, "Fixing computers to read the year 2000 will become the single most expensive problem of all time."[39] The Gartner Group has estimated that it is going to cost some $600 billion to make the world's computers Year 2000 compliant. In reviewing this estimate, the investment and securities firm of J.P. Morgan originally thought it was way too high. But several months later, they changed their opinion: "We continue to view our 1996 estimate of $200 billion as conservative and now feel that the Gartner Group's $600 billion estimate may not be as outrageously high as we originally thought."[40]

Moreover, the longer an organization waits to get started, the more it's going to cost. "Refusing to believe that the cost estimates for complying with the year 2000 requirements can really be so huge, many corporate executives seem to be in a state of denial. But guess what? The true costs will almost certainly be even higher than current estimates."[41]

Consider the federal government. In mid-1997, only 302 of over 7,000 federal government systems—4 percent—were compliant.[42] This is truly amazing given the size of the problem and the amount of time left to deal with it. When the Office of Management and Budget (OMB) made its Y2K budget public, it was ridiculed by nearly everyone who commented on it. William D. Rabin and Terrence P. Tierney of J.P. Morgan Securities said, "We consider the $2.3 billion to fix the problem laughable, and we believe the cost will almost certainly increase substantially as more thorough assessments are completed."[43] And increase it did. It went from $2.3 billion to $3.8 billion in less than six months.[44] Most experts still believe that the revised budget is extremely conservative. Given the government's record on exceeding budgets, they are likely right.

Compare this budget to big business. Chase Manhattan Bank said it planned to spend $250 million over the next three years to repair some two hundred million lines of code. AMR (parent of American Airlines), Hughes Electronics, and a number of other Fortune 500 companies have announced $100 million–plus Year 2000 liabilities. Federal Express, a relatively "modern" computer user, has budgeted more than $500 million to solving its Year 2000 problems.[45] J.P. Morgan responded: "We believe these initial estimates are conservative and likely to increase as we get closer to the deadline."[46]

Amazingly, in mid-1997, the IRS was still in the assessment phase. But the IRS expects to move three hundred full-time employees from other assignments to assist with the repair of more than one hundred million lines of code in more than fifty thousand applications.[47] Just to put this into perspective, it took the Social Security Administration (SSA) five years, using four hundred full-time programmers, to repair six million lines of code. Does the IRS really believe it can repair one hundred million lines in less than eighteen months, plus have a full year for testing? Other government agencies are in even worse shape, as we will see in Chapter 6. But what it really comes down to is this: "our enemy is time, not cost."[48]

## Triage

Many corporations and government agencies have come to the conclusion that they can't fix everything. There is simply not enough time or money. As a result, most corporations are applying the principle of "triage" to their systems. *Triage* is a medical term that refers to sorting injured people into one of three groups: (1) those that will live regardless of the medical treatment applied, (2) those that will die regardless of the medical treatment applied, and (3) those that require medical attention in order to survive. In an emergency, scarce medical resources are applied to the last group first. The same is true of the Y2K Crisis.

As government agencies and companies take inventory of their software, they are applying the concept of triage. They are being encouraged by consultants and others to fix the "mission-critical" applications first. Everything else can wait.

> We recognize that the remediation effort ceases to be one of "fix everything" and becomes one of "fix the most important things first." We begin to think in terms of active prioritization and technology "triage."... We must recognize that this is one of the most important planning aspect[s].[49]

Even the governor of New York issued an executive order mandating that state programmers cease all new development work and focus on repairing the state's noncompliant applications. We will likely see more and more of this kind of activity as we move closer to the deadline.

## Conclusion

Am I saying that it will be impossible to get the vast majority of our computers and computer programs compliant by midnight, January 1, 2000? No. Am I saying it is highly improbable? Yes.[50] The more I read, the more discouraged I become. It seems that human beings have an amazing capacity to avoid reality and hide from the facts. In Greek mythology, Cassandra, daughter of Priam, king of Troy, was endowed with the gift of prophecy but fated by Apollo never to be believed. It seems that the "Y2K prophets" have been similarly cursed. As Dr. Gary North commented, "What will amaze historians of the future is that anything this huge could have been ignored for so long and then, when discovered, been denied so universally."[51]

My greatest fear, however, is that we will move quickly from *denial* to *panic*. If that happens, we are in real trouble.

# Chapter Three

## One Bad Apple Spoils the Whole Bunch

### *How Noncompliant Computers Will Affect Compliant Ones*

For want of a nail, the shoe was lost;
For want of the shoe, the horse was lost;
For want of the horse, the general was lost;
For want of a general, the battle was lost;
For want of a battle, the kingdom was lost;
And all from the want of a horseshoe nail.

—Proverb

If you've ever caught a computer virus, you know what a miserable experience it can be.

Recently, for no apparent reason, the CD-ROM on my laptop stopped working. I tried everything I knew to fix the problem, including calling the manufacturer's tech support department. I spent about thirty minutes on hold waiting for a technician (which, sadly, is not an unusual experience). The technician walked me through several trouble-shooting procedures, but none of them worked. Finally, he suggested, "Perhaps it's a virus."

"A virus! How do I check that?"

"Do you have an antivirus program installed?" he queried.

"No. I don't think so."

"You might want to buy one and run it on your hard disk," he suggested.

So, out of options, I went to the store and picked up a copy of *Norton AntiVirus.* I brought it home and installed it. Almost immediately, it found the culprit—a virus lurking in the boot sector of my hard disk—and removed it. I was impressed, but a little anxious. Now the real test: would my CD-ROM work? Sure enough, once I rebooted, everything worked fine, including the CD drive.

**Some estimate that 50 percent of companies won't fix the problem in time, and many will be driven out of business.**

That got me thinking: *I wonder if the machines at the office are infected?* They were. All of them. None of them was showing the ill-effects of being infected, but it was only a matter of time. As I have since learned, a virus can remain dormant on your hard disk, waiting for just the right set of circumstances to be activated. Once activated it can wreak havoc—everything from stopping certain hardware from working to completely erasing your hard disk!

I'm sure the viral infection was my fault. In our small office, I'm the one that does the bulk of the Web surfing. And, up until that point, I was not practicing "safe surfing." Now that I look back on it, it seems stupid. But I was naive. I failed to realize the potentially catastrophic damage that can be done by computer viruses.

## Mixed Metaphors

In many ways, the Year 2000 Problem is similar to a computer virus—only worse. As the Gartner Group points out:

> A program can fail in one of two ways. The first is simply when a program stops working and the failure is recognized immediately. The second, more insidious, is for the program to continue to run, generating false information, thus spreading the equivalent of a "virus."[1]

By now it should be apparent that not all of the computer programs are going to be repaired in time. Ann Coffou, managing director of the Year 2000 Relevance Service at the Giga Group, a Boston research company, predicts:

> We believe about 50 percent of all companies just aren't going to make it. Of those, we believe that about a quarter will be driven out of business [12.5 percent of the total], between the costs of resolving the problem technically and the legal fallout resulting from their failure to fix it.[2]

The job is just too big, and the time is too short. Of the computers that are not fixed in time, some will simply stop working. Others—and this is the scary part—will start spewing out corrupt data and infecting computers they come in contact with. Just like a computer virus, infected computers (those still having uncorrected Y2K code) will transmit their corrupted data to compliant, noninfected computers. Potentially, therefore, if *all* the computers aren't fixed, then *none* of them is safe.

If you work in the private sector, your company is probably linked to:

- customers
- suppliers
- sales agents
- financial service providers
- insurance carriers
- research sources (e.g., various content providers on the Internet)
- federal government agencies
- state government agencies
- local government agencies
- electric utilities
- water utilities
- telecommunication networks

- postal and parcel carriers
- security providers (including the local police, fire department, and even the military)
- charities
- competitors

Many of these relationships are computerized. You either feed data to one of these entities or are fed data from them; oftentimes both. What happens when that data is corrupt?

## All Fall Down

In *Datamation*, an Internet magazine, C. Lawrence Meador and Leland G. Freeman paint a troubling scenario. Imagine for a moment you are the chief information officer for your company:

> It's the first week of the year 2000, and you're heaving great sighs of relief. All of your systems are functioning properly. The big bucks you spent on analyzing, fixing, and replacing your million lines of code was money well spent.
>
> But what you don't realize is that one of your suppliers didn't fare so well, and just-in-time [JIT] shipments of parts that should have left that supplier's factory on Monday didn't. Tomorrow, three of your plants will shut down for want of that part. Your JIT shipments to your biggest customer won't happen, causing your customer to default on an important government contract.
>
> Excuse me, but the CEO wants to see you—*now!*[3]

We don't have to create imaginary scenarios or "fast forward" to the future to see examples of systems failing because one item failed. Consider the following real-life, recent examples:

- A seventeen-day strike at two Dayton, Ohio, brake manufacturing plants in March 1996 shut down twenty-six of twenty-nine General Motors plants in North America, as well as eighteen other parts plants. More than 177,000 workers were furloughed. It also stopped work at countless other suppliers and hurt companies such as restaurants that depend on autoworkers. The strike ended up costing GM about $900 million.[4] A similar strike at GM's PowerTrain Division transmission plant idled more plants in July 1997.[5]

- An Idaho power line short-circuited in July 1996 when electricity jumped to a tree that had grown too close to the transmission line. The outage on that one line, combined with a record heat wave, caused a ripple effect that cut power to fifteen western states and parts of Canada and Mexico.[6] Commenting on the outage, Lynn Baker, spokeswoman for Bonneville Power Administration, which oversees the power grid in the Pacific Northwest, said, "Having an interconnected system really makes for more efficient use of our natural resources and keeps the cost down. But it means when something goes wrong, it can cascade through the system."[7] And cascade it did. "In California, hundreds of thousands lost power. Thrill seekers at Del Mar Fair outside of San Diego were surprised when the rides suddenly shut down. Subway cars in San Francisco's Bay Area Rapid Transit system stopped in their tracks. Los Angeles briefly shut down seven of its giant water pumps. Some stores, banks, and restaurants closed; others operated without cash registers, computers, lights, and refrigeration. In Northern Nevada, police in Reno and Sparks reported so many traffic lights out of service that they ran out of temporary stop signs. Casinos in Reno briefly lost power.... In

Boise, Idaho, most offices and state agencies sent workers home and banks locked their doors during a two-hour outage."[8]

- The faulty installation of new system software shut down America Online for an entire day in August 1996. The outage left AOL's then six million members, including many small businesses and home-office workers, without e-mail and other key communications services. In addition, the crash caused dozens of AOL's information providers—for example, Motley Fool and Health ResponsAbility—to lose thousands of dollars in lost access fees or advertising revenues.

- In August 1997 the Teamsters staged a fifteen-day walkout on United Parcel Service. Although the strike had no apparent impact on big business, it had a significant, negative impact on small businesses. (Small businesses account for more than 50 percent of all jobs.) For some it was simply an annoyance; for others, it ate severely into their profits. And for a few, it threatened the viability of their enterprise. In the midst of the strike, more than thirty retail executives signed a letter to President Clinton warning that "the ramifications of the strike are alarming" and urging him to intervene. Other parcel carriers were overwhelmed and begged for relief. In the end, the Teamsters "won"; but UPS ended up laying off more than fifteen thousand workers because the demand for their services had been transferred to other carriers.[9]

While some of these examples aren't computer-related, they do demonstrate how our modern division of labor creates interdependencies that make each component vulnerable to the failures of others. The damage from each of these *single-cause*, *single-system*, *regional*, and *sequential* failures was significant. At the least, people were inconvenienced. At the worst, millions of dollars were lost and thousands of individuals and businesses were adversely affected.

What happens when, because of unresolved Y2K issues, we begin to experience *multiple-cause*, *multiple-system*, *global*, and *simultaneous* failures?

## Multiple-system Failures

Let's imagine what could happen if Year 2000 computer problems were not fixed in time, or if noncompliant computers managed to crash compliant ones. Leon Kappelman and Phil Scott in *ComLinks.Com* magazine warn:

> At the present rate of progress [in fixing the Year 2000 Problem], there will be interruptions of public and private services, business failures, shareholders actions, and regulatory intervention. And that's not the worst of it because telephone and transportation systems, water and sewage treatment facilities, chemical plant and oil refineries, and even nuclear power plants and weapon systems are also at risk.[10]

The authors go on to note:

> The world has become extremely dependent on computer technology. Many benefits have resulted, but this dependency is not without its risks.... Computer failures have been responsible for seriously interfering with, and even stopping, the delivery of products and services in health care, banking, security exchanges, retail, manufacturing, telecommunications, air traffic control, and electric utilities, to name but a few. *What*

> *would happen if suddenly all of those computers began to malfunction? The global economy would come to a screeching halt* [emphasis added].[11]

Let's consider several entities and how a failure there might cascade into multiple systems.

*The Social Security Administration (SSA).* The SSA probably has the best chance of any government agency of finishing its Y2K conversion project. But what if it doesn't? The SSA sends out approximately forty-three million checks a month to American citizens.[12] What happens if, because of malfunctioning computers, it can't send out accurate checks, or, worse, can't send out any checks at all?

**What's truly scary is that noncompliant computers will start spewing out corrupt data and infecting computers they come in contact with.**

Or assume for a moment that the SSA does finish its repairs. What if one or more of its key suppliers doesn't make it? What will it print checks on if its paper suppliers don't finish in time? How will it deliver the checks if the U.S. postal service experiences problems? How will it cover the checks that are sent if the IRS can't collect revenue and make a deposit in the SSA's coffers?[13]

The SSA has reported that even a *1 percent error rate* in its checks would generate 430,000 phone calls from confused or angry recipients, starting the day after the checks are mailed. If these problems are not resolved immediately, they generate more phone calls the next day, and the day after that, until the only thing the callers can count on is a busy single.

*Financial Institutions.* Financial service providers share massive amounts of information with other financial institutions and government agencies. Testifying before the Senate Subcommittee on Financial Services and Technology, David Iacino of BankBoston, the fifteenth largest bank in the United States, identified at least four problems that would have resulted if their computers had not been made compliant.[14] He observed:

- we would have not been able to mature our customer's Certificates of Deposits in the year 2000 and beyond;

- our Negotiable Collateral system would have lost expiration dates and review dates on collateral used to secure loans in the event of loan default;

- the system processing a daily volume of $800 million of Controlled Disbursements for our corporate customers would have been inoperable for up to ten days while the problem was corrected in January 2000, resulting in massive overdrafts to the bank, and;

- our Precious Metals business would have been inoperable for up to two weeks while systems changes were being made to correct erroneous date processing. And keep in mind that had these situations not been identified in advance, our ability to respond to all of them simultaneously in the year 2000 may have been hampered by the availability of computer resources and the pressures brought on by the demands of our customer base.[15]

Near the end of his testimony, Iacino sounded a sober warning:

> Knowing that all financial institutions must address the very same issues that we have faced with much less time remaining, I am concerned with the general preparedness of the rest of the financial services industry. In my discussions with other banks, customers, and service suppliers, I feel that unless comparable programs to

> BankBoston's are put into place within the next few months, *the effect will adversely impact even those that are adequately prepared* [emphasis added].

Ed Yourdon, a renowned mainframe programmer and author of various computer science textbooks, paints this hypothetical scenario:

> ...consider XYZBank, which has 300 million lines of legacy code. Assume that XYZ has the time and resources to convert 200 million lines, and it has done a triage to ensure that the mission-critical systems are converted. That leaves 100 million lines of unconverted code that won't run at all, or will spew out gibberish. Since this unconverted code is associated with noncritical systems, it won't have a fatal impact on XYZ though it could incur a nontrivial cost. My real concern is the applications XYZ considers noncritical might be very critical to some of XYZ's customers, partners, suppliers, etc. So it's quite possible that XYZ's failure to convert some of its software will cause little, tiny ABCWidget Company to go bankrupt, which causes slightly larger DEFCorp. to fold, and so on.
>
> Meanwhile, XYZ can't operate entirely alone; without electricity, phone service, and water, the offices can't function; without transportation services, none of its employees can come into work, and none of its customers can visit the bank to transact business. Let's assume for a moment that these basic utilities do continue operating properly after January 1. But what if the Federal Reserve Bank, S.W.I.F.T., and all the other banks that XYZ interacts with are having problems? What if XYZ's ability to print monthly financial statements depends on PQRPaper Corp. supplying laser-printing paper on a "just in time" basis? And what if PQR has a staff of three overworked programmers who maintain an ancient legacy system

> written in assembly language? If PQR stops shipping paper, then XYZ stops sending bank statements. Not forever, perhaps just for a month or two, but that's enough to cause a lot of confusion.[16]

Indeed. But perhaps all of this still seems remote—as if it were someone else's problem. Let's bring it a little closer to home. Think about the statements you get from your bank or other financial services provider on a monthly basis: checking account statements, passbook savings account statements, investment account statements, and so on. What happens if you can no longer be sure these statements are accurate? Straightening out a bank error can be difficult even when the computers *are* working. What happens when they are not? If you make decisions based on the statements you receive, and those decisions end up being bad because of inaccurate data, whom are you going to call? Your banker? Your attorney? And what happens when you can't get through to your bank because of similar worried callers?

**A major dilemma is that we won't be able to respond to all the problems simultaneously in the year 2000.**

***Farming.*** Most of us don't think much about farming anymore. Fewer than 2 percent of American citizens are actually involved in farming. Through the use of hybrid seeds and computers, we have experienced a "green revolution" in farm productivity. Today, according to the U.S. Department of Agriculture, 24 percent of crop farmers use computers in the business of raising crops.[17] They use these computers to manage seed inventories and the research of crop data, and for bookkeeping, accounting, sales, and marketing. In addition, embedded computer chips drive many of the high-tech farm machines, including tractors, grain combines, and irrigation systems.

Geri Guidetti moderates a computer forum on Nonhybrid Gardening. Recently she discussed Y2K's possible impact on farming:

> What happens if, down on the farm, the embedded computer chips and application software in those super high-tech tractors, grain combines, and other sophisticated farm machinery crash on January 1, 2000? Do you think the average farmer, however sophisticated, is fretting about finding and fixing lines of code in his machinery today? I'll bet my money that he's worried more about the weather.
>
> If the crops *do* make it to and from the fields that year, where will the farmer sell them? Markets used to be local and regional, but now they are global and very complex. They are dependent on international loans, payments, and the electronic exchange of money.... If the crops *do* make it to market with limited chaos, will they make it to the food processors, alcohol and sweetener producers, [and] industrial chemical manufacturers with minimal disruption? If they make it to the processors, will the food make it to each supermarket across the nation dependably? Every day?[18]

The typical supermarket turns its inventory over every seventy-two hours! This inventory is computer-managed. It is delivered by trucks whose routing and schedules are run by computers. And the plants that process and package our food are computer-managed. One little slip in this "food chain" and thousands, perhaps millions, of people are inconvenienced or, worse, go hungry.

## Filters, Windows, and Extensions

Perhaps you are wondering: why can't compliant computers simply convert the data that comes into them from noncompliant sources? Well, they can. Sort of. But the process is by no means fail-safe.

The solution—such as it is—involves creating a "filter" or "bridge" program that detects date patterns in the input stream. When a two-digit format is discerned by the system, it is converted before it is allowed into the system. This is similar to how antivirus programs work on microcomputers or how software "firewalls" work on computers that are connected to the Internet.

The problem is that filtering technology is still in its infancy. Given that so many of the programs that need protection are custom applications, these filters can be constructed only on an application-by-application basis. And, time spent writing and testing filters is time *not* spent converting and testing the actual code itself to make it Year 2000–compliant.

Filters won't solve all the problems. Donald Rife, a principal at American Management Systems in Fairfax, Virginia, a systems integration and consulting firm, notes:

> There will be a lot of situations in which the dates look fine—they have the right format and number of digits—but they are wrong because the computer has misinterpreted them. They may use different pivot dates to determine which century they are in. They may use European date formats which are different from U.S. date formats.[19]

### *Pivot Concept*

Once the date pattern is discerned it is often converted using a *pivot* concept or "windowing" mechanism. "The windowing option allows programmers to preserve the two-digit date format by designating a 'pivot date' to differentiate the centuries."[20] Some personal computer programs (like the popular *GoldMine* contact management system) use a similar concept called an "epoch setting."

Regardless of the terminology, the idea is simple. Let's assume the programmer selects a pivot date of "50." Any two-digit dates that are greater than 50 but less than 99 would be assumed to be a 1900 date. For example, "61" would be interpreted as "1961." Conversely, dates that are greater than 00 but less than 50 would be assumed to be a 2000 date. For example, "05" would be interpreted as "2005."

Unfortunately, there are no agreed-upon standards for pivot dates. Some applications may use 30 as the pivot date; others may use 40 or 50. As a result, there will be an incompatibility between applications that make different assumptions. Once again, even with pivot dates or filters, a compliant system is not protected from corrupt data coming into the system in the wrong format or being incorrectly interpreted.

### *Date Extension Solution*

Once the date is brought into the system, the programmer must decide how to store it. He can continue to store it in a two-digit format, using an internal pivot routine to translate it correctly, or he can use a *date extension* routine. In the latter routine, the program expands the actual date field to allow for two more digits in order to accommodate the century indicator. Instead of storing January 1, 2000, as 010100, for example, the field is extended to 01012000. This approach is certainly the most effective over the long term. However, date extension is also the most expensive to implement. It is "time-consuming because it requires changing each date-sensitive line of code, often by hand."[21] And, not only do the programs themselves have to be converted, but all the enterprise's data, input screens, and reports have to be changed as well.

Unfortunately, there are no agreed-upon standards for storing extended dates either. For example:

> ...the U.S. takes the *mm/dd/yy* approach, which makes sense when you consider the way most North Americans express the date: "Today is July 4, 1998," or 07/04/98. That's the standard (including the slashes separating the elements) approved by the National Institute of Standards and Technology (www.nist.gov). Canadians and Britons reverse the month and day, so they would represent the same date as 04/07/98. In some other countries, periods take the place of our slashes, and some peoples—such as the Scandinavians—start with the year, which in the case of our example would give 98-07-04, the reverse of the

> American system. The International Organization for Standardization, also known as the ISO (www.iso.ch), has set the standard as 1998-07-04, which includes the four-digit year. Too bad programmers didn't have the foresight to use this standard, which is inherently sort-friendly and which would have prevented the Y2K problem.[22]

There are other problems created by date extensions as well. When I first began talking about the Y2K Problem with my computer consultant brother-in-law, he did a quick "spot check" on his current client's computer system. He came back and informed me that there was nothing to worry about. "They are already storing their dates in an eight-digit format," he said proudly.

"Okay," I replied, "what about the input screens, do they allow for a four-digit year?"

He rubbed his chin. "I don't think so," he admitted.

"So, then, at the very least, you are going to have to recode all the input screens, right?"

"I'm afraid so," he admitted.

"What about the reports?" I asked.

"I'm not sure about those," he said thinking, "I guess I need to have a look at them."

The point is that it's not enough to fix one part of the system. Every part of the program that deals with dates has to be made "Y2K-OK." Even this may introduce problems when sending data to other systems. If the receiving system expects a two-digit date format and gets a four-digit one, unless it has a filter that can handle it, we are right back where we started. According to American Management Systems, even if all the Year 2000 problems are repaired, the resulting format inconsistencies will create 1,768 ambiguous dates that computers could misinterpret in the first decade of the next millennium.[23]

## Conclusion

In the early 1990s I went through a business failure. My company employed fifteen people and had relationships with some 150 different suppliers and vendors, as well as over 2,500 customers. When the business closed its doors in February 1992, my partner and I were devastated. The impact of the failure cascaded into our personal lives, of course, causing personal financial hardship that took several years to recover from. In times like those it is easy to become self-centered, seeing only what affects you and failing to see the effect your decisions and mistakes have on others.

We weren't the only ones hurt. We were the first "dominos" to fall, but definitely not the last. Suddenly, thirteen other people were out of work. Some of these people found immediate employment elsewhere; some didn't. Many struggled to make ends meet. In addition, our business failure had a significant impact on our suppliers. When we couldn't pay them, some were unable to meet their obligations, ultimately contributing to their own business difficulties.

Perhaps on a small scale, this example illustrates the power of the domino effect down the line. Magnify it a thousand- or a millionfold and you can see why the Year 2000 Problem could potentially cause some of the greatest problems Western civilization has faced in recent centuries.

# Part Two

## Against the Clock

### *The Implications of the Year 2000 Computer Crisis*

# Chapter Four

## When the Bottom Falls Out

### *The Impact of the Year 2000 Computer Crisis on Our Primary Infrastructure*

**A smell of burning fills the air—**
**The electrician is no longer there!**

—Hilaire Belloc

I got my first taste of a prolonged power outage in the winter of 1994. My family and I live just outside of Nashville, Tennessee. Typically, we have four moderate seasons. In the winter it can get cold, but we generally have only three or four snowfalls a year, and even those don't usually stick. For example, I bought my kids a couple of sleds in 1988 in the midst of one huge snowfall; we haven't been able to use them since.

In January 1994, however, after a brief warm spell, a massive cold front blew through. Just after the cold air hit, it began raining. Hard. The television weatherman warned us that it would soon turn to freezing rain and that it wasn't going to be pretty. He was right. My wife and I woke up in the middle of the night to what we thought were gunshots. We sat straight up in bed. Disoriented, it took us a few minutes to figure out what was going on. Our house is on the edge of a large wooded area. What we were hearing were large tree limbs breaking off under the weight of heavy ice, every ten minutes or so. Some of them were distant bangs and cracks;

others sounded like nearby explosions. We tried to sleep, but it was impossible. To make matters worse, at about 3:30 AM the power went off. Even that didn't initially alarm us. We are used to losing power in Middle Tennessee. Often in a heavy rainstorm we will lose power for an hour or two. But this was different.

**Because the U.S. electrical grid is one giant, interconnected system, local shutdowns could quickly become regional or even national.**

When we finally decided to get up at about 5 AM, the house was already growing cold. We threw on a second layer of clothing and went to check on the children. Amazingly, they were still asleep, so we threw a couple more blankets on them and went in search of some candles.

A few years before, we had remodeled part of the house and installed a separate heating and air conditioning unit. This part of the house was my office, and the heater there was gas. *Great!* I thought. *At least we can keep part of the house warm*. Wrong. We couldn't turn the heater's fan on without electricity.

*Hmmm*. I thought some more. *Okay, what about the fireplace?* Another bad idea. We had no wood in the house (of course). The only wood was outside, and it was now wet and frozen like everything else. *Now what?* I wondered. I was getting increasingly worried, as the house grew colder still.

I went back into the master bedroom where I kept an emergency weather radio in the drawer next to my bed. I brought it to the kitchen so my wife Gail could hear, too. The National Weather Service five-day forecast called for continued temperatures in the teens with intermittent freezing rain mixed with snow. "Oh, great," I said out loud. "Just what we need. More ice."

"What should we do?"

"I don't know."

"Why don't we call the electric company and see if they have any idea how long we'll be without power," Gail suggested.

"Good idea."

Gail looked up the number. I reached for the phone, checking to make sure there was a dial tone. Fortunately, it still had power. I dialed the number as Gail called it out to me.

"Shoot. It's busy," I said, frustrated.

"Well, then let me call a few of our neighbors."

"Okay. I'll check on the kids." While Gail started making calls, I walked to the back of the house. Megan, my oldest, was already awake.

"Dad, why is it so cold in here?"

"The power went off a few hours ago. We had an ice storm."

"I'm freezing," she said, irritated.

"I know. Me, too. You might want to put on a sweat suit and just stay in bed."

I checked on the other girls and then went back to the kitchen.

"Nobody has power in our neighborhood, but I called my parents, and they do!" Gail exclaimed. (Her parents live in a nearby community about ten minutes away.) "Do you think we should wake up the kids and go over there?"

"The only problem is going to be the roads. I bet they're slicker than glass," I said, thinking out loud.

"I know, but I don't think we have much choice. The house is already cold. It won't be long before it's *freezing* in here."

"Okay, let's give it a shot."

The roads were slick, and we had to drive very slowly, but, fortunately, there wasn't any traffic to contend with. We felt as if we were driving through a battle zone. Tree limbs were lying everywhere, and in some places entire trees had fallen over from the weight of the ice. We could see why the electricity was off—some of the trees had taken the power lines down with them.

We made it to my in-laws with no problem. Getting into a warm house was great. You don't realize how much you take heat and lights for granted—until you don't have them.

As it turned out, the power was off in our community for more than three days! Some outlying communities were without electricity for more than a week. It was a mess. I tried to work in my office at home for a few hours each day. My phone was still working, and the batteries on my laptop would last for about three hours. After that I was nearly frozen anyway. I honestly don't know what people did who had no relatives in town. I imagine it was pretty miserable.

## Power Games

A power outage can bring everything to a grinding halt in a heartbeat. Electricity is one of those invisible necessities that, in the modern age, is almost impossible to live without. Like Samson's hair, cut the juice, and our strength is gone. We are virtually helpless to do *anything*. Our tools go limp until the power can be restored. Unfortunately, computers are used extensively by utility companies to generate electricity. If the computers shut down, so does the power plant. And if the power plant goes down, we can't even keep the computers running so we can fix them!

Think of the *personal* consequences:

- No electricity means the bank's computers can't run.
- If the bank's computers can't run, deposits and payments can't be made.
- If deposits and payments can't be made, you can't be paid.
- If you can't be paid, you'll eventually run out of money. (Even if you are wealthy, how much cash do you have on hand? If the bank's computers aren't running, forget about withdrawals.)
- If you run out of money, you won't be able to purchase food and other basic necessities.

Or this:

- No electricity means the water department can't pump clean, safe water to your home.
- If the water department can't deliver clean water to your home, you have to find an alternative source.
- If you can find an alternative source, you will have to purify it.
- If you can't purify it, you run the risk of getting sick. If you can't find an alternative, you will eventually die. (You can only go about three days without water.)

Or this:

- No electricity means you can't heat your home with conventional means.
- If you can't find alternative means, you will be very uncomfortable. If you live in a region of the country where the winters are harsh, you might possibly freeze to death.

Or this:

- No electricity means you can't run your most basic tools, whether a computer, a vacuum cleaner, or a power saw.
- If you can't run your most basic tools, you might not be able to work.

- If you can't work, you can't get paid. (I won't continue the scenario because it ends up being the same as the first one.)

### *Use of Computers*

To grasp what is at stake, you need to understand just how dependent the modern electric utility is on computers. From the production side—generating and delivering electricity—to the business side, computers run the show. For example, they control:[1]

- security computers
- plant processes (data scanning, logging, and alarms)
- emergency response systems
- preventative maintenance
- radiation monitoring systems in nuclear plants
- dosimeters/readers in nuclear plants
- plant simulators
- engineering programs
- communication systems
- inventory control
- technical specification surveillance systems

Any or all of these systems may be affected by Year 2000 problems. In addition, computers are used in the *business* side of the utility. They are used for processing accounts payable and receivable, payroll, and purchase orders; tracking customer service requests and scheduling site inspections; generating budgets, income statements, balance sheets, cash flow projections, and a host of other management reports; and monitoring assets, investment accounts, and inventory stocking levels. Clearly, the modern utility is thoroughly computer-driven.

### *The Electrical Grid*

The U.S. electrical infrastructure includes some six thousand generating plants, more than five hundred thousand miles of bulk transmission cable, some twelve thousand major substations, and innumerable lower-voltage distribution transformers.[2] The entire grid is controlled by mainframe computers. The system itself is "divided into four electrical grids supplying Texas, the eastern states, the midwestern states, and the northwestern states. They are all interconnected in Nebraska."[3]

This grid is one giant, interconnected system. It's similar to the telephone system in which there are numerous long distance carriers, switching systems, and local phone companies. But essentially it is one interdependent system.

> Electric utilities generally have the responsibility for routing power from generating stations to distribution facilities owned by a power interchange. Power interchanges are companies that are typically a joint venture between neighboring electric utilities, and their facilities act as the distribution point for routing electricity to end users. And on a regional basis, several power interchanges may form a regional compact, and buy and sell power on an "as needed" basis. The entire arrangement is more commonly referred to as the national power grid or infrastructure.... If one link in the chain breaks, it becomes rather painful and expensive (and sometimes impossible) to reroute electrical power.[4]

Embedded systems and microcontrollers are used in every facet of the electrical generation process.

> Within a typical electric utility, embedded chip logic control is prevalent in every facet of the operation; from load dispatch and remote switchyard breaker control to nuclear power plant safety systems and fossil plant boiler control systems. Whole generating units (generally, gas turbines) are controlled from miles away by personnel adjusting system loads in response to peak demands.

> Embedded logic control is the dirty little Y2K secret of all production facilities (manufacturing and utilities) that has the most significant potential to bring whole companies to their knees.[5]

And, I might add, the potential to bring entire regions if not *nations* to their knees.

## *Power Outages*

Power outages are not that unusual, of course. They can result from harsh weather, equipment malfunctions, environmental causes, or, yes, even a computer failure. Regardless, they can cause a ripple effect throughout the grid.

As noted in the last chapter, a July 1996 power outage in Idaho caused fifteen states in the west and parts of Canada and Mexico to lose power. A similar blackout occurred in Oregon just a month later, on August 10, 1996. David Foster, an Associated Press writer, described this second power outage as "a case study in the domino effect":

> At 2:01 PM Saturday, a sagging transmission line sent an arc of electricity into the trees sixty miles east of Portland, Ore. The line short-circuited, and the resulting surge of electricity knocked out two other lines in Oregon during the next fifty minutes.
>
> At 3:42, another sagging line short-circuited over a filbert orchard just west of Portland. Five minutes later, two units at the McNary hydropower dam on the Columbia River sensed the system's instability and shut down automatically. One minute after that, voltage fluctuations shut down the main connection from Oregon to California.[6]

Although both outages were initially *local*, they quickly became *regional* in their impact.

Can a Year 2000 Problem cause this kind of shutdown? The answer is, yes. Recall that in Honolulu the electric utility's systems simply stopped working when it ran Year 2000 tests. If the problem had not been addressed prior to January 1, 2000, then some customers would have lost power, while others would have received a power spike, getting their electricity at a higher frequency than normal, in which case, "the clocks would go faster, and some things would blow up."[7]

What's important to remember is that Hawaii, because of its geographical isolation, is not part of one of the major power grids. If mainland utility companies have a major line go down, they could potentially drag the rest of the utility companies on the same system down with them.

> A unique aspect of the electrical grids, as with communication grids, is that most built-in computerized security is designed to anticipate no more than two disruptions concurrently. In other words, if a primary line went down, the grid would ideally shut off power to a specific section while it rerouted electricity around that problem area. If it ran into two such problems, however, the grid is designed to shut down altogether.[8]

### Nuclear Outages

In the case of nuclear power plants, it doesn't take a malfunction to shut them down. Merely, the *prospect* of a malfunction can force a shutdown. Approximately 20 percent of the total electricity in the United States is generated by nuclear energy. In some portions of the country the percentage is much higher. This is particularly true on the eastern seaboard, where nearly 40 percent of the region's juice comes from splitting atoms. And it was in the east that an incident occurred that forever changed the way nuclear power plants are regulated.

On March 28, 1979, an accident occurred at Three Mile Island, a nuclear plant just southeast of Harrisburg, Pennsylvania. A partial meltdown released radioactive material into the air and forced the evacuation of thousands of nearby residents. The ensuing crisis lasted for fourteen days before it was brought under control. As a result, the government tightened its regulations and many existing reactors had to engage in expensive refurbishment efforts in order to bring their systems into compliance. "The end result was that the plant which cost $250 million to build in the 1970s suddenly ballooned to $4 billion in the 1980s."[9]

The Nuclear Regulatory Commission (NRC) requires that plants cease operations when encountering an "unreviewed safety question" (USQ). This means that "any existing circumstance that could potentially place the plant in a condition adverse to safety must be reviewed for adverse impact as soon as the condition is discovered."[10] Or in short, "when in doubt, shut it down." The consequences stemming from a nuclear accident make this the only logical procedure.

**Nuclear power plants could be shut down, suddenly depriving the U.S. of 20 percent of its power.**

There are a variety of situations that could cause a plant to generate a USQ or "unanalyzed condition." Apart from the threats to embedded chips that control various aspects of the reactor itself, consider simple "event logging," or the concurrent recording of events which are kept by the computers themselves. According to Rick Cowles, an Information Technology expert who has worked in the electrical utility industry for over twenty-five years, this could be a serious problem.

> In the days following 01/01/2000, let's assume that a plant has some type of transient [event] that causes an automatic shutdown (a relatively routine event). What would happen if the event recorder (computer) completely and unrecoverably crashed during a routine SCRAM or plant trip? If you've been in the control room during a garden variety SCRAM, you know that things are happening much too fast to analyze everything that's occurring while it's occurring. Event logging is the only way to understand the big picture (while it's happening), and reconstruct the event (after it's over). If

> you don't have event logging, you can't understand what's happening in your plant. Even making the rash assumption that everything else worked O.K. and Y2K didn't raise its ugly head in some embedded chip logic somewhere that no one knew about (Murphy's Law is not scheduled for revocation prior to 01/01/2000), if event logging is inoperable, the plant is in an *unanalyzed condition.* Period....
>
> Current federal regulations and individual plant operating licenses require cessation of operations when operating in an "unanalyzed condition." A USQ represents an unanalyzed condition. And Y2K, as previously stated, is undoubtedly the most challenging generic USQ the nuclear industry has ever faced.[11]

Cowles then discusses the implications of this kind of situation:

> There is growing concern within industry working group circles that every nuclear power facility in the U.S. which has not conclusively proven Y2K compliance may be required to shut down prior to the end of 1999. The NRC has already issued an information notice, 96-70, regarding Year 2000 and nuclear facilities, and is expected to issue more guidance or rulemaking in the very near future. Given the General Accounting Office's (GAO) recent harsh criticism of NRC oversight, it can be expected that the eventual NRC response to the Y2K issue will indeed be significant.[12]

Proving compliance will not be easy. Not only do nuclear power plants have to ensure that all their business systems are compliant—the same challenge every other business faces—they also have to make sure all their electrical generating systems are compliant: safety systems, reactor control, turbine control, event logging, safety-related embedded control systems, emergency core cooling systems, and so on. The NRC will undoubtedly leave no stone unturned. The risks are simply too high. If a nuclear plant can't demonstrate compliance, it will be taken off-line.

What do you think would happen were the U.S. suddenly to lose 20 percent of its electrical generating capacity? According to Cowles, "this possibility is not farfetched."[13] At the very least there would be widespread "brownouts" and, potentially, blackouts. At the most, this kind of disruption could cause a cascading effect through the entire power grid, taking down system after system until, essentially, none is left standing.

**Everything from your telecommunications system to your water and sewage systems is susceptible to the Millennium Bug.**

This, of course, assumes that the NRC will have its own Y2K problems under control and can find the resources to supervise the plants under its jurisdiction. But the NRC is way behind the eight ball in its Y2K renovations. In September 1997, when Congressman Stephen Horn (R-California) issued his second annual "report card" that graded government agencies on their Year 2000 progress, the NRC received only a "D"; as of that date, the commission had still not completed its Year 2000 assessment. The only thing worse than shutting these plants down is letting them *melt down* when they encounter unresolved Y2K problems that cause their reactors or other utility equipment to malfunction.

### *Solar Flares*

If the Y2K Crisis isn't enough to contend with, the utility industry will also face a rash of solar flares in the Year 2000. According to geophysicists, "the sprawling North American power grid resembles a large antenna,"[14] and will attract electrical currents induced by giant solar storms. These storms have the ability to cause large-scale blackouts throughout the world.

> What drives space weather is the solar wind, a never-ending gush of magnetized gas spewed out by the

> corona, the sun's glowing outer shell. The gas is so hot (two million degrees Fahrenheit) that atoms of hydrogen and helium are homogenized into a dilute plasma, composed mainly of negatively charged electrons and positively charged protons. Yet the solar wind is a gossamer thing, far less substantial than a whisper. "What you have... is a million tons of matter moving at a million miles per hour. But it's density is so low that essentially you're dealing with the physics of a vacuum.[15]

When this so-called space wind encounters the earth's magnetic field, it creates a kind of funnel effect, channeling huge quantities of solar plasma into the earth's magnetosphere. This disturbance can scramble broadcast signals. "These surface currents can corrode buried pipelines, interrupt transatlantic phone conversations, and overheat electrical transformers."[16] This is not mere speculation. In 1989, at the peak of the solar cycle, currents generated by a geomagnetic storm shut down the power grid that supplies Canada's Quebec province. More than six million customers were plunged into a blackout.[17] It threatened to spill over into the United States as well.

Solar activity runs in eleven-year cycles. The last "solar maximum"—when solar activity is at its peak—was 1989. Guess when the next one is due? That's right.

> The next solar maximum, due sometime around the Year 2000, could create worse nightmares. For one thing, modern societies, with their cellular phones and satellite navigation and communications systems, have become more vulnerable than ever to electronic disruptions. Equally worrisome is the fact that electrical utilities have created enormous, interconnected power grids in an attempt to save money.[18]

### Blackouts

Power outages are a nightmare for the utility industry. Not only are they expensive in terms of customer relations, lost revenue, and expensive repairs, but, short-term, they are difficult to overcome. Once power is interrupted, especially in large cities, the delicate balance and diversity of electrical use is destroyed. For example, let's say you live in a subdivision with one hundred homes. In the late spring, at any given moment, the air conditioning is running in 30 percent of the homes. As the thermostats in some homes turn the systems on, others turn them off. The total load level increases or decreases in response to the outside temperature, and this occurs gradually without stressing the system. But when power is restored after a blackout, there is a surge in demand as all the thermostatically-controlled electrical devices and appliances come back online *at once*. As a result, loads can surge to 600 percent of their normal levels in the span of a few minutes.

When this happens, it can often "cause transient voltage stresses and permanent damage to network equipment such as high-voltage breakers, transformers, and generation plants, which makes them unavailable for restoring power. Hours or days may pass before power can be restored."[19] In other words, the system goes back down again as quickly as it came up.

As we have seen in so many other cases, the real problem is the interdependency among systems. If these systems aren't *all* fixed, then unresolved Year 2000 problems may cause multiple system failures. If that happens, potentially the entire electrical grid can come down.

## "Who Ya Gonna Call?"

The Year 2000 Problem in the telecommunications industry is huge. AT&T has 500 million lines to review.[20] Sprint has 100 million lines.[21] MCI has declined to make its numbers public, but they are no doubt somewhere between AT&T and Sprint. Considering the size of the problem, Bichlien Hoang, executive director of Year 2000 network solutions at Bellcore, a communications software, engineering, and consulting firm in Morristown, New Jersey, commented, "This is a problem of gigantic dimensions and with so many complexities that it's very hard to think something will not slip."[22]

In addition, the telecommunications industry makes extensive use of embedded chip systems. This is especially true in call-center equipment and telephone switching devices that are used to relay calls to their destination. Dataquest, a market research firm in San Jose, California, has estimated that as much as 25 percent of all call-center equipment may need to be replaced in order to be Y2K–compliant.[23] These systems can be date-sensitive in a variety of ways. For example, some systems use past experience to predict future workloads. "On Monday and Tuesday afternoons, calls reaching one center may be automatically routed to a center that has more staff working that day, even if it's located across the country."[24] The problem, of course, is that the correspondence between the date and the day of the week in the Year 2000 is different from what it was in 1900. If the embedded chip system thinks the year is 1900, then it will use the wrong day of the week to route calls.

**Frighteningly, many utilities don't realize how vulnerable they are to the Millennium Bug.**

"Call-center managers [also] tend to be risk-adverse [*sic*]... if their technology works, they don't upgrade until they have to."[25] As a result, the average call center upgrades only every six years. What this means is that there are a lot of old systems being used by businesses. Many of these will not be Year 2000–compliant.

Unfortunately, the major long distance carriers are lagging woefully behind the financial industry, according to Bruce Hall, a research director for the Gartner Group.[26] Like the electrical utilities industry, the telecommunications industry has to repair the code on two levels: (1) the product delivery side and (2) the business side. There must also be coordination between the long distance carriers (e.g., AT&T, MCI, Sprint, etc.), the local service providers (e.g., BellSouth or your local "baby bell"), and the suppliers (e.g., Lucent

Technologies, Nortel, and Siemens AG). Add to this the Internet infrastructure, including Internet service providers, "backbones" (e.g., Agis, Atlantic, and others), and commercial content providers (e.g., CompuServe, America Online, Delphi, and commercial Web sites, etc.). Bill Nichols, director of service planning at the General Services Administration's Federal Telecommunications Service, said that a system may work fine on its own. Connecting it to another system, however, can result in other problems:

> "You may have products in compliance, but the interfaces with other equipment may not be in compliance," Nichols said. "It may result in dropped calls. *We don't know what will happen*" [emphasis added].[27]

As of this writing, there is little coordination among service providers and vendors. Each entity appears to be immersed in its own Y2K conversion efforts with little attention given to monitoring other entities for compliance. As a result, it will not do AT&T any good to become compliant if the switching devices maintained by Lucent Technologies are not repaired. One can't work without the other.

Telecommunications companies in other countries are perhaps even further behind and yet have enormous projects under way. British Telcom is reportedly spending $500 million (U.S.) to renovate its computer systems. Telstra, the largest phone company in Australia, has just increased its Y2K budget from $80 million to $400 million (U.S.).[28] South Africa's Telkom did not get started until January 1997, but is planning to spend an amount comparable to Australia.[29]

And what about the interconnection *between* countries? According to David Harrington of Britain's Telecommunications Managers Association, "there is evidence that the level of cooperation and coordination between the world's [telephone] operators is not good."[30] There is no international standard. It's basically every man for himself. If the whole thing works, it will be a miracle.

## Water, Water Everywhere

Recently, I had a disconcerting experience. As part of my research for this book, I called my local water utility in mid-September 1997 and asked to be connected to the person in charge of information technology. (I live in a small municipality outside of Nashville, Tennessee, with a population of about thirty-five thousand.) When I was transferred to the appropriate person, I asked him what his utility was doing to address the Year 2000 Computer Problem. There was a long pause, so I asked him if he was even *familiar* with the Year 2000 Problem. There was another pause, and then he said, "Well, I've heard of it, but I'm not sure exactly what it is." I was shocked, to say the least, so I double-checked to make sure I was speaking to the head of the computer department. "Yep, I'm the right guy," he assured me.

I explained the Year 2000 Problem and asked if his systems were Year 2000–compliant. "Well, I don't know, but it sounds like this is something we ought to check into." I explained how the problem affects embedded chips and programmable logic controllers, which I knew were used extensively in the water treatment process. I told him that some of these date-sensitive systems will simply fail when they try to roll over to the Year 2000.

His response: "I don't know anything about that stuff. I think engineering handles that."

"Okay. Who should I talk to?"

"I don't know. They're in a different building. You might want to call back on the main number and have the operator connect you."

I wonder how many other small municipalities are in the same boat.

### *Modern Plumbing*

We take water for granted, of course. No wells to dig. No buckets to carry. No fear of contamination. Just turn the faucet on, and out flows clean, safe water (or at least *relatively* safe water). And as an extra bonus, most water utilities throw in a little fluoride to keep our teeth and gums healthy, too.

Most water departments are also responsible for "waste management" as well. (That's why many water municipalities are referred to as the "Water and Sewer Department.") No latrines. No outhouses. No potential for disease to spread. Wth a simple flush, the waste problem is eliminated (no pun intended). We rarely give it another thought. Until something goes wrong.

### *Water Treatment*

The water treatment process is fairly complicated.[31] First you have to have a water supply. In my neck of the woods, the water comes from the Cumberland River. The water from the river is first screened to remove large objects such as logs and debris. Coagulants such as alum and other chemicals are added to the water and mixed. These chemicals do not remain in the water. Instead, mud and algae cling to them, forming larger particles that can be screened out. The water then slowly moves through settling tanks where large particles sink to the bottom. The water in these tanks passes through filters made of gravel and sand. At the end of this process, the water is crystal clear. But before the water is distributed, chlorine is added to keep bacteria from growing. A small amount of fluoride is also added in order to prevent tooth decay. Most of the steps in this process are handled automatically by embedded chip systems.

Once the water is cleaned, it is ready for distribution. In Nashville this means pumping the water to some 142,000 customers through 2,600 miles of water mains and 2,517 miles of sewer lines. And guess what? All valves regulating the flow of water through the system are controlled by embedded computer systems, some of which are date-sensitive. When Dick Brich, the City of North Platte, Nebraska's, sole programmer, began tackling his city's Y2K Problem, he discovered:

> Two areas of city water operations are affected by the problem of Y2K. All valves regulating water flow are controlled by SCADA [Supervisory Control and Data Acqui-

> sition] software. The software vendor, Canon Technology, has initiated corrective action (the only case we found where a vendor notified the city and provided upgrades to the software). The water system now has year 2000 compliant software controlling its valves.
>
> In contrast, software that controls valves to prevent backflow of lawn fertilizer through residential sprinkler systems, waste in hospitals, and sewer runoff into the drinking water, has not been updated. The software which records inspections of these systems will not accept dates past May 25, 1995! Worse yet is that the software supplier, Liaison Computer Systems, is out of business. This software is obviously useless to the city and records of inspection are kept manually at this point.[32]

Keeping records manually may work temporarily in smaller municipalities (North Platte has only twenty-five thousand residents), but it is unlikely to work in larger cities where there may be ten times as many inhabitants. The systems are simply too big.

## Conclusion

We are completely dependent upon our invisible, pervasive infrastructure. Without electricity, telecommunications, and water, nothing else works in our "wired-up-the-wazoo" civilization. Each of these three areas is seriously dependent upon computers, not only to conduct the business aspects of their enterprises, but also to produce and deliver their products. Like their business and government agency counterparts, these companies typically have massive amounts of code to review and repair. But unlike their counterparts, they also have to deal with the impact of the Year 2000 Problem on embedded computer systems and programmable logic controllers. Many of these companies admit that they don't really know the extent to which they are at risk with these systems. Much of the computer code is inaccessible. It is either stored as unalterable "firmware" or written in a proprietary language known only to the vendor.

Unfortunately for many utilities—and ultimately for us—they will not know just how vulnerable they are to the Millennium Bug until the clock rolls over on January 1, 2000.

# Chapter Five

## Hot Checks and Cold Bankers

### *The Impact of the Year 2000 Computer Crisis on the Banking and Credit Card Industries*

**It is no accident that banks resemble temples, preferably Greek, and that the supplicants who come to perform the rites of deposit and withdrawal instinctively lower their voices into the registers of awe. Even the most junior tellers acquire within weeks of their employment the officiousness of hierophants tending an eternal flame. I don't know how they become so quickly inducted into the presiding mysteries, or who instructs them in the finely articulated inflections of contempt for the laity, but somehow they learn to think of themselves as suppliers of the monetarized DNA that is the breath of life.**

—Lewis H. Lapham

If you are like most Americans, you've probably overdrawn your checking account once or twice. There's nothing that will make your heart sink quite like going to the mailbox and pulling out an overdraft notice from your bank—except, perhaps, pulling out more than one.

Several years ago, my wife went to the mailbox and pulled out *fourteen* such notices! She, of course, did what any rational person would do: she panicked, ran into the house, and confronted me with the envelope.

"Honey, we just got *fourteen* overdraft notices! What did you *do*?"

"What do you mean, 'What did *I* do?'" I fired back. "I didn't do anything! What did *you* do?" Neither of us was going to accept the blame if we didn't have to.

**Even the Federal Reserve System's own computer programs aren't compliant.**

After a few minutes of wrangling and getting nowhere, I loaded Quicken and showed her the balance. "Look, I just balanced the checking account last weekend after I got paid. We still have more than $1,000 in that account."

"Hmm," she said. "Let's call the bank and see what's going on." She went downstairs to use the phone.

Before she had a chance to get to the phone, I heard it ring. She picked it up. I was still upstairs; all I heard was her response. "I am very sorry, Mr. Kawasaki, I don't know what's going on. My husband and I were just trying to figure it out when you called." I headed downstairs. As I entered the kitchen I heard her say, "Yes, I'll come by this afternoon and give you another one." She hung up, sighed, and gave me a worried look.

This time I picked up the phone and dialed the bank. To make a long story short, when I deposited my paycheck, the bank credited the wrong account. The deposit receipt had the right account listed, but somehow the money ended up in a second account that we used only for groceries and various household items. Initially, the bank insisted that it must have been our fault—they thought I had simply used the wrong deposit slip. I finally had to go down to the bank in person, meet with the branch manager, and show him my deposit receipt. "You're right," he said. "Somehow, we messed up. I'm very sorry." He then instructed his assistant to credit our account for the cumulative total of the overdraft charges. (We found out later that they had bounced an additional eight checks for a grand total of *twenty-two!*)

"If you'll give me a list of everyone who received a bad check," he said, "I'll call them personally and apologize. We'll also take care of any returned check charges."

"Great!" I replied. I don't know if I was so much impressed with his customer service as I was relieved that, for once, it wasn't my fault. In any event, it took a little over three weeks for the problem to be completely resolved and for all the loose ends to be tidied up. I never thought we would get it behind us.

## The Big Picture

Certainly you can understand a banking crisis on a small scale. It can be a nightmare to straighten out when the computers *are* working. What happens when they aren't working or, worse, when they are the *cause* of the problem? And what happens if the banking errors affect not only you personally, but banking at a global level?

To understand the global financial implications, you need to grasp the concept of *fractional reserve banking*. Entire books have been written on this subject, but I recently read an excellent, succinct explanation of how the system works in CompuServe's Year2000 forum. It was written by Mike Phillips and is worth quoting at length:

> There's really only one point you need to grasp to understand everything you need to know: *the money's not there.* The average person generally thinks that if he deposits $1,000 in his bank, the bank keeps it until he needs it. A more sophisticated person probably realizes that in order to pay interest, even on his checking account, they must lend it out to earn the interest. Having heard about reserve requirements and that they're about 20 percent, he assumes they keep $200 and lend out $800.
>
> Both are wrong. What the bank actually does is send the entire $1,000 to the Federal Reserve. Then having reserves of $1,000, they proceed to make loans of $5,000, which are shown as a deposit in the borrower's checking account. Thus, the loan is both an asset and a liability to

the bank and the books balance. This is the mechanism that the government, in conjunction with the banks, uses to create money. They don't run the printing presses anymore. The purpose of the Federal Reserve is to coordinate this process, making sure all banks create money, or inflate, at the same rate.

If this is your first exposure to this subject, you probably think, *This is crazy. How can this work? I don't just deposit money in my checking account to leave it there. What happens when I spend it?* The key is that it works as long as the money never leaves the system. Consider what happens when you deposit your paycheck. A computer debits your employer's account and credits yours. The same thing happens when you write a check to the phone company. Credits and debits flow back and forth within the banking system, but nothing ever leaves it. Therefore the fraud, the inverted pyramid, remains hidden from view.

"OK," you say, "but what happens when I go to the ATM and withdraw cash? Doesn't money leave the system then?" The answer is yes and no. Right now, no. There's a certain amount of "slosh" at the bottom of the banking system. You go to the ATM and withdraw $20. Then you gather your family and head to McDonald's where you spend it. Later that afternoon, a Brinks truck shows up at McDonald's and takes the cash back to the bank. The cash never really leaves the banking system, at least permanently. The government prints just enough paper money to support the demand for cash, and it's constantly recycled in and out of the banks. Over 90 percent of our fiat money is computer entries and because of the fractional reserve banking system, even that isn't there. It's been lent out at the rate of five dollars for every dollar of deposits.

So, what would happen if lots of people decided to withdraw their money in cash and not spend it? That's when the system will collapse. First of all, there isn't that much paper money in existence, just enough to support the current demands. Before it could be given out, it would first have to be printed. But, even that wouldn't solve the problem. The banks have allowed for the current small amount of currency usage, but the rest of the money is over at the Federal Reserve acting as deposit for the pyramid loan structure. In order to pay money to its depositors, it would first have to call in loans, five dollars for every dollar a depositor wanted. But, they really can't do this either. The banks have committed the cardinal sin of banking, borrowing short and lending long. If you have a four-year car loan, you don't have to make payments to the bank any sooner than you agreed to do when you took out the loan.

Proclaiming that a fiat money system will collapse does not really qualify as much of a prediction. The informed response would be, "Well, Duh!" Every fiat money system in recorded history has collapsed. One of the earliest recorded examples of a debt collapse was the Assyrian Empire. The Jews who were living among them at the time were affected by it and that's how all that anti-money stuff got in the Old Testament of the Bible; "Neither a lender nor a borrower be." This is not a new phenomenon, but it is a long-term cycle. No one experiences a complete cycle within their lifetime. Most of us have to go back three generations to our grandparents to find someone who experienced a banking collapse in the 1930s. We'd have to go back even further, four generations, to get someone similar to ourselves, middle-aged adults in the roaring '20s.

Back then, the stock market was booming and the party was going full blast. At the time, no one saw the 1930s coming. They were blindsided by it. Well, a few people did. One financier said he knew the end was coming when he started getting stock market tips from his shoeshine boy. Of course, "This time it's different" (a familiar refrain). Now it's the Beardstown Ladies.

However, the closest example to now is not the 1920s but rather the South Seas Bubble of the 1720s. Only that can be compared, albeit feebly, to the bubble we've got going now. No wonder so many of us think it's different this time. We weren't around the last time it was the same. Most of us have spent our entire adult lives in the end stages of a bull market cycle. Our beliefs are formed by our experiences and we know nothing else. It is this factor which makes these cycles possible in the first place—that plus stupidity and greed.

Anyway, it's one thing to predict the collapse of a fiat money, fractional reserve banking system. "When" is something else. Our money system is like one of those cartoon characters that have run off a cliff and are still going in mid-air. Our fiat money is still convenient, consistent, easily divisible and most important, accepted. However, it is accepted out of habit, not because it has any inherent value. Unless human nature makes some dramatic change, people will not knowingly and willingly accept nothing for something forever. This acceptance is a state of mind and it can change in a heartbeat.

It did in the 1930s. People went from drinking and dancing at the speakeasies to lining up at the doors of closed banks in a short period of time. The catalyst was the failure of a bank in Austria of all places! They began calling in loans, other European banks followed and eventually they started calling in loans with American banks. Once an inverted pyramid begins to collapse, it takes on a life of its own. The problem is predicting the triggering event.

That's where Y2K comes in. It has the potential, in many ways, to put an exact time on what heretofore has been unpredictable. It seems clear from published articles… that any initial Y2K impact will not originate with the major New York banks. They should be compliant. However, there are hundreds of banks in this country, many of which don't appear to be on track to compliance. Once one bank gets cash demands which exceed its ability to pay, it must begin calling in loans or close. Either action tends to spread the problem to other banks, regardless of whether or not they are computer compliant.

Okay, what about the FDIC? Don't they guarantee deposits? Yes, and they have been very good over the years at swooping in to small banks in trouble and making a public show of paying off the depositors. However, it's largely a bluff. They only have enough to cover about 1 or 2 percent of the deposits in the banking system. Y2K has the potential to affect much more than this.

Even worse, Y2K doesn't have to directly impact the banking system in order to cause problems. Suppose a large number of small and mid-sized businesses have difficulty dealing with the banking system, even temporarily, because of Y2K computer problems. In order to stay in business, they turn to cash. Their customers, wanting what they have to offer, go to their banks and demand cash from their accounts in excess of previous demands. This is enough to start unwinding the debt pyramid, even if the banks are 100 percent computer compliant.

Y2K might exert its influence through the military. I think the chances are zero that a Y2K glitch could fire a missile or anything silly like that, but the military exists to protect our interests. It is a giant bureaucratic logistic enterprise with hundreds of thousands of people to pay and feed, and supplies and hardware to position where needed. It was the military that invented the term SNAFU (Situation Normal, All Fouled Up. This was WWII, they actually used the word "fouled" in those days). Y2K could take the term SNAFU to undreamed of heights.

Suppose for a period of time, however brief, we were unable to get troops, ships, and supplies where needed or use them with confidence. Would China take advantage of such an opportunity to retake Taiwan as they've indicated they wished? Would North Korea try to retake South Korea? If that happened, what would be the effect on Japan, who has depended on us since WWII for military defense and is currently in a six-year recession? They presently hold over one trillion dollars of our national debt! Would they want to pull their money out? If so, bye-bye banking system.

There are other abuses that await a day of reckoning. Today, there are trillions of dollars floating around in the derivatives market. You've got county treasurers and other yo-yos playing the futures market with highly leveraged tons of other people's money. We've seen some of the preliminary tremors from this earthquake in Orange County, California, and Daiwa Bank. A banking crisis will bring many more such abuses to light and intensify the effect.[1]

## Electronic Alzheimer's

Alzheimer's is a degenerative disease of the brain that produces memory loss, impaired judgment, and disorientation. It is also a good description of what might happen to many computers that are not Year 2000–compliant. For computers in financial institutions, the effect could be devastating. Consider just five of the problems that might occur.[2]

*1. Loss of faith by the public in the banking system.* If there is one thing that holds the entire system together it is *confidence.* If that confidence is lost, one result could be a "bank run" in which people rush to their banks to withdraw the cash value of their accounts. If enough people do this, the demand will exceed the bank's available cash. And it can become a compounding problem, spreading through the entire system.

Note that the "trigger" that could set this kind of collapse in motion could be based either on the *fact* that a bank (or banks) is not Y2K–compliant or on the *belief* that it is not. As Jeff Jinnett, a Y2K expert, testified before Congress:

> ...even if almost all of the U.S. financial institutions become fully Year 2000 compliant, a highly publicized computer system failure of one institution, together with the resulting litigation, may prompt stock market analysts and investors to "short" the stocks of other companies in the affected business sector.... [Also,] depositors may become concerned about their ability to access their funds if a "run" on their bank ultimately occurs. "Doomsday" articles alleging that federal government agencies and/or state agencies are unlikely to become Year 2000 compliant may add "fuel to the flames."[3]

Based on this, is it any wonder that government and business officials have been silent on the Year 2000 issue? And for those that haven't been silent, all we have heard is the oft-repeated mantra: "We will be finished with our Year 2000 repairs by December 31, 1998, so that we will have a full year for testing." This will be particularly difficult—especially for those that haven't yet even finished their "assessments"!

***2. Rise in security problems as a result of hackers taking advantage of Y2K disruptions.*** It is likely that banks and other financial institutions will have to turn to outside contractors to assist them with their Y2K projects. And, as we move closer to the deadline, they will have fewer and fewer third-party options, since most of these firms will already be engaged in Y2K projects for other companies. That, coupled with a growing sense of urgency, if not outright panic, may cause security procedures to be abbreviated or discarded altogether. William J. McDonough, president of the Federal Reserve Bank of New York, warned:

> Security also is likely to be of increasing concern. As time pressures mount, there is a risk that shortcuts will be taken. The checking of credentials for new staff or outside contractors or consultants may be rushed and less vigorous. Date-dependent security applications may be turned off to facilitate testing.[4]

As a result, this situation will give *outside access* to a financial institution's most sensitive data: *its customers' personal records.* It is possible that unscrupulous programmers could either modify this data, steal it, or—even more insidious—build "back doors" into the system, so that they can skirt the company's security procedures in the future, and gain full access to the system whenever they want. Jinnett agrees: "In addition, computer hackers may attempt to take advantage of general system disruptions caused by the Year 2000 computer problem to gain unauthorized access to the institutions' systems."[5]

*3. Increase in bad debt from businesses that fail and that are unable to repay their loans.* Financial institutions aren't the only ones struggling to get their computers Year 2000–compliant, of course. Nearly all of their customers are racing the clock as well. As I cited in Chapter 3, the Giga Group estimates that nearly 50 percent of all companies won't get their computers repaired in time. They also estimate that 25 percent of the companies that don't make it will go out of business altogether.[6] These companies will obviously default on any outstanding loans or lines of credit they may have. But even companies that do make it may have depleted their working capital to such an extent that they go into default or have to restructure their debt. Some companies will no doubt have to borrow just to complete their Y2K projects. In any event, the banks will bear the brunt, and so, of course, will their owners or shareholders.

*4. Increase in litigation stemming from Y2K problems.* As we shall see in Chapter 8, experts estimate that litigation stemming from Year 2000 problems could exceed $1 trillion worldwide. Some of this litigation will, of course, be directed toward banking customers and hinder their ability to repay outstanding loans or keep current with their payments. Banks and other financial institutions could themselves be sued.

*5. Possibility that some of these losses won't be insured.* Some losses that a financial institution incurs as a result of the Year 2000 Problem won't be covered by existing insurance policies. "For example, insurers may decline to cover business interruption losses under the institution's property and casualty policy on the grounds that a loss due to the Year 2000 computer problem is not an insurable 'fortuitous event'."[7] In addition, it may be difficult for companies to recruit independent directors to their board unless they can assure these prospective board members that they will be covered by a company's directors and officers liability policy. Many underwriters are changing the terms of their policies specifically to exclude Year 2000 losses.

But it is not simply financial institutions that are at risk; consumers are, as well.

## *Impact on Consumers*

As important as these financial institutions are to the health of our society, the effect of the failure—if they do fail—will ripple down to all of us. There are at least *five* ways you and I will be affected if the banks don't make it.[8]

*1. Errant transaction records or their complete destruction.* Many computers are programmed automatically to delete records that are older than a certain, predefined age. The programmers assume that the bank is maintaining regular backups of this data and that they are archiving them offsite. If your bank's computer isn't compliant before the year 2000, it may interpret any transactions made in that year as having been made in the year 1900. Consequently, from the computer's point of view, these records will be nearly one hundred years old. If the computer is programmed automatically to delete records that are more than twelve months old, it will automatically delete these records—possibly before they can be backed up.

**As of March 1997 only 40 percent of U.S. banks had even begun to assess their Year 2000 situation.**

*2. Miscalculated savings, checking, and brokerage accounts transactions.* At least if the computer deletes your records, you and the bank both know there is a problem. But what happens if the bank's computer miscalculates some of your transactions? It could introduce subtle errors or more obvious ones. For example, suppose you have a variable-rate mortgage. The amount of interest fluctuates according to the value of T-bills, or some other agreed-upon standard. If the mortgage company's computer is noncompliant, and it interprets the year 2000 as 1900, then any interest calculations based on dates in the next century will be wildly inaccurate. The computer could determine that you owe interest on a balance that is ninety-nine years past due.

*3. Inability to access funds when needed.* If you receive your income by receipt of a physical check, at least you can take it to a compliant bank and cash it (assuming there are compliant banks that have not been impacted by corrupted data from noncompliant ones). But if you receive your paycheck by electronic transfer and your bank is not compliant, you are out of luck. In either case, you could be prevented from withdrawing money, because:

- Records jumbled by Y2K problems could show you

overdrawn or with a smaller balance than you actually have.

- The bank's computers could completely shut down because of an unresolved Year 2000 Problem.

- The bank may be so overrun with computer-generated problems that it simply cannot both conduct normal business and attend to the problems created by the misbehaving computer.

- If there is a "run" on your bank, the bank (or the government) may shut it down temporarily, giving the market a chance to "cool off," which, unfortunately, will probably have the opposite effect.

And don't forget: bank employees have no way of verifying your current balance apart from looking it up on the computer. The days of green visors, arm bands, and handwritten ledgers are *long* gone.

*4. Reduction in the value of stock market holdings.* Individual companies that are not Year 2000–compliant will suffer business losses that will, in turn, reduce the value of their stock. But if the Millennium Bug bites hard, the entire market could experience a downturn.

*5. Disputes with the IRS over underpayment of taxes because of incorrect filings by noncompliant third parties.* Erroneous income reported by your employer or erroneous interest by your bank could get you in trouble with the IRS, particularly if the only records you have are electronic.

## The Wizard of Oz

The Federal Reserve System (the Fed) is the nation's central bank—arguably the most important central bank on the planet. It has encouraged its member banks to work quickly to ensure Year 2000 compliance. Large banks "appear capable of renovating their critical operating systems by year-end 1998, and will have their testing well under way by then."[9] Small banks, on the other hand, including the U.S. offices of foreign banks, are in a far different place. "Many of these organizations appear to have underestimated the efforts necessary to ensure that their systems will be compliant."[10] How does the Fed know this? It conducted a survey of its 13,000 supervised banks and received back 1,000 responses. The Fed's conclusion: "the banking industry's awareness level has improved substantially during 1997." I suppose this is a step in the right direction, but the bottom line is that we are running out of time. By now, we need *far more* than awareness. As one Y2K pundit observed:

> Awareness is dandy; but what is needed is a cure. The awareness of the pilot and his co-pilot that their 747's hydraulic system has just failed is important; the problem is, without the hydraulic system, they can't land the plane. I ask: Will they admit this to their passengers?[11]

Edward W. Kelley, Jr., one of the Fed's governors, informed Congress of some of the Fed's efforts:

> We have inaugurated a Year 2000 newsletter and have just published our first bulletin addressing specific technical issues. Copies of our recent newsletter and the bulletin are provided as Attachments 1 and 2, respectively. We have also established an Internet Web site to provide depository institutions with information regarding the Federal Reserve System's CDC [Century Date Change] project. The site can be accessed at the following Internet address: http://www.frbsf.org.fiservices/cdc. [12]

Gee, a newsletter *and* a Web site. I guess they *are* on top it. They've even produced a ten-minute Y2K awareness video for banks to use with their directors. The Fed has also promised (threatened?) to conduct on-site examinations of every bank under its jurisdiction by mid-1998 to review their progress.[13]

There's one additional problem: the Fed's own computer programs aren't compliant.[14] This is particularly disturbing when you consider that the Fed operates the nation's payment system, moving $1 trillion a day among financial institutions.[15] FedWire, the Fed's electronic transfer system, is used by 11,600 customers. In 1995 more than twenty-seven million transfers (over $220 trillion) were made using this computerized payment system.[16] Errors in just 10 percent of these transactions could cause unbelievable chaos in the world's banking systems.

**Focusing on converting to the Euro dollar, European bankers have simply ignored the Year 2000 Problem.**

The Fed faces the usual obstacles. But "in the case of the Federal Reserve, management of this project is particularly challenging in that it requires coordination among Reserve Banks, the Board of Governors, government agencies, numerous vendors and service providers, and approximately 13,000 customers."[17] And just how much progress has the Fed made? In April 1997, Senate Banking Chairman Alfonse D'Amato (R-New York) warned that "the Federal Reserve may not be taking adequate precautions to ensure that its technological systems and those of the banks it regulates will function properly in the Year 2000."[18] He sent a letter to the Fed asking for additional information: "Congress expects detailed plans and concrete actions to prevent possible future catastrophes which could endanger the financial well-being of hundreds of millions of Americans. We can't wait around. Timing is critical."[19] Evidently, the letter got the Fed moving in the right direction, but not by much. In July the Fed told Congress, "We have completed an initial inventory of vendor components used in our mainframe and distributed computing environments."[20] In other words, the Fed has a *list* of what needs to be fixed. According to the experts, that is approximately 1 percent of the overall project.

Does the Fed have a contingency plan if it doesn't get its computers repaired in time? Edward Kelley, Jr., admits:

> ...preparation for contingencies in the century date change environment does offer some new and significant challenges. For example, in the software application arena, the normal contingency of falling back to a prior release of the software is not a viable option [since the prior release will be infected with the Millennium Bug as well]. This underscores the importance of the rigorous assessment and testing to which all applications must be subjected.[21]

In other words, although the Fed understands what is at stake, it doesn't have a contingency plan. The Fed has some experience with disasters. The Los Angeles earthquake, hurricane Hugo in the Carolinas, and hurricane Andrew in south Florida threatened to disrupt banking services in the affected regions. How did the Fed meet the challenge? According to Governor Kelley, "In these cases we worked closely with financial institutions to ensure that *adequate supplies of cash* were available to the community [emphasis added]."[22] In short, they simply printed money. Not very comforting. Unfortunately, this is too often the central banker's solution to most economic problems.

## Don't Take It to the Bank

Financial institutions—particularly banks—face unique challenges in reviewing and repairing their computers. First, "information systems are often complex and have developed over many years through a variety of computer languages and hardware platforms."[23] Second, because these systems are so transaction intensive, they are exceedingly large. For example, Citicorp, the nation's second largest bank, has a staggering four hundred million lines of code to correct. This is *four times* as much code as the IRS has to correct. And these systems are interdependent in a way that defies the imagination.

> Financial institutions are extremely dependent on one another as well as common service providers for the interchange of electronic commerce.... The retail consumer is dependent on the use of credit and debit card

> conveniences offered internationally through suppliers such as Visa, MasterCard, and American Express which have extensive electronic networks linking a transaction from its point of sale to the consumer's financial institution. The corporate customer, heavily dependent on Electronic Data Interchange (EDI), Wire Transfers, and Letters of Credit, uses the nation's financial institutions as their financial intermediaries. The increasing globalization of the business enterprise radiates these dependencies beyond our borders to include financial institutions worldwide. *It should be clear from these examples that there are significant risks associated with such tightly woven interdependencies* [emphasis added].[24]

### A Late Start

Despite the risks, as of March 1997 "only 40 percent of U.S. banks had begun an earnest assessment of their Year 2000 impact." And even some of those "are now recognizing that they are late in commencing Year 2000 corrective work and may not have sufficient personnel and other resources to correct 100 percent of their computer systems by January 1, 2000."[25]

Fixing these financial institutions' computers will not be inexpensive. One consulting group has estimated that correcting the Y2K problem in U.S. commercial banks will run at least $7.2 billion. Add to this $4 billion to repair computers in the securities industry.[26] These estimates do not take into account

> ...the added potential cost to the financial services industry of productivity losses resulting from computer shutdown due to the Year 2000 problem. One study has estimated that U.S. securities firms each typically suffer 6.9 on-line system failures per year, which collectively resulted in $3.4 billion in productivity losses in 1992.[27]

## Some Will and Some Won't

The larger banks have been working on the Year 2000 Problem for some time. BankBoston is generally regarded as being the banking industry's leader in aggressive Y2K repairs. The company manages $65 billion in assets and is ranked number fifteen in the United States with 475 branches and 275 offices located in twenty-four countries around the world.[28] It has fifty thousand lines of code in about 273 different applications.[29] It began its Millennium project in the spring of 1995.

Initially, the bank thought it could turn the whole project over to an outside consulting team. But then, according to Mike Lezenski, the company's chief information officer, "What we found was terrifying."[30]

> Fixing this particular problem seemed simple. Then, last year [1996], BankBoston acquired BayBanks, a local rival. BayBanks stored its data about certificates of deposit in a different way. When BankBoston integrated the two systems, *a rash of computer failures followed* [emphasis added]. It had to solve that particular millennium problem all over again.[31]

BankBoston says that it anticipates spending "tens of millions of dollars" on the problem by the end of 1999. As Lezenski points out, "For an institution that earned $650 million after tax last year, that is no insignificant sum."[32] Nevertheless, if any financial institution is likely to finish its Y2K project on time, it is BankBoston. Other large banks may not be so fortunate.

Chase Manhattan Bank—the nation's largest with $336 billion in assets—started working on its Year 2000 Problem in 1995 when it realized that its $1 trillion-a-day-plus transaction processing system was at risk. Steve Sheinheit, senior vice president, corporate systems and architecture at Chase, says:

> ...we're pushing between one and two trillion dollars a night. Millions of transactions go to make that up. You can't handle these things manually anymore. We are completely reliant on technology to make the business work.[33]

If the business is this dependent on the computers to process the volume of transactions it does, then there really is no fallback position. As Sheinheit explains, "That's why, rather than thinking in terms of contingencies, we think in terms of guaranteeing that it's done early enough that we're sure it's fixed."[34] But this is no small task at Chase. The company has 200 million lines of code running in 1,500 applications on more than 60,000 desktops, 100 midrange computers, and scores of mainframes.[35] The company expects to spend from $200 million to $250 million on its Y2K project over a three-year period.[36] The company is attacking the problem with the help of outside consulting firms and some eight hundred programmers on the Chase staff.[37] It plans to add several hundred more programmers to the bank's payroll in the next two years—assuming it can find them.

Finishing a job this big is not going to be easy. The Social Security Administration (SSA) got started six years earlier than Chase, had a project one-sixth the size, and half as many programmers, and is still not finished. Nevertheless, Chase is continuing to chant the by-now-familiar mantra: "The plan calls for many mission-critical applications to be converted this year [1997], with the rest finished in 1998—leaving an entire year for testing."[38] Unfortunately, the odds are against them. As I pointed out earlier, according to Standish Group International, 84 percent of all corporate software development projects are late. Why should we think Chase will be an exception, particularly when this project is likely to be far larger and more complex than anything the bank has *ever* attempted before? To quote an old slogan: "I wouldn't bank on it."

Citicorp, the nation's second largest bank, has an even bigger job. The company has four hundred million lines of code to review and correct. To give you a sense of perspective, this is twice as many lines of code as Chase Manhattan, four times as many as the IRS, and *more than thirteen times* as many as the Social Security Administration. Citicorp estimates that between 5 percent and 10 percent of the code will need to be *repaired*—that's as much or more code than the Social Security Administration had to *review!* Like Chase, they got started in 1995. It is hard to imagine Citicorp completing this project in time, given the magnitude of the problem.

**The failure of only *5 to 10 percent* of the world banks' payment systems could create a global liquidity lock-up.**

But, if anyone is going to make it in the banking industry, it is going to be the larger banks. They have more resources and they got started early compared to their smaller counterparts. The small- and medium-size banks are lagging far, far behind.

In a survey conducted in the summer of 1997 of banks with assets between $50 million and $1 billion (medium-size banks), 33 percent of the CEOs responded that they are "not at all prepared" for the Year 2000 Problem.[39] Worse, 88 percent said they had no documented plan for tackling the Year 2000 Problem, and 95 percent said they did not even have a budget to correct the Year 2000 Problem![40] By the first week in September 1997, another survey was done, this time by the American Bankers Association (ABA). Of those surveyed, 17 percent said they were still in the awareness stage (i.e., they have not begun their Year 2000 projects). Another 63 percent said they were still in the assessment stage. Only 20 percent had actually started making repairs. Commenting on the survey, Howard Amer, assistant director of the division of banking supervision and regulation at the board of governors of the Federal Reserve System, said, "a significant portion are behind the curve, and that is of great concern to us."[41] And well it should be, given the interdependencies within the banking industry. Unless and until each part is brought into line, the whole system is at risk.

## Where Credit Is Due

One of the first places consumers began encountering the Millennium Bug was in credit card expiration dates. As soon as banks began issuing cards with a "00" expiration, the problems began. Either the credit card company's computers thought the card was already expired (having been issued in 1900) or rejected the date altogether. As a result, point-of-sale systems locked up and cardholders were denied credit. The first Year 2000 lawsuit was over just this issue.

Visa International has spent more than four years helping to prepare the credit card industry for the Year 2000. MasterCard has spent three.[42] The risk is so big for these two companies that, contrary to their competitive posture, they have actually been exchanging information.[43]

In October 1996 Visa instructed its member banks to refrain from issuing cards with Year 2000 expiration dates.[44] MasterCard followed suit.[45] Both companies were set to issue cards in October 1997 with expiration dates of 2000.

But credit card companies rely on some thirteen million point-of-sale terminals to process purchase approvals,[46] and millions of these are not yet compliant. As a result, as of this writing, both companies have been forced to delay their plans to introduce new cards.

Once again, this shows how interdependent these systems are and why becoming compliant is just not enough. Until a company's vendors, service providers, and partners are compliant, the job is not done and the company is still at risk.

The expiration date problem is only one of many facing the credit card industry. Once Visa is finally able to issue cards that have an expiration date of 2000, it doesn't mean its Y2K problem is solved.

> [Visa's people] haven't stated that their systems will process transactions made after the Year 2000. They don't promise that their systems will accept batches of transactions which include pre and post Year 2000 charges [as will

> be necessary to process monthly statements]. They don't know if card re-issue runs made after the Year 2000 will renew cards. They don't know if interest charges and fees will be calculated correctly during the 1999 to 2000 transition. They don't know if their computer systems will work at all. All this must be tested and re-tested, and they haven't said that they've done this.... The well-publicized credit card expiration date problem is a trivial problem compared to the others.[47]

In other words, credit card companies are basically in the same position as the large banks. They have made a good start, but they still have a lot of work to do.

## Around the World

As it relates to the Y2K Crisis, the banking problem extends far beyond the borders of America. It's really a global problem. And unfortunately, banks in other countries are even further behind. Testifying before Congress, Larry Martin, president of Data Dimensions, warned:

> The lack of concern and action on the part of the international banking community is particularly distressing. The ability of international banks to operate effectively after the Year 2000 is, in our estimate, *seriously in question.*[48]

As noted, part of the problem is that European banks are already in the process of rewriting all their software in order to handle the conversion to the common Euro currency late in 1999. This by itself is a *massive* project. Experts estimate that the Euro conversion will cost about $100 billion worldwide.[49] (Banks in non-European countries will also have to be able to accommodate the Euro and will therefore require recoding.) Not wanting to face another gargantuan project, European bankers have, so far, simply ignored the

Year 2000 Problem. Many are only now realizing that they have a problem and that they do not have the resources to tackle both jobs at the same time. Tom McCallum, director of the Scottish Software Federation, urged the European Commission to delay the introduction of the Euro by three years:

> There are currently 33,000 unfilled IT [Information Technology] jobs in the UK, with perhaps 10 percent of these in Scotland. The shortfall stems from the strain placed on the industry by the millennium time bomb crisis, coupled with general industry growth. Add the pressures of changing computer systems to cope with the introduction of the Euro, and it's clear the industry doesn't have enough resources to cope.[50]

Problems in other areas of the world could have a severe impact on the U.S. banking system. Perhaps the biggest threat comes from Japan, because that country is so heavily invested in the United States. At this writing, Japan's Kyodo News Agency reports that Japan is just beginning to deal with the Year 2000 Problem. No specific timelines or action plans have been announced.[51] Latin America is even further behind. In early October 1997 Jim Cassell of the Gartner Group made a presentation of the Year 2000 Problem to one hundred technology executives from Latin America. They responded in "shock." Most are not upgrading their computers because they simply do not have the resources.[52] Not only have they not completed their assessments, there seems to be very little awareness.

## Conclusion

Most of us grew up hearing stories from our parents or grandparents about bank runs during the Great Depression. The Millennium Bug could have a similar impact on our lives. As Robert Lau, managing consultant at PA Consulting in Hong Kong, warned in an interview with Reuters News Service:

> It is our prediction that it will only take 5 to 10 percent of the world banks' payment systems to not work on that one day [January 1, 2000] to create a global liquidity lock-up. I don't think the markets have quite grasped the implications of what will happen if the entire system goes down.[53]

# Chapter Six

## The Tax Man Cometh—*Not!*

### *The Impact of the Year 2000 Computer Crisis on Federal, State, and Local Governments*

> **Those who govern, having much business on their hands, do not generally like to take the trouble of considering and carrying into execution new projects. The best public measures are therefore seldom adopted from previous wisdom, but forced by the occasion.**
>
> —Benjamin Franklin

Even when government computers are supposedly working, they can wreak havoc. I recently sent yet another letter to the IRS, attempting to explain why I wasn't responsible for a certain tax liability dating back to 1994. My partner and I own a business that happens to use our last names as the company name. In 1994 a certain corporate customer paid us for some work we had performed. But rather than making the check out to the company, the accounting department made it out to me personally and reported it as a charge to my social security account. (I used to be an employee at this company, which probably explains how they got access to this tax identification number.) Evidently, my secretary deposited it to our corporate account, not noticing that the check was made out to me *personally*. And the bank didn't care either.

After the first of the year, I received from the customer a Form

1099, indicating the amount paid. I turned it over to my accountant to deal with. But by the time he processed my tax return, the customer was either unwilling or unable to cancel the 1099. Consequently, we included it in the tax return and attached a note explaining what had happened, as well as the fact that I had never had access to the money personally, and that it had been deposited directly into our corporate account.

**Nearly 71 percent of the federal government's "mission-critical" systems must be replaced or repaired.**

Early in 1996 I received my first notice from the IRS, stating that they had found unreported income for the 1994 tax year and were charging me approximately 30 percent of the amount in question—which was several thousand dollars. My tax accountant wrote them a polite letter, over my signature, explaining exactly what had happened. We heard nothing for approximately six months. Then I received a second letter, reprimanding me for not responding to the first letter, and making certain ominous threats if I didn't immediately send them a check. There was no mention of the first letter.

So, once again, we sent them a letter, which included a copy of the first one. And again, about six months passed without any response. Then, just as before, I received a letter that was even more threatening than the last. And again, they chastised me for not responding to their previous notices and promised swift action if I didn't comply and send them a check for the full amount due. And I sent them yet another letter with copies of the previous two. At this writing, the matter is still unresolved.

Evidently, I am not alone in my experience. In September 1997 Senator William V. Roth, Jr., chairman of the Senate's Finance Committee, held hearings in Washington, D.C., regarding alleged IRS abuses. He charged that within the IRS "a subculture of fear and intimidation has been allowed to flourish."[1] The agency issues or conducts roughly four million liens, levies, and seizures each year,[2] which have given rise to plenty of horror stories. The committee spent three days hearing about abuses from expert witnesses, four aggrieved taxpayers, four former IRS employees, and seven current IRS employees,[3] who testified anonymously behind a white screen in order to protect their identity and ward off any retaliation from agency superiors.

During these sessions, taxpayers recounted with tears "years-long nightmares at the hands of the IRS."[4] These included a Delaware businessman who paid $50,000 in taxes that the IRS later admitted he didn't owe and a California woman who fought the IRS for seventeen years because it illegally confiscated $11,000 of her money. A Senate finance staff member said that "the examples cited were merely the tip of the iceberg."[5] One explanation for the horror stories was the IRS's highly publicized computer troubles. Perhaps you could add your own experience with the IRS to this section. In any event, these kinds of inconveniences, abuses, and outright harassment are happening when the government's computers are supposedly *working*. What will happen when they shut down or begin spewing out bad data on or before January 1, 2000?

## Tweedledee and Tweedledum

The federal government has a big Year 2000 Problem. The Defense Department (DoD) has in excess of one billion lines of code to review and repair.[6] The IRS has more than one hundred million lines.[7] International Data Corporation, in a study done for the federal government, reported that 83 percent of the government's mainframe sites had "moderate or high degrees of date sensitivity for mainframe-based applications. Only 3 percent reported no date sensitivity."[8]

Estimates on the total cost to make the federal government's computers Y2K–compliant range from $3.8 billion to $30 billion.[9] Perhaps the worst problem, however, is that, overall, the government is running seriously behind schedule. According to Congressman Stephen Horn, "The good news is that every federal government agency knows there is a problem. The bad news is that only a few of them have specific, realistic plans to solve the problem."[10]

Only 21 percent of the federal government's mission-critical systems are reported as Y2K–compliant. An additional 8 percent will be retired or scrapped. This means that of the 7,649 systems that the various agencies have classified as "mission-critical," nearly 71 percent must be replaced or repaired.[11] Fifteen of the twenty-four agencies do not plan to finish their Y2K projects until November or December of 1999.[12] That leaves them with only *one or two months* to test these very complex and extensive changes to their systems! Since most experts agree that 40 percent to 60 percent of the project's time should be spent in testing, this seems to be a grave and reckless course of action.

**A congressional subcommittee gave less than one-fifth of government agencies acceptable grades for Y2K repairs.**

The Office of Management and Budget (OMB) declared June 1, 1997, as a deadline for all federal agencies to complete their preliminary assessment phase. Six agencies failed to meet the deadline: Defense, Transportation, Treasury (including the IRS), Veterans Affairs, the Agency for International Development, and the Nuclear Regulatory Commission.[13] This is particularly troublesome when you consider that these six entities will likely represent about 70 percent of the federal government's total Y2K costs[14] and the "assessment phase" is generally considered to be only 1 percent of the total work involved in a Year 2000 project. "I see a lot of denial and procrastination," said Nancy Peters, director of business development for Software AG Federal Systems, a company in Reston, Virginia, that consults with government agencies. "It can take longer to fix things than they think."[15] Thomas D. Oleson of International Data Corporation, a Year 2000 consulting firm, agrees: the federal government is "way behind the eight ball." Fixing it "is nearing the point of impossibility."[16] The Gartner Group has gone so far as to say that "about half of all government agencies in North America won't solve the year 2000 problem in time so you have to plan for failure."[17]

Like everything in Washington, it is hard to get at the truth because everything has political consequences. Suffice it to say, there is a significant amount of "spin doctoring" going on about the size of the problem, what it's going to cost to fix it, and whether the projects are on schedule. Worse, apart from the work being done by Congressman Horn's Subcommittee on Government Management, Information, and Technology, there seems to be a good deal of silence about the issue:

> "There is a weird and ominous silence," said Bert Concklin, president of the Professional Services Council, a Vienna [Virginia]-based industry association. "The government is not talking because the government does not know what to do."[18]

And this silence will be *deadly* if the federal government is not fully compliant by January 1, 2000.

> Unless this problem is resolved ahead of time, widespread operational and financial impacts could affect federal, state, and local governments; foreign governments; and private sector organizations worldwide. At the federal level, scenarios like these are possible:
>
> - The IRS's tax systems could be unable to process returns, which in turn would jeopardize the collection of revenue and the entire tax processing system.
> - Payments to veterans with service-connected disabilities could be severely delayed because Veteran's Affairs' compensation and pension system either halts or produces checks that are so erroneous that the system must be shut down and the checks processed manually.
> - The Social Security Administration's disability insurance process could experience major disruptions because the interface with various state systems

fails, thereby causing delays and interruptions in disability payments to citizens.

- Federal systems used to track student education loans could produce erroneous information on loan status, such as indicating that an unpaid loan had been satisfied.[19]

### *The White House*

With a problem of this magnitude—especially when the consequences are potentially catastrophic—you would expect the president to be taking more leadership. Congresswoman Constance Morella (R-Maryland) has said, "Maybe we need more reality—maybe we need a year 2000 czar, someone in charge of this."[20] Congressman Horn has said he thinks President Clinton should use the "bully pulpit" of the presidency to "galvanize the government and the nation about the urgency of the Y2K problem."[21] "The president," he continued, "needs to appoint an individual who will step up to the plate and directly address the nation's computer problem." And he went on, "The American people deserve nothing less."[22] But as of this writing, no such leadership has been forthcoming from the White House.

In a speech at the "The White House Millennium Event" in August 1997, the president made the following promise:

> Now, as the millennium turns, as we have seen from countless reports, so do all the dates on our computers. Experts are concerned that many of our information systems will not differentiate between dates in the twentieth and the twenty-first century. I want to assure the American people that the federal government, in cooperation with state and local government and the private sector, is taking steps to prevent any interruption of government services that rely on the proper functioning of federal computer systems. We can't have the American people

> looking into a new century and a new millennium with their computers—the very symbol of modernity and the modern age—holding them back, and we're *determined* to see that it doesn't happen [emphasis added].[23]

Determination alone won't solve the problem. The deadline is fixed into millions of lines of computer code. He cannot wave a magic wand and produce hundreds of thousands of additional COBOL-skilled programmers needed to get every mainframe in the country Y2K–compliant. This problem *will* come to light. There is a judgment day coming, and we know exactly when it will occur: January 1, 2000.

The ironic thing about the president's lack of leadership is that his administration has boasted about its technological savvy. When his administration came into office, the White House IBM-compatible PCs weren't good enough, so they ripped them out and replaced them with Macintosh computers. The vice president wrote a book about the Information Superhighway and went on the talk show circuit discussing how the Internet would change our lives. Unfortunately for Clinton and Gore, history will judge them with regard to how they have handled—or mishandled—the Year 2000 Computer Crisis. It is likely that Al Gore will spend the entire 2000 campaign explaining to the media and the American people why his administration didn't have the foresight to address this problem when it could still be solved. And, just as Herbert Hoover's name is synonymous with the Stock Market Crash of 1929, so Bill Clinton's name will become synonymous with the Computer Crash of 2000. Everything else will be swept away and forgotten.

## Making the Grade

As noted in Chapter 4, in September 1997 Congressman Stephen Horn, a former college professor, released his second annual "report card" on the government's Year 2000 progress. "When it comes to preparing for the test of the century, Uncle Sam has shown he is not a very good student."[24] Here's how the report card looked:

| | Agency | 1996 | 1997 |
|---|---|---|---|
| Agriculture | Department of Agriculture | D | D- |
| AID | Agency for International Development | A | F |
| Commerce | Department of Commerce | D | D |
| DOD | Department of Defense | C | C- |
| DOE | Department of Energy | F | D |
| DOT | Department of Transportation | F | F |
| Education | Department of Education | B | F |
| EPA | Environmental Protection Agency | D | C |
| FEMA | Federal Emergency Management Agency | F | C |
| GSA | General Services Administration | D | B |
| HHS | Department of Health and Human Services | D | B- |
| HUD | Department of Housing and Urban Development | D | C |
| Interior | Department of the Interior | D | C |
| Justice | Department of Justice | D | D |
| Labor | Department of Labor | F | C |
| NASA | National Aeronautics and Space Administration | D | D- |
| NRC | Nuclear Regulatory Commission | B | D |
| NSF | National Science Foundation | C | B |
| OPM | Office of Personnel Management | A | D |
| SBA | Small Business Administration | A | B |
| SSA | Social Security Administration | A | A[25] |
| State | Department of State | B | C |
| Treasury | Department of Treasury | C | D- |
| VA | Department of Veterans Affairs | D | C |

According to Congressman Horn, "Less than one-fifth of these government agencies have acceptable grades for the year 2000 computer problem.... Some agencies received worse grades than last year because they made little progress as they kept finding more and more computer programs requiring modification."[26]

By December 1997 things had become even worse. Horn's subcommittee warned that fourteen of the above federal agencies will not be successful in repairing their mission-critical applications prior to January 1, 2000.[27] Based on current rates of progress, these agencies will not complete their Year 2000 Projects until:

| | |
|---|---|
| 2019: | Department of Energy |
| 2019: | Department of Labor |
| 2012: | Department of Defense |
| 2010: | Department of Transportation |
| 2010: | Office of Personnel Management |
| 2005: | Department of Agriculture |
| 2004: | Department of Treasury |
| 2002: | General Services Administration |
| 2001: | Department of Health and Human Services |
| 2001: | Department of Justice |
| Mid-2000: | Department of Education |
| Mid-2000: | Agency for International Development |
| Mid-2000: | Federal Emergency Management Agency |
| Early 2000: | National Aeronautics and Space Administration |

In a report dated February 6, 1997, Sally Katzen, administrator of the OMB's Office of Information and Regulatory Affairs, said that the Year 2000 Problem would cost the federal government $2.3 billion.[28] By May 15, 1997, her estimate rose to $2.8 billion. As noted in Chapter 2, the estimate escalated a few months later to $3.8 billion—a 65 percent increase over the original projection. Budgets were not the only thing that went up. Katzen increased the number of mission-critical systems by nearly a thousand, from 7,649 to 8,562. And at the

OMB itself, things were getting worse, not better. In June 1997 the OMB reported that 270 of its thousands of computer systems had been repaired. But in September 1997, when Ms. Katzen was asked to explain why more than half of the computers that were supposed to be fixed actually weren't, she said, "I will have to check on that."[29] Not too reassuring, given that she is the person in charge.

### *National Institute of Standards and Technology*

Federal computers interface with myriad other federal computers, as well as state and local agency computers. They even share data with scores of businesses in the private sector. Unfortunately, there is no agreed upon format for the representation of dates across these various entities.

**The IRS is in deep, deep trouble; it won't even come close to fixing its Year 2000 problems.**

The National Institute of Standards and Technology (NIST) has adopted a standard of an eight-digit format represented as CCYYMMDD, where "CC" is a two-digit representation for the century, "YY" is a two-digit representation for the year, "MM" is a two-digit representation for the month, and "DD" is a two-digit representation for the day. So, for example, January 1, 2000, would be formatted as 20000101. The NIST, however, can only *highly recommend* this standard; it cannot enforce it.

As a result, the SSA has adopted its own "standard." It, too, has an eight-digit format, but it is different from the NIST's. It uses the following format: MMDDCCYY. So, for example, January 1, 2000, would be formatted as 01012000. The century and the year digits come at the end of the data rather than at the beginning. Imagine what happens when a computer expecting the date to be represented in one format receives data from another supposedly compliant computer in a different format. In this particular case, the SSA's computer would interpret a date in the NIST format as something radically different: January 1, 2000, suddenly becomes the "00" day in the twentieth month of the year 101. (If this isn't confusing enough, the British typically represent their dates as DDMMCCYY, with the day and month reversed from our approach.)[30]

As Dr. Gary North aptly observed:

> Does anyone seriously think that there will not be chaos in the year 2000 when standards are this confusing and not even enforceable? If all the government can do is "highly recommend" a standard, then there is no standard. If there is no standard, there will be chaos. Now multiply this across every government, bank, and computer-driven system on earth.[31]

## Three and a Half Blind Mice

### *Treasury Department*

The U.S. Treasury represents "the crossroads of financial activity for the federal government."[32] It pumps money in and out of various sectors of the economy, keeping everything running smoothly. It does this through the use of large, complex computer systems:

- The Treasury collects $1.4 trillion annually through IRS, customs, and ATF, representing over 97 percent of the total federal revenues. Last year, 250 million returns were processed.

- The Treasury Financial Management Service (FMS) oversees a daily cash flow in excess of $10 billion and issues over 800 million payments totaling over $1 trillion each year for all executive agencies.

- The Customs Service collects over $20 billion in duties, taxes, and fees. They assist in the administration and enforcement of some 400 provisions of the law on behalf of more than 40 government agencies and process 456 million persons and 127 million conveyances a year.

- Public Debt auctions $2 trillion [in] marketable Treasury securities annually. They issue and redeem 150 million savings bonds annually, and they account for the $4.9 trillion federal debt and over $300 billion in annual interest charges.[33]

The Treasury has a huge inventory of legacy systems with homegrown routines adapted for specific agency requirements. Assistant Secretary of the Treasury George Muñoz told Congress that the software is "monstrously complex and run[s] on outdated hardware."[34] He concludes, "Neither the government nor industry has ever attacked a computer systems problem this massive or pervasive."[35]

Now add to this enormous Y2K project the Treasury Department's initiative to move to a completely "checkless system" by December 31, 1998. The Treasury wants to eliminate the flow of paper checks in and out of its offices and institute a fully computerized, electronic transfer system.

> A checkless U.S. Treasury will affect tens of millions of individuals who receive government payments or in-kind benefits, millions of businesses that withhold taxes from their employees, and the small and large banks that service all of the above. An annual flow of a billion electronic payments worth a trillion and a half dollars—one-fifth the value of the gross domestic product—will speed the economy's transition to a new era of paperless transactions, digital cash, and "wallets" embedded in plastic cards.[36]

Under this program, all federal payments to individuals or businesses will be made electronically; paper food stamps will be replaced by debit cards; and virtually all businesses will be required to pay their taxes electronically.

Imagine what must be involved in making this transition. It is an enormous project. Is it any wonder that the Treasury Department received a grade of D-minus on its last Y2K report card?

### *Internal Revenue Service*

The Internal Revenue Service (IRS) is, of course, but one department within the Treasury Department. But it is one *very* large department. You might recall that in early 1997 the agency publicly admitted that its eleven-year program to integrate all of its computers had failed. As a result, the government had to write off more than $1 billion.

**Most state governments are in worse shape than the federal government.**

The IRS knows it is behind the eight ball. In June 1997 the agency told Congress it needed an additional $258 million to make its computers century–date compliant. This was up from a previous request of $84 million. Susan Marshall, who studied the issue for Federal Sources, Incorporated, of McLean, Virginia, said she is not surprised: "They found out that every single platform—all IRS applications and databases—is in danger of non-compliance." She concluded, "This is an iterative process. Their costs are going to escalate as each year passes."[37] They escalated well before the year passed. In September, three months later, the IRS asked for $[illegible] million,[38] conceding that simply repairing some code wouldn't fix the problem. Instead, entirely new software is needed for some applications, which in turn will require purchasing new hardware.

Moreover, the IRS doesn't have enough programmers to do the work. But, on the other hand, hiring outside programmers could also be a problem. A posting on one of the Internet newsgroups for people who do Y2K repairs had this story:

> Another problem that has not been widely addressed in public yet is the fact that many of the programmers needed for the Y2K fix feel absolutely zero loyalty to the system they are serving. They have long been disrespected

by an administrative culture that viewed them as expendable nerds doing pedestrian technical tasks, and expended they were when it came time for corporate restructuring and downsizing. Nor have they ever gotten any breaks from tax-collectors, with more of their income going to the government instead of into their own pockets. With your typical codehead being treated like an unwashed techno-serf over the past twenty years, should it be any surprise when they decide that the Y2K is not so much a problem as it is an opportunity to screw a bunch of technophobic executives, lawyers, bureaucrats, and other parasitic life-forms?

Now mind you, I'm not advocating that anyone sabotage their employer's code; I'm just noting that there is a volatile combination of wounded pride and subversive libertarian sentiments among programmers that make it dangerous for management to cavalierly hire a bunch of strangers to come in to deal with their Y2K crisis for them (assuming, of course, they can find enough technical competence in the first place). With men of intelligence having been objects of contempt and government extortion for so long, does anyone really think they will be eager to sustain an uninterrupted flow of funds to the Internal Revenue Service and kiss up to management?

Of course, we also have to consider that even the most servile order-obeying type will think twice about finishing the project he is working on. Once he realizes that he has a big enough pile of money to take care of his needs, he won't stick around major urban centers waiting for doomsday to strike even if his employers offer him $300 per hour. What good is putting more paper money into a bank account when most of the banks are going to turn illiquid in the near future? Anyone with any sense at all will convert his assets to gold and useful survival items and, if he can afford it, head for the hills. Indeed, a friend

> of mine who owns a coin-shop in the San Francisco Bay Area reported to me that he already has codeheads coming in to buy gold from him. One of these customers was an employee of a major west-coast electric utility. Do you begin to see the picture yet?[39]

The consequences of the IRS not meeting the Year 2000 deadline are enormous. We may dislike the IRS and the notion of paying taxes, but what's the alternative?

### *Social Security Administration*

Of all the federal agencies and departments, the SSA is the one that started early and has worked hard. In 1989 the SSA knew it had a problem and began taking a full inventory of its systems and developing an assessment of the work that needed to be done. It determined that it had approximately thirty million lines of code to review and repair. Because its applications are so date-sensitive, it determined that "20 percent of the lines of code would be affected by the millennium change."[40] It began the actual renovation process in 1991, planning to be finished by December 31, 1998, in order to have a full year of testing. As mentioned, it assigned four hundred full-time programmers to the project. By June 1996 the agency reported that it had completed the work on six million lines of code.[41]

Now stop and think about this for a moment, because it has enormous implications for every other agency and private enterprise working on a Year 2000 project.

- It took the SSA *two full years* to complete the inventory and assessment phase before the actual renovations could begin. As I write, there are some government agencies that still have not completed even this initial phase. What *reasonable* chance do they have of finishing in time?

- It took the SSA five full years to fix six million lines of code—20 percent of the project. Some government agencies—particularly the IRS and the DoD—have far more code and got started years later. What *reasonable* chance do they have of finishing?

- The SSA assigned four hundred programmers to work on the project full-time. Many government agencies and private sector companies have far fewer resources. I personally know of one multi-billion–dollar, publicly held company that has still not completed its assessment phase. The chief information officer hasn't yet received the funding to put *even one person* on the project full-time! Other companies find themselves in similar circumstances. What *reasonable* chance do they have of finishing?

I know of no other entity on earth that has more experience in Y2K repairs than the SSA. By its own admission, the work is arduous, and other organizations should take note:

> Although the problem is easy to describe, it is very difficult to solve for a number of reasons, and can be likened to looking for a needle in a haystack. The visual image of looking through hay is not difficult to conjure up, but the painstaking execution of the solution is awesome. The sheer size of the problem is the first of these. Dates are everywhere, which means that all program code must be examined to determine if change is necessary. Most large corporations and government agencies have thousands of programs containing millions of lines of code.[42]

The agency has a lot at stake. Kathleen M. Adams, coordinator for the agency's Year 2000 project, says, "We send out 43 million checks each month, and we have to have as close to zero defects as we can.

Even with a 1 percent error rate, we'd have 430,000 people calling in or calling our district offices; so we do everything we can to avoid risk in our core functions."[43]

In November 1997 the SSA admitted that it was not as far along as it had previously announced. Rather than having thirty million lines of code to review and repair in its main systems, it actually had thirty-four million. And, worse, there were an additional thirty-three million lines of code in its state offices that it had completely overlooked.[44]

### *Medicare*

Some thirty-eight million people are covered by Medicare today.[45] By the year 2000, Medicare is expected to process over one billion claims per year. It will pay out over $288 billion in benefits.[46] Today, seventy private contractors manage the Medicare program at forty-five different sites throughout the country.[47] The Feds were in the process of implementing a new $1 billion computer system called the Medicare Transaction System when they became aware of the Year 2000 Problem.

On September 15, 1997, the government cancelled the new computer system:

> The Clinton administration has terminated the contract for a vast new Medicare computer system that had been promoted as a way to speed payment of claims, improve customer service, and combat fraud in Medicare, the United States' largest health-insurance program.... In a letter to GTE, Bartlett Smetana, a contract officer at the Department of Health and Human Services, ordered the company to "stop all work, make no further shipments, place no further orders, and terminate all subcontracts."[48]

When asked about the issue, "Medicare officials said... they planned to try a more gradual approach to overhauling their computer systems."[49] In other words, it's back to the drawing board.

Unfortunately, at this late date, Medicare does not have time for anything "gradual." If they don't get their computers compliant, then there is the distinct possibility that they could end up sending out millions of bad checks in the year 2000. And forget about using a manual system as a backup. Processing one billion claims would require that over four million checks be written by hand every single day the government is open for business.[50] This would take a veritable army of check-writers, not to mention the sea of people required to process the claims. And, oh, by the way, with the computers down or unreliable, how will these people look up the information they need to *approve* the claims?

## Meanwhile, Back at the Ranch

After reading the above information on the federal government, it's probably difficult to imagine that the situation could be worse elsewhere. Perhaps you're thinking, *I'm not surprised the federal government is so screwed up, but surely the states—my state!—are on top of this problem.* Well, I hate to be the bearer of more bad news, but it's likely your home state is in *even worse shape* than the federal government. And, unfortunately, your state does not have the federal government's resources—it can't simply print more money if it gets in a jam. And make no mistake about it: *Y2K repair costs are going to cost the states a fortune.*

Capers Jones, in his often-quoted white paper on the Year 2000 Problem, attempts to come up with a state-by-state cost estimate. These figures are listed in Table 6.1.

**Table 6.1:**
**Software Repairs by State for the United States[51]**

| State | Amount |
|---|---|
| California | $ 9,552,960,000 |
| New York | $ 6,036,120,000 |
| Texas | $ 5,142,800,000 |
| Illinois | $ 3,741,640,000 |

| | | |
|---|---|---|
| Florida | $ | 3,666,384,000 |
| Pennsylvania | $ | 3,588,920,000 |
| Ohio | $ | 3,283,480,000 |
| Michigan | $ | 2,672,600,000 |
| New Jersey | $ | 2,624,400,000 |
| Massachusetts | $ | 2,143,260,000 |
| North Carolina | $ | 2,009,280,000 |
| Virginia | $ | 1,839,264,000 |
| Georgia | $ | 1,811,475,000 |
| District of Columbia | $ | 1,687,888,000 |
| Maryland | $ | 1,469,664,000 |
| Indiana | $ | 1,460,800,000 |
| Washington | $ | 1,445,850,000 |
| Wisconsin | $ | 1,374,480,000 |
| Tennessee | $ | 1,369,666,000 |
| Minnesota | $ | 1,271,394,000 |
| Missouri | $ | 1,248,486,000 |
| Alabama | $ | 1,207,040,000 |
| Louisiana | $ | 1,179,816,000 |
| Connecticut | $ | 1,094,715,000 |
| Kentucky | $ | 1,038,644,800 |
| Oregon | $ | 1,014,768,000 |
| Colorado | $ | 1,012,690,000 |
| Arizona | $ | 1,011,770,000 |
| South Carolina | $ | 916,320,000 |
| Oklahoma | $ | 832,324,000 |
| Iowa | $ | 741,854,000 |
| Mississippi | $ | 697,164,000 |
| Kansas | $ | 662,240,400 |
| Arkansas | $ | 650,686,400 |
| New Hampshire | $ | 483,000,000 |
| West Virginia | $ | 455,838,000 |
| Utah | $ | 439,070,000 |
| Nebraska | $ | 416,162,000 |
| New Mexico | $ | 398,068,000 |

| | | |
|---|---|---|
| Hawaii | $ | 337,464,000 |
| Maine | $ | 318,628,800 |
| Rhode Island | $ | 284,325,000 |
| Idaho | $ | 271,410,000 |
| Montana | $ | 208,081,000 |
| Nevada | $ | 208,081,000 |
| Delaware | $ | 196,627,000 |
| South Dakota | $ | 178,760,000 |
| Alaska | $ | 170,694,000 |
| North Dakota | $ | 159,408,000 |
| Vermont | $ | 154,560,000 |
| Wyoming | $ | 136,752,000 |
| **United States Total** | **$75,337,768,800**[52] | |

The biggest challenge many states face in making their computers Year 2000–compliant is securing the necessary funding. State legislatures must first be convinced of the necessity of making the repairs. "Part of the problem is making people believe that [the Year 2000 Problem] is real," says Camaron Thomas, director of the New York governor's task force on information resource management and the state's chief information officer. "The public has become incredibly dependent on these systems, and it's part of our responsibility to make sure they work."[53]

This job is particularly difficult, given that *there will be zero return on investment*—no new programs, no hoped-for efficiencies, no improved services—just the ability to stay in business after January 1, 2000. Steve Kolodney, CIO of Washington State and head of the National Association of State Information Resource Executives' (NASIRE) Year 2000 working group, says, "This is a tough call politically, because after you spend the money [on Year 2000 fixes], all you've got is what you had before. It's a hard sell."[54]

The North Carolina legislature, for example, has allocated only $7.7 million to the state's Y2K project, although State Controller Ed Renfrow now estimates that it will cost $333.5 million.

Governor Jim Guy Hunt has proposed spending $50 million over two years. He is not willing to ask for more until he is convinced that Renfrow's numbers are reliable.[55]

There is an enormous risk to the public if the states do not get their computers compliant in time. As Pennsylvania's Lieutenant Governor Mark Schweiker has observed, "This is more than an information technology problem. It's a matter of huge public interest. States should be prepared for tremendous economic losses if they fail to make fixes."[56]

Unfortunately, many states are off to a slow start. According to a survey conducted by NASIRE in March 1997, only thirteen of forty-four CIOs said their states were in the implementation or testing phase of Year 2000 repairs. "Twenty respondents [nearly half!] didn't know how many lines of code they needed to convert; eleven hadn't set a target completion date for conversion; and twenty didn't have an estimate on how much year-2000 fixes would cost." At this writing, seven states are claiming compliance: Arkansas, California, Georgia, Illinois, Missouri, Oklahoma, and Wyoming.[57] Please note: these claims have not been independently verified.

## Conclusion

Many government officials are pessimistic—and even fearful about the government's chances of repairing its computers in time. In early 1997 a "Year 2000 Conference and Expo" in Washington, D.C., attracted some six hundred government bureaucrats. Cory Johnson, reporting on the conference, said this:

> To the assembled bureaucrats, though, the impending deadline simply seems to imbue fear. For that emotion is the one thing that all of these attendees seem to share—that, and a remarkable propensity for bad hair and more Sears suits than a Dean Witter sales meeting. Some were near tears. "I just don't know how we are going to do this," says the Y2K "expert" from the Veterans Hospital Administration. "I'm 75 percent of my

> department's Y2K office, and I don't even know what I'm doing."
>
> At times this conference represented an AA meeting, with one sad-eyed participant after another testifying about the escalating scope of the Y2K problem they are supposed to solve. Many are heartbroken to find out that it is not just a database issue, but a monster computer problem that could cause air conditioners to fire up in the middle of the winter and stop elevators from moving. Basically, everything on earth that gets juice from a socket will start blinking stupidly like a VCR.[58]

Particularly telling was a comment from Julia McCreary, Year 2000 coordinator for the IRS. "If you don't have a contingency plan, you're gonna be in trouble. But I've got a contingency plan. I plan on taking up pottery in October 1999 and moving to Montana, where you can drive as fast as you want and they don't pay taxes." I'm sure Ms. McCreary meant these comments tongue-in-cheek. But I'm having a hard time laughing.

# Chapter Seven

## Dropping Our Guard

### *The Impact of the Year 2000 Computer Crisis on Those Institutions That Are Supposed to Protect Us*

**History shows that there are no invincible armies.**

—Josef Stalin

The modern military is a computerized military. Nearly every facet of its operations involves sophisticated, high-tech computer systems. The first time most of us realized this was in watching the Gulf War unfold on television.

Iraq invaded Kuwait on August 2, 1990, and then refused to withdraw. After months of negotiating, the United Nations finally gave Iraq an ultimatum: Get out of Kuwait by January 15, 1991, or face the consequences. Saddam Hussein ignored the resolution, allowing the UN deadline to pass. The United States, along with a coalition of other states, decided to attack. In the early morning on January 17, 1991, the combined forces began a massive, high-tech air strike on Iraqi targets that involved scores of computers and embedded chip systems.

> The initial attacks included Tomahawk cruise missiles launched from warships in the Persian Gulf, F-117A Stealth fighter-bombers armed with laser-guided smart bombs, and F-4G Wild Weasel aircraft loaded with

> HARM anti-radar missiles. Timed to eliminate or reduce the effectiveness of Iraq's ground radar defenses, these attacks permitted the F-14, F-15, F-16, and F/A-18 fighter bombers to achieve air superiority and drop TV- and laser-guided bombs. The A-10 Thunderbolt, with its Gatling gun and heat-seeking or optically guided Maverick missiles, provided support for ground units and destroyed Iraqi armor. The AH-64 Apache and the AH-1 Cobra helicopters fired laser-guided Hellfire missiles, guided to tanks by ground observers or scout helicopters. Also essential to the allied air fleet were the E-3A Airborne Warning and Control System (AWACS), and an aging fleet of B-52Gs.
>
> Over 2,250 combat aircraft, including 1,800 U.S. craft, participated against Iraq's approximately 500 Soviet-built MiG-29s and French-made Mirage F-1s. By the end of the fifth week, more than 88,000 combat missions had been flown by allied forces, with over 88,000 tons of bombs dropped.[1]

Like millions of other Americans, I watched the Gulf War on television as if it were some kind of world championship sporting event. "Smart bombs," pinpointing targets as small as a door or window, struck with deadly accuracy, thanks to their on-board computerized navigation systems. From the safety of my own home, I sat in amazement and watched the coalition forces decimate the Iraqi military and much of the civilian infrastructure.

The air strikes broke the back of Iraq and set the stage for the coalition's land invasion on February 20. Again, high-tech computers led our troops to victory. The tanks positioned themselves and fired on the enemy with exacting accuracy, thanks to the navy's twenty Global Positioning Satellites. Two days after the land war began, it was over. On February 28, having accomplished its goals, the coalition declared a cease-fire.

We had always been told that we had the most advanced military on earth, but seeing was believing.

## Military Nonpreparedness

With the demise of the Soviet Union, the United States and its allies have assumed the *de facto* responsibility of preserving the world's peace. They are able to do so, in large part, because they possess the necessary force. And this force is, of course, dependent upon the widespread use of computers and embedded chip systems. If these systems fail because of a computer malfunction owing to the Millennium Bug, then there will be serious consequences.

**The Department of Defense—the most heavily computerized government agency—is completely dependent on computers.**

What's at stake? Globally, a failure in the military computers could upset the delicate balance of world peace and give the advantage to those countries that are less dependent upon advanced technology. China, for example, might suddenly find itself in a position of military superiority over the rest of the world. Would it use that advantage responsibly? Given their history of human rights violations and the current level of violence they are exercising toward their own people, there is no reason to believe they would treat outsiders any better.

In addition to world peace, our ability to suppress terrorism, though not perfect, is a result of our sophisticated intelligence and security systems, most of which are computer-driven. If these defenses are dropped for a single day, let alone weeks or months, we can expect international terrorism to rise. If it does, then we put at risk the current level of free access to other countries and the international trade we enjoy.

Institutionally, the Year 2000 Problem threatens both the military's ability to do its job and the confidence of its personnel. It is clear that the U.S. military understands these risks to some extent. In March 1997 General Dennis J. Reimer, United States Army and chief of staff, and Togo D. West, Jr., secretary of the army, sent an internal memorandum to virtually everyone within the army who was in a position of authority. In it, they said:

> Our army's ability to shoot, move, and communicate effectively—both within our service and in conjunction with Joint and Combined forces—has come to rely heavily on automation. The increasing importance of information dominance, with its continual introduction of more sophisticated technological weaponry to the inventory, has made this reliance critical. Consequently, the Year 2000 (Y2K) Problem must not be allowed to pose any risk to the warfighter [*sic*]. This is a matter that affects the credibility of the army and its soldiers and the public we serve.[2]

But in addition to the army's *ability*, it could also affect their *confidence*—both of which are necessary to win battles.

> We must deal with Y2K now so that our soldiers can continue to place well-founded confidence in their weaponry and automation tools through the change of the millennium.[3]

And what does this mean for you and me? If the military is not able to make its computers Year 2000–compliant by January 1, 2000, then our ability to go about our normal business is threatened. This ability assumes a peaceful environment wherein there is no threat of foreign invasion, civil war, or attacks from terrorists. Without this environment, we face the constant interruption in the flow of goods and services, not to mention the threat to our personal safety. Like the military, without the ability to conduct business as usual, our confidence in the future is impaired or destroyed.

### *Command and Control*

Of all the government agencies, the Department of Defense (DoD) is the most heavily computerized, and it is completely dependent upon those computers.[4] It operates an incredible array of high-tech weapons systems. Not only does it use mainframes and personal computers in its command and control centers, it makes extensive use of embedded chips in missiles, tanks, planes, ships, and satellites. Some of these chip systems are date-sensitive. Regardless, they *all* have to be checked.

> Fortunately, weapons systems are, for the most part, much less date-intensive than most business information systems, so there are fewer Year 2000 fixes which need to be made in them. *Nevertheless, we still have to check all weapons systems for the Year 2000 Problem.* When we are dealing with weapons and their delivery systems, we must leave nothing to chance [emphasis added].[5]

Tony Valetta, a DoD employee working on the Year 2000 Problem, has tried to reassure other federal agencies that there is no cause for concern: "Now don't worry, we're not going to have any problems with our weapons systems functioning properly."[6] But, at this writing, the DoD has still not completed its inventory of systems, so the military doesn't really know how big its problem might be.

Part of what makes the U.S. military's weapons systems so powerful is the navy's Global Positioning System (GPS). This system consists of twenty four satellites that transmit signals to earth, which are in turn picked up by electronic receivers to determine a vehicle's exact location and velocity. They are installed in both military and civilian vehicles and devices, including fighters, bombers, commercial and private airplanes, helicopters, trains, ships, submarines, tanks, jeeps, missiles and other "smart" weapons, police cars and ambulances, and some newer-model cars.

Each satellite carries four atomic clocks that are extremely accurate. The GPS system works by computing the difference between the time a signal is sent from each of four different satellites and the time it is received. This enables the receiver to determine its precise latitude, longitude, altitude, and time. It is completely date- and time-driven.[7] And therein lies the problem.

The GPS has a date-related error in its receiver technology.[8] (The satellites are compliant; the problem is with the receivers.)

One programmer reviewing the GPS ground station code for potential Year 2000 problems found

> ...no less than ten types of manifestations of the problem in a survey of a randomly selected sample of 10 percent of the code. The occurrence of the literal value "19" was only one of these ten types. Other types included type overflow problems at various dates throughout 1999, Y2K arithmetic that implicitly assumed no dates later than 31 Dec 99 were possible.[9]

The GPS receiver code had even more significant problems:

> [The] date [field], in the GPS standard, uses exactly thirteen bits (these bits represent a time-unit offset from a conventional epoch date). This allocation is burned into the proms [programmable read-only memory] on all existing GPS user equipment. On about August 20, 1999, the actual date value will overflow this 13-bit type, *and the equipment will fail to produce correct time or position information.* Best estimate is that there are ~$10^6$ [i.e., ten million] pieces of user equipment that will be immediately affected. Everybody who depends indirectly on those pieces of equipment [meaning all the rest of us] will also be affected [emphasis added].[10]

The DoD has confirmed that this problem exists and recommends that civilian companies that use the system—and there are many that do—obtain Year 2000–compliant systems from their private GPS vendors. In other words, the navy will not take responsibility when these systems fail. After August 20, 1999, planes, trains, ships, and automobiles (especially police cars) that use the system to determine their location and help them navigate will be left in the lurch, unless they replace their GPS receivers—all ten million of them.

### *Keeping the Troops Working*

Like most other government agencies and all private-sector enterprises, the military has the usual computerized business systems. These computers generate financial statements, track budgets, process payrolls, and cut hundreds of thousands of checks each month to government contractors, consultants, vendors, and service providers. They assist military personnel in making their purchasing decisions, managing their inventories, and ensuring that supplies and equipment are delivered on time and in conformity with contractual terms. They also generate and maintain "executive information systems," so that those in authority can make accurate and timely decisions regarding the ongoing health of the operations under their command.

**At its current rate of progress, the Department of Defense won't finish repairing its "mission-critical" applications until 2012.**

> If our personnel and payroll systems process dates incorrectly, current employees, members of the armed services, and our annuitants cannot be properly paid. If our logistics and transportation systems process dates incorrectly, people and equipment cannot be delivered to the correct place at the correct time. This, of course, could have catastrophic consequences should it happen during a time when our fighting forces are being called upon to react to national security crises or lend emergency assistance. Some of our weapons systems would not function properly. Our databases would be greatly corrupted.[11]

### *Massive Problem*

The military has thousands of mainframe computers, tens of thousands of programs, hundreds of thousands of microcomputers, and millions of embedded chips to assess, review, and repair. Congressman Stephen Horn's subcommittee has estimated that the DoD has

358 million lines of code to examine.[12] But Robert Molter, a DoD computer scientist, estimates that the total will be *in excess of one billion lines of code!*[13] This, of course, does not even include the DoD's embedded chip problem. It is no wonder that the problem has been described as "potentially catastrophic,"[14] "overwhelming,"[15] "a particularly difficult challenge,"[16] and "a very serious situation."[17]

The DoD faces significant obstacles in trying to complete its Year 2000 program on time. Among these are the following:

***1. It is difficult to inventory all the computer code and locate the documentation.*** When you have a system as massive as the DoD's—spread across numerous government agencies, departments, and other entities, as well as around the world—it takes a significant effort just to figure out what you have. And once you have it, you might discover you no longer have the source code. Or worse, you find that much of the documentation is obsolete or missing altogether.[18]

***2. Many defense programs are written in obsolete computer languages.*** While some of the DoD's systems are written in COBOL, most are written in arcane languages like CS-1, CMS-2, JOVIAL, NELIAC, and Ada. Because these languages are either not used elsewhere or not widely used, there are few or no automated tools available to assist programmers in their Year 2000 conversion efforts.[19] Even the COBOL code is problematic because the department has a lot of *old* COBOL, which is not supported by the COBOL Y2K tools that are available.[20] And, as a matter of fact, there are not many programmers who still understand these languages.

***3. There are hundreds of thousands of personal computers to examine.*** The problem with PCs in large organizations is that they can sometimes proliferate outside of anyone's direct control. A variety of configurations abound as do the number of commercial and homegrown applications. Again, according to Assistant Secretary Paige, "much hardware and systems software must be replaced or upgraded, including *the majority of hundreds of thousands of personal computers* [emphasis added]."[21]

***4. Embedded chips and other types of firmware are used extensively throughout the military.*** This is perhaps the biggest problem of all. The military makes extensive use of embedded chips in its weapons systems as well as its planes, tanks, ships, and innumerable electronic devices. One of the major obstacles to routing the Millennium Bug out of these systems is that these chips may no longer be in production. Some of them were made to fulfill specific military requirements (e.g., a chip used in a particular missile); when the contract was fulfilled, the manufacturers stopped making the chips. These embedded systems will thus have to be identified, tested, and either replaced or retired.

***5. Internal systems are often heavily dependent upon one another, and remediation efforts need to be coordinated.*** As a result, information must be examined as it both enters and leaves a system. If programmers are not careful, their fix may become someone else's problem. As a result, programmers will have to analyze carefully the systems affected by the one they are currently working on and make sure that they coordinate their efforts with those of others. And, when one system becomes compliant, its testing must be synchronized with other applications to ensure that the larger system works. Because the military's systems are so interdependent, the domino effect poses a particularly serious threat.

***6. The military is dependent on civilian infrastructure.*** Like every other government agency and private sector entity, the military is dependent upon utilities, financial institutions (including banks), transportation, and telecommunications. "Disruption in these civilian resources would directly affect the DoD's ability to fulfill its missions."[22] Without electricity, for instance, the DoD can't even run its computers, let alone repair the ones that are still infected with the Millennium Bug. Without the banking system, it can't pay the troops and other vendors who supply necessary equipment and supplies. Without telecommunications it can't communicate with its far-flung operations around the world. Thus, the national infrastructure is very much a national security issue.

These aren't the only obstacles, of course, but they are certainly significant ones. Each of them must be addressed and overcome if the government is going to fulfill its responsibility to "provide for the common defense" after January 1, 2000.

### *A Status Report*

So then, we have seen that the Year 2000 Problem affects a broad range of military systems and that these systems collectively represent an enormous, if not impossible, management challenge. How is the DoD progressing? In a word, poorly.

**The Millennium Bug directly threatens our personal safety because our police forces are so computer-dependent.**

In Congressman Horn's 1997 report card, the DoD received a grade of C-minus, down from a C the previous year. Given what's at stake here—namely our national and personal security—this is simply unacceptable. The DoD should have begun this project years ago. Instead of sinking billions of dollars into the B-1 Bomber, for example, it should have been doing the difficult, less glamorous work of making sure its existing systems would function into the next century. As it is, it is doubtful whether the B-1 will even be able to fly after the year 2000. And if it is able to fly, how will it navigate or deploy its arsenal of weapons if the GPS is on the blink?

Amazingly, the DoD does not plan to put its Y2K–compliant systems into production until November 1, 1999. This leaves only one month to make sure all systems are functioning correctly and to make any last-minute repairs. Either the DoD thinks it has programmers that write error-free code, or it just doesn't get it. The truth is that there is really no way it can project a completion date on the project until its people know how much work has to be done.

And at this writing, they are still in the assessment phase.[23] It is one of the twelve agencies reprimanded by the Office of Management and Budget (OMB) in its August 1997 report for being too far behind schedule.[24] Until it knows how big the job is, it really can't tell us when it will be done.

Here's an account of the progress to date:

- As of February 10, 1997, only 302 computer systems were fully compliant; 7,000 were not.[25]

- As a result, on March 31, 1997, General Reimer and Secretary of the Army West postponed all new enhancements to nonessential computer systems.[26]

- On August 1, 1997, the DoD's Global Command and Control System failed when, as a test, the date was rolled over to the year 2000. The failure occurred at the end of a Joint Warrior Interoperability Demonstration. According to *Government Computer News*, the cause of the failure was the SunSoft Solaris operating system running on Sun workstations.[27]

- On August 15, 1997, the OMB reported that only 43 percent of the DoD's 2,593 mission-critical systems were in the assessment phase.[28]

- According to a report released by the General Accounting Office the DoD's method of tracking potential Y2K problems throughout the military "is not a reliable and accurate tool for managing [its] Year 2000 efforts."[29] The DoD acknowledged that its Defense Integration Support Tools (DIST) system isn't working as well as it needs to.

- On September 5, 1997, a source on Capitol Hill told

a reporter for *ComLinks* that the DoD is still not through the inventory stage. He said that the DoD is "somewhat behind schedule" on its Y2K conversion.[30]

- On September 13, 1997, *Science News* reported that the DoD's Defense Logistics Agency had accidentally removed ninety thousand items from inventory in a Y2K-related failure. Correcting the problem took four hundred hours![31]

- On September 16, 1997, *TechWire* reported that the DoD had upped its count of systems to 13,897. Of these "more than 8,000 are still in assessment, more than 1,500 are scheduled for or undergoing repair, 189 are validated but not certified, and more than 1,100 will be eliminated before the year 2000."[32]

- On October 1, 1997, the General Accounting Office said that the army's Logistics Systems Support Center (LSSC) has not adequately dealt with competing workload and staff priorities as they relate to its Y2K conversion project. It also has not developed testing plans or communicated with "outside partners" to ensure that data can be properly exchanged. The LSSC does not have a contingency plan.[33]

The DoD was not scheduled to have completed even its assessment of the problem until December 31, 1997.[34] But if, as the experts say, the "assessment phase" accounts for only 1 percent of the work involved in a Y2K conversion project, the DoD cannot possibly fix its Y2K Problem in time. In fact, as noted, in December 1997 the House Subcommittee on Government Management, Information, and Technology projected that the DoD, based on its current rate of progress, would not finish repairing its "mission-critical" applications until the year 2012.[35]

## Where Are the Police When You Need Them?

While the national defense is, of course, extremely important, many of us face more imminent threats closer to home. At the national level we face the threat of attack from foreign countries and terrorists. At the local level we face threats from organized crime and individual criminals. We also count on the police (and the highway patrol) to maintain safe highways and streets, so that we can come and go without fear of being run down or car-jacked.

**What will happen to health care when date-driven diagnostic equipment shuts down or spews out inaccurate information?**

As in the case with the military, there is a great deal at stake. We can expect the police to experience serious difficulties in apprehending criminals if they do not have access to the advanced computer systems they now use to trace fingerprints and track suspect profiles. Criminals will be able to commit their crimes with less fear of being caught. As a result, we can expect to see crime and violence increase—perhaps significantly—as criminals take advantage of the situation.

You and I will be at risk if the police computers fail. We can expect slower response time to emergencies. (If you live in a large city, for example, and the police are accustomed to depending on the GPS to navigate to your home when you make an emergency call, they will then have to find you by other, slower means.) We can also expect higher crime rates which, of course, threaten our personal security and safety. Across the board, this will have a negative impact on society. It will cost us financially as well as in terms of the personal freedoms we now enjoy.

### *Robocop*

The police use computers extensively in law enforcement. Like everyone else in society, the police have become increasingly computer-dependent in the last thirty years. Embedded chips are of particular concern. They are used by police departments in:

- electronic locks
- elevators
- vehicle management systems
- radios
- radio substations
- conventional telephones
- mobile phones
- maintenance scheduling systems
- burglar and fire alarms
- CCTV cameras/monitors
- radar speed detectors
- speed cameras
- photo surveillance equipment
- traffic light controllers
- pagers
- personal organizers
- heating and ventilation systems
- sprinkler systems
- time clocks/stamps
- faxes
- telex machines

It is important to recognize that "this risk may not depend upon whether the particular device has any explicit date-dependent functions to perform in the particular device concerned. As just one example, a major international burglar alarm supplier has estimated that approximately 20 percent of the alarm systems which it has supplied and which are still in use will suffer problems... at the date change."[36]

Mary Ann Agler, a supervisor with the North Platte, Nebraska, Police Department, encountered an early Y2K failure with a program she uses to dispatch police, file reports, track personnel, and assign expiration dates to documents like handgun permits. When she attempted to enter a "00" date, she received an error message:

"Date must not be in the past." Obviously the computer assumed that "00" stood for "1900." For the moment, she is entering "99" when she has to enter 2000 or beyond. "But all those entries will eventually have to be fixed," she said. "Right now, it's a minor inconvenience. But it's going to get worse."[37] In addition:

> Disruption of 911 telephone services worries Mary Ann a lot.... [There were] three events in the last year or so in which service was interrupted and citizens were unable to report emergencies. Worst of all is that the 911 dispatchers did not realize that the system was broken, and citizens trying to report a fire heard the phone ringing as usual, also not realizing the system was nonfunctional.[38]

Like the military, the police also use computers to run the business side of their operations. They must pay vendors, suppliers, and various service providers. Most importantly, they must pay their own detectives and police officers. In the larger cities especially, this is all done by computer. They also use computers to process traffic tickets, post payments of fines, issue warrants, and move cases through the criminal justice system.

### *Clueless*

No one is giving much attention to the impact of the Year 2000 Problem on police work. When I did a search on the Internet for articles that included both the words "Y2K" and "police," I only came up with one hit: a white paper prepared by a police organization in Great Britain.[39] Regardless, most police departments will face at least *four* obstacles in making their computers Y2K–compliant:

*1. They have a problem with awareness.* This is true in organizations across the board, but it is especially true of police departments.

*2. They assume that third-party vendors are taking care of the problem.* Like many small- to medium-sized businesses, they are having a difficult time taking responsibility for Y2K compliance.

*3. They are dependent upon other federal and state agencies.* Local police departments are often tied in with larger state and federal systems, like the National Crime Information Computer System, which is operated by the FBI.

*4. They have inadequate funding.* While federal agencies are able to command enough attention to gather the resources they need to address the problem, it is more difficult for state and local agencies to do so. There simply isn't the awareness, the concern, or the available resources.

It is uncertain whether local police departments will successfully complete their Year 2000 conversion projects. There just isn't enough information available. It's one thing if our military is not able to protect our allies and keep the peace in faraway foreign countries. It is quite another thing if our local police are not able to guarantee our personal safety and well-being at home.

## The Real Health Care Crisis

While the military and police have the responsibility of holding our external enemies at bay, our health care system is responsible for keeping our internal enemies in check. The health care system in the United States is arguably the most advanced in the world. Nearly all of this is owing to our sophisticated medical technology. And, of course, at the heart of this technology are vast computer systems and embedded chip systems.

### *Patient Care*

The embedded chip problem within the health care industry offers alarming prospects. Consider, for example, the disturbing possibilities for a simple piece of medical technology: an automated, intravenous drip machine.

> Infusion pumps in intravenous drips are calibrated to deliver the correct drug and fluids dosage to the patient, but become inaccurate over the passage of time and need recalibrating every three months. An embedded chip registers when the last calibration took place, and compares it with the current date in its internal time-clock.
>
> If no calibration has taken place, the pumps "issue an alert and shut down altogether after six months on the basis that they are probably dangerous," said Ian Hugo, author of the British Standards Institutions year 2000 code of practice and chairman of the Visual User Group.
>
> When the millennium arrives, the date calculation will indicate that the last recalibration took place nearly 100 years ago, causing the pump to shut down. "It's very easy to fix, but you have to check every one," warned Robin Guenier, executive director of Taskforce 2000. "There could be five in every ward—in every hospital."[40]

This is, of course, only the tip of the iceberg. Consider what would happen if:

- A physician fails to perform a caesarian section in a timely fashion because the diagnostic equipment malfunctioned as a result of the Millennium Bug. Because he failed to detect fetal distress, the infant's brain is damaged.

- A physician examines and releases a patient complaining of chest pains because his diagnostic equipment fails. The patient dies a few hours later from heart failure.

- A physician administers too much medication, not enough medication, or the wrong medication, which kills the patient. The equipment he was trained to use and rely upon did not yield accurate data.

- A nurse anesthetist administers a fatal does of anesthesia because the biomedical equipment in the operating room is unreliable as a consequence of its dependence on a date-coded microchip.

- Health care professionals, unaware of the Millennium Bug and its manifestations, are not trained in detection techniques or how to treat the patient without their high-tech resources, and therefore make repeated errors in patient care.

If critical medical equipment stops working when the century rolls over, you and I will be deprived of the quality of health care we are accustomed to receiving. Worse, if this medical equipment malfunctions by reporting inaccurate or errant data, we are in even greater danger. It's one thing to be denied treatment because of a computer glitch. At least in this situation, everyone knows there is a problem, and you can receive alternative treatment. But it is another thing to receive wrong or harmful treatment.

### *Legal Liability*

As a result of these inevitable equipment failures, the health care industry will face enormous legal liability. If electronic life support systems or other crucial medical equipment fails, then the victims—or their families—will undoubtedly sue. Already, government agencies and health care trade associates are concerned about the problem.[41] And well they should be, says Chris Dowd, editor of *Health Informatics Journal*:

> This issue is a serious one for the industry. If electronic equipment in hospitals fails, someone will be held responsible. If my daughter was on a life support machine which failed because no one checked if it was year 2000 compliant, I would want to sue somebody.[42]

As is the case with all lawsuits, it is not just those that lose their cases that must pay. If the litigation is widespread—as it could very likely be—you and I will also pay in the form of higher prices for health care and health insurance.

### *The Business Side*

Apart from the issues related to patient care, the Year 2000 Problem threatens the health care industry's ability to manage the business. If you've ever received a hospital bill—and who hasn't—you know how complex and detailed these documents are. A two-day stay can result in several pages of detailed transactions. Every piece of medical equipment, medicine (including aspirin), and procedure is accounted for. And behind every one of those transactions is a computer record that someone, somewhere in the health care system had to complete and process. (As a result, it is not unusual to find data files that have a billion or more records each.) If those records cannot be completed thoroughly and accurately, then patients—or the appropriate government agency—cannot be billed.

If patients can't be billed, and if health insurance claims can't be filed, cash flow will come to an abrupt halt. And if these health care entities, whether individual doctors or hospitals, cannot generate income, they cannot pay their vendors and service providers, and perhaps most importantly, their employees. If this happens, the consequences of the Year 2000 Problem will ripple through the entire industry, affecting medical equipment manufacturers, pharmaceutical companies, and anyone else who sells goods or services in this market segment.

### *Lack of Awareness*

On February 25, 1997, the information technology law firm of Gordon & Glickson, P.C., released its Third Annual Health Care Technology Survey.[43] According to this nationwide survey of 1,700 hospitals, fewer than one-third of the respondents had developed a Year 2000 compliance plan and only one in five had implemented such a plan. Worse, and most alarming, *18 percent of these hospitals are planning no action to protect their systems.* Pity the patient who checks into one of these hospitals on January 1, 2000.

## Conclusion

We take our national and personal safety for granted. Whether it is external enemies or internal ones, help is only a phone call away. Military, law enforcement, and medical professionals stand ready to protect us, giving us the peace of mind that we can conduct our vocational and personal lives without fear of being invaded, attacked, or infected. And currently, if the system breaks down at some point, we have access to quality health care that, while not perfect, affords us a quality of life heretofore unknown.

As we have seen, however, this protection, whether military or medical, is highly dependent upon advanced computer technology. Without that technology, we are left vulnerable to our enemies. And it is precisely that vulnerability that threatens each of us on January 1, 2000, unless the military, the police, and the health care industry repair their computers and their embedded chip systems.

# Chapter Eight

## See You in Court

### *The Impact of the Year 2000 Computer Crisis on Litigation and the Legal System*

**A lawyer with his briefcase can steal more than a hundred men with guns.**

—Mario Puzo

It's already started. In August 1997 the first-ever Year 2000 lawsuit was filed.[1] A fruit and vegetable store in Warren, Michigan, got tired of credit cards with expiration dates of 2000 crashing its systems. As a result, the owners filed a lawsuit against the company that sold them their "high-tech" cash register system.

The co-owner of Produce Palace, Mark Yarsike, said that he and his partner, Sam Katz, paid about $100,000 in April 1995 for the system, which included ten registers that not only handle purchases but also keep up with the company's inventory. The problems surfaced last year, when customers began using credit cards with the expiration date 2000. Earl Pratto, the store's manager, said the system would crash for four or five hours at a time. "Here we have a hundred people in the store, and all of sudden we can't take charge cards," he said. "The lines get very long." And he added that many customers would leave full carts and walk out.

Yarsike estimated the system cost him more than $50,000 in additional wages plus hundreds of thousands of dollars in lost business.

At this writing, the outcome of the lawsuit has not been determined. But one thing you can know for sure: this is only a taste of things to come.

## Ready, Aim, Fire

Experts estimate that the Y2K Crisis will provide the biggest litigation opportunity of all time. This is saying a lot considering that in 1995 Americans filed more than 14.8 million civil lawsuits and paid $121.7 billion in legal fees.[2] Amazingly, litigation stemming from the Year 2000 Problem could dwarf that by comparison.

According to *USA Today*, “Litigation resulting from Year 2000 meltdowns will be more costly than asbestos, breast implant, and Superfund cleanup lawsuits combined.”[3] Estimates range from a low of $100 billion[4] to in excess of $1 trillion[5] in the United States alone. (Just to put this into perspective, the total output of the U.S. economy is about $7 trillion per year. [6]) As Vito Perainoi, an attorney specializing in catastrophe litigation, said in his testimony before Congress, “the Year 2000 Problem is a litigation catastrophe waiting to happen.”[7]

It is important to understand why the Millennium Bug creates such enormous legal liability. “At its most basic level, the Year 2000 Problem threatens the integrity of financial information.”[8] Every day millions of people make decisions based on the assumption that the financial information provided to them is accurate. Whether you are a small investor or a professional broker, your decisions are only as good as your information. If your information is inaccurate, your decisions are going to be bad, and the impact on your personal financial health—or that of your clients—will be negative. As a result, inaccurate information is going to generate an avalanche of lawsuits. These lawsuits will stem from one of seven causes.[9]

***1. Unresolved Y2K Problems will generate lawsuits from clients against banks, brokers, and money managers whose finances or investments were damaged or diminished.*** Imagine that you are the owner of a small business. On January 15, 2000, you hand out bimonthly paychecks to each of your employees. But the day after, one of your employees informs you that her check has bounced! She is respectful but clearly upset. Soon, all of your other employees make the same report. Caught completely off guard, you are flustered. You immediately call your banker. Unfortunately, all you get is a busy signal. You hit redial. Same thing. You try it again. Still busy. For the next forty-five minutes you keep trying to get through. Your anger level is rising by the minute.

**Experts estimate that the Y2K Crisis will provide the biggest litigation opportunity of all time.**

Finally, you get through. The clerk is apologetic. "Yes, sir, I know the phones have been busy. I'm very sorry. Our phones have been ringing off the hook. No, you're not the only one. It seems that we've been bouncing everyone's checks. Your account is currently $90,000 overdrawn, but we know that can't be right. Evidently, our computers are messed up. All I can do is take your number and call you back once we figure out what the problem is."

"What am I supposed to do in the meantime?" you demand. "My employees are camped outside my door!"

"Well, sir, I don't know what to tell you. We're working as fast as we can, but we don't know what the problem is yet. I'll call as soon as I know something." You hang up more frustrated than ever.

You explain the situation to your employees, but it doesn't alleviate their worry and concern. And for good reason. Over the next two days, their checks begin to bounce and they start receiving calls from their creditors. They have nothing to offer and neither do you. And neither does your bank. You are all victims of the Millennium Bug. As a result, you—and a host of other bank customers—file a law suit.

In his testimony before Congress, Vito Peraino painted a similar scenario:

> A bank that cannot open because of a Year 2000 failure could face huge liabilities. A bank needs to track customer

deposits; it needs to service loans; it needs to track payments and receipts; it needs to clear checks; it needs to maintain trust accounts; and, it needs to report to state and federal regulators. Let's consider how my business—a law firm—might be affected by the Year 2000 bank failure. Hancock, Rothert & Bunshoft needs access to funds to pay our employees. We need to pay our vendors. We need a credit facility. We need to have our clients' settlement checks cleared to pay litigants. We need to maintain trust accounts or we can be sued and we can be disciplined by the State Bar of California. If my bank can't open for several weeks, our firm is out of business. We will sue and we are no different than millions of other businesses in the country.[10]

According to attorney and Y2K litigation specialist, Warren Reid, "If you recommend that your clients invest in companies that cannot ship or receive goods, pay their payrolls, or provide promised or mandated employee benefits because of Year 2000 defects, you may be liable for not performing due diligence, meeting industry standards, malpractice or much worse."[11]

*2. Unresolved Y2K problems will generate lawsuits from shareholders whose stock value was reduced because of the company's failure to repair its computers.* Imagine for a moment that you have invested in XYZ Corporation. The company is not a high-tech startup with a lot of risk; it's simply a conservative, moderate-growth stock that has performed quarter in and quarter out. Steady growth and predictable results—until the Millennium Bug bites. Unfortunately the company was late in getting started on its Y2K repairs. When the company finally comes face-to-face with the fact that it has virtually no chance of completing the remediation efforts in time, it is forced to disclose the information to the Securities and Exchange Commission. When it does, the press picks up on it, and immediately the company's stock plummets. As a result, before you hear about it, you have lost over $15,000 in diminished stock value. And you are one angry investor.

What was the CEO thinking? Was he just hoping this problem would go away? And what about the board? What were they doing? Couldn't they see this problem coming?

There will probably be as many answers to these questions as there are companies. Some will claim ignorance. They will insist that they were simply unaware of the Year 2000 Problem or (perhaps more plausibly) that they didn't think it applied to them. But this argument will likely carry little weight with the court. Attorney Warren Reid warns, "Most decision makers are aware of the Year 2000 Bug and doing nothing about it will not be a defense, even if the argument is, we… didn't know how bad it was going to be."[12] Lawyer Ronald Palenski agrees: "Given widespread publicity about Year 2000 issues, failure to at least assess exposure could be a breach of fiduciary duty."[13]

**Defendants in Y2K lawsuits can't claim ignorance: it is a known problem that can be corrected.**

Others will also be accused of negligence or incompetence. Many managers and CEOs are in a state of denial. They are hoping the problem will go away. No matter how many people within the organization are telling them they have a problem, they simply aren't listening. Again, Vito Peraino's experience is instructive:

> In my work in the Year 2000 speaking circuit I come across thousands of dedicated IS [Information Systems] professionals who are attempting to raise their management's awareness of this problem. Far too many report a similar story: management just won't listen. Part of it is an education problem—a view that the problem can't be real. Part of it is a funding problem—a view that the problem is too expensive to fit into an already tight budget. Part of it is old fashioned denial—a view that if the problem is ignored long enough it will go away. For companies that fall into this category, they will face

> directors and officers liability. Shareholders and customers will sue.[14]

Finally, some will be guilty of out-and-out *fraud*. At least two governing bodies require publicly held companies to disclose anything that could affect their corporation's assets. One of the "generally accepted accounting principles" promulgated by the Financial Accounting Standards Board is the "Statement of Financial Accounting Standards No. 5." It says that contingencies that are reasonably possible must be disclosed in a note to the financial statements.[15] In other words, shareholders have a right to know if something threatens the value of their stock. The Securities and Exchange Commission also requires disclosure. Regulation S-K, Item 303, says that each annual report and quarterly report must include a section entitled "Management's Discussion and Analysis of Financial Condition and Results of Operations." This regulation basically obligates management to disclose any "material events and uncertainties" that negatively affect future operations.[16]

Clearly, many companies have not yet made these disclosures and some never will. Why? Because CEOs are evaluated on the basis of what happens to the stock price. In this kind of environment the goal is simple: maximize shareholder values. The strategy? Maximize corporate earnings. And therein lies the problem.

A major Y2K repair project does nothing to enhance the company's value. It won't make the company more productive. It won't make the company more competitive (except indirectly). It won't reduce costs. All it does is maintain the status quo—and at an *enormous* cost. Moreover, the "Emerging Issues Task Force" of the Financial Accounting Standards Board has ruled that Year 2000 costs must be expensed in *the year incurred*, rather than allowing companies to amortize the cost.[17] In other words, if a company incurs $4 million in actual Year 2000 repair expenses in a given year, they can't be written off over several years. The expenses must be subtracted from the bottom line in the same year. For some companies, this will put them in the red—or, at a minimum, slash expected profits.

Is it any wonder that CEOs and directors are reticent to tackle this problem head on? There's no upside. It's only a question of what is worse: dealing with the problem now and taking the hit on the bottom line or putting it off until later.

*3. Unresolved Y2K problems will generate lawsuits from victims (or families of victims) who suffered injury or death as a result of the Year 2000 Problem.* Because of the embedded chip problem, we will undoubtedly see a variety of appliances and devices fail that have a direct impact on people's safety and health. Some will be injured when these failures occur, and some, unfortunately, could die.

Imagine that you had a close relative that dies in a plane crash sometime shortly after the dawn of the next millennium. At the trial, the family of the victim's attorney introduces into evidence the fact that certain parts in the plane were supposed to have been replaced in January 2000 according to a pre-set maintenance schedule. The parts were not replaced, however, because the airline's noncompliant maintenance computer failed to calculate accurately each part's "time in service." Although it is unclear as to whether the parts involved were the actual cause of the plane crash, the jury takes the new testimony as evidence of the airline's reckless attitude toward safety and imposes punitive damages in addition to compensatory damages in order to "send a message."[10]

If you doubt this could happen, just think about the legal fallout from breast implants, diet drugs, or the tobacco industry. The Year 2000 Problem could make these look small by comparison.

*4. Unresolved Y2K problems will generate lawsuits from customers against software companies for delivering or failing to replace defective software.* In the first class-action lawsuit regarding the Millennium Bug, Atlaz International, a New York–based computer hardware company, filed a $50 million lawsuit in California State Court against Software Business Technologies and its subsidiary SBT Accounting Systems for failing to provide free Year 2000 compliance upgrades. The claim charges the vendor with breach of warranty, fraud, and fradulent and unfair business practices. According to Atlaz, SBT was improperly requiring customers to pay substantial fees to purchase upgrades that corrected the Year 2000 Problem in its software.[19]

**Because the Millennium Bug affects the entire economy, the cost of litigation will be enormous.**

Many contracts contain a *force majeure* paragraph that protects the software vendor from an "Act of God" or other event that is beyond his reasonable control. This could be a fire, loss of electrical power, hardware malfunction, or any other force that inhibits the vendor's software from working correctly. However, "It is unlikely that the Year 2000 Problem would be viewed as an Act of God, since it is a known problem, which can be corrected with enough planning and resources."[20]

*5. Unresolved Y2K problems will generate lawsuits from organizations against out-source vendors, contractors, consultants, or commercial Year 2000 software tools providers who failed to get the organization fully Year 2000–compliant.* Many outside the software industry have claimed that the Year 2000 Problem is just a bunch of hype generated by consultants looking for work. There is no question that hundreds of companies and thousands of consultants have jumped into the fray, hoping to get their piece of the action. In some cases, retired COBOL programmers have been enticed out of retirement to help fix this massive problem.

Like anything else, some of these companies are competent and some are not. Some have sufficient experience and some don't. The better ones were typically booked early and simply don't have the time to take on any new projects. That means that as we move toward the Year 2000 target, companies will grow increasingly desperate and be forced to hire less-qualified Y2K specialists. Inevitably, these consultants will over-promise and under-deliver. They simply may not make the deadline. Or worse, they will make it, but because of inadequate testing, they will allow undetected bugs to linger in the system, where they will cause more damage than if the computers had just shut down altogether.

Other programmers have written software tools that help automate the process of hunting down errant code and repairing it. I have been amazed at how many of these programs are advertised as "silver bullets." While they are helpful, to be sure, they by no means solve all the problems associated with the Year 2000 Problem. At best, all they do is automate a manual process, taking out of it some of the tedium and possibility of error.

Some of these programs are, of course, better than others. Some of them are very clever. Some of them are a total waste of money. I read a message from a Y2K project leader on CompuServe's "Year 2000 Forum" that said he ended up discarding the automation tool he had purchased because it was more trouble than it was worth. "The program didn't catch every instance of date code, and we found ourselves manually having to go back and double-check every instance ourselves. After cataloging several such errors, we just lost confidence in the program. The vendor didn't help either. Evidently, this was a case where the marketing department was writing checks the programmers couldn't cash! We found that it was taking more time with the tool than without it, so we sent it back for a refund and went back to our manual process. As a result, I'm very skeptical about the claims made by any vendor."

What happens if a company buys one of these programs and makes it a central part of their Year 2000 remediation efforts? And, what if (as in the case above) not every instance of bad code is caught and repaired? Even if the software vendor has a disclaimer in its license, it may not protect the company from customers looking for someone to blame. And in this country, even if you are technically right, you can still get sued, and you can spend a good deal of money defending yourself.

*6. Unresolved Y2K problems will generate lawsuits from businesses that are damaged as a result of a vendor failing to fulfill a contractual obligation.* When computers shut down and make it impossible to deliver goods or services as contracted, and when this failure has a significant financial impact on clients and customers, there will be little sympathy. These companies should have known about the problem and they should have taken action while there was still time to fix it.

> When your customers' backs are up against the wall. When they feel that they have been wronged. When they begin to lose money because your computer systems are down and you cannot fulfill your contractual obligations—they will be looking for someone to blame, someone to fire, and someone to SUE.[21]

*7. Unresolved Y2K problems will generate lawsuits from software developers and publishers against customers who they feel violated their intellectual property rights by modifying their program to make it Year 2000–compliant.* Some software vendors will be either unwilling or unable to make the needed repairs to their software. As a result, their customers will be placed in the difficult position of trying to decide whether to go ahead and make the repairs themselves, knowing that if they do so, they may be violating the vendor's software license and infringing upon his intellectual property rights. In these cases, companies will have to decide where they have the most exposure: a lawsuit from the vendor, or lawsuits from their own customers when they fail to provide the goods or services they have promised. They will, no doubt, be forced to make the modifications just to stay in business. Nevertheless, they might also find themselves in court defending their decision.

## Full Court Press

As you can see, the Year 2000 litigation potential is enormous. "Because the Year 2000 problem is so pervasive and affects virtually every sector of our economy, if the litigation hits, it will hit like a fireball. It will hit several industries and it will come from all directions."[22]

It will also be enormously expensive. "If companies think that the cost of the Year 2000 fix is expensive, they haven't begun to consider the cost of Year 2000 litigation."[23] The challenge of trying to absorb the cost of Year 2000 repairs into our economy without triggering a major recession—or worse—is significant. The additional cost of litigation could have a catastrophic impact on the economy, grinding investment and productivity to a halt. But even assuming that won't happen, there will be a significant impact on our system. Here are some possibilities:

- *Damage awards may be lower than anticipated.* "With so many potential claimants looking to recover such expenses—usually from small vendors, some of which may have gone out of business or be unable to pay"[24]—there simply may not be the dollars available. In addition, the courts may have to reduce damages just to allow some companies to stay in business and keep a bad situation from getting worse.

- *Disputes may be resolved more slowly than claimants wish.* Even today, it seems that it takes forever to bring a case to court. But what happens when you quadruple the volume of litigation? How will our courts process this additional amount without the system grinding to a halt?

- *Litigation costs will be passed on to consumers in the form of higher prices.* Ultimately, it is the consumer who must "foot the bill" for this debacle. Companies will not be able to absorb all these costs and still stay in business. As a result, prices will inch up and we will undoubtedly pay the piper.

- *Key suppliers and vendors will go out of business.* Many businesses will be ruined as a result of failing to make their computers Y2K–compliant. Many more will be ruined as a result of the litigation that ensues. The result is that you and I will have fewer choices and we will pay more for the ones we have left.

- *Much-needed Y2K repairs will not be made because companies will be forced to expend their limited resources on defending themselves.* Certainly, many companies will go into the next millennium with their Y2K repair projects unfinished. Some will be close to finishing and others might have the option of employing consultants or programmers that have finished other projects. But if all their resources are tied up defending themselves in court, this will not be an option. And everyone loses.

Analysts predict that hundreds, if not thousands, of Y2K-related lawsuits are looming on the horizon. According to Steve L. Hock, an attorney who specializes in technology law, lawyers are "actually slobbering" over the prospect of Year 2000 lawsuits.[25] With $1 trillion in judgments to collect, few litigators will be able to resist the temptation to secure their share of the pie. And ultimately, even if we aren't directly sued, you and I will be among the losers.

# Part Three

## The Day After

*Preparing for Life After the Year 2000 Computer Crisis*

# Chapter Nine

## Seeing Through a Glass Darkly

### *Three Scenarios That Could Result from the Year 2000 Computer Crisis*

**I do not believe in a fate that falls on men however they act; but I do believe in a fate that falls on them unless they act.**

—G.K. Chesterton

On April 11, 1970, Apollo 13 "slipped the surly bonds of Earth" on what everyone thought was a routine space flight to the moon. American astronauts had successfully landed on the lunar surface twice, and by the time this third mission was launched, the public had grown bored with it. In fact, the mission was initially *so* routine that a television broadcast from the spacecraft scheduled for prime time viewing was cancelled because there was not sufficient interest.

During the first two days of space flight, it was "business as usual." Everything went according to plan. But as the three astronauts approached the moon, an explosion occurred that caused the Command Module to lose its oxygen, electricity, and other systems, including its ability to abort the mission and return to Earth. It was then that commander James Lovell, Jr., informed Ground Control, "Houston, we have a problem." For the next three days, the astronauts and their colleagues at NASA worked around the clock to cheat death and bring the crew safely back to earth. On April 17, after five nerve-wracking days in space, Apollo 13 successfully reentered the earth's atmosphere and landed in the Pacific Ocean.

In many ways, life at the end of the twentieth century has become routine. Some things are so taken for granted that we never think about what it would mean if we were suddenly deprived of them. Things like electricity, water, telephones, transportation, banking—and most of all—computers. What I have been trying to say throughout this book, in one way or another, is similar to what Commander Lovell said when he saw the oxygen from Apollo 13 venting into space: "Friends, we have a problem."

## Facts versus Speculation

Up until this point, I have presented to you the facts about the Year 2000 Problem. I have documented my sources and presented what I have found in a manner that is as objective as I know how to make it. However, what I have written so far is much different from what you are about to read. We are about to move from the world of *facts* (what we know) to the world of *speculation* (what may or may not happen based on the facts as we understand them).

History is littered with the unfulfilled predictions of would-be prophets. This should give every seer—including me—reason enough to pause. Scores of speakers, authors, and futurists are nevertheless willing to stare into the crystal ball and tell us what they see. Whether it stems from alleged apparitions of the Virgin Mary or complex mathematical formulas supposedly drawn from holy writ, many religious mystics are predicting the literal end of the world. (It is interesting to note that these sorts of predictions were also circulating widely in the years preceding the dawn of the second millennium.) Ecologists are warning of the potentially catastrophic effects of global warming, solar flares, and El Niño. Conversely, New Age prophets are predicting the dawn of enlightenment and a new age of awareness. And some secular futurists are promising that new technologies will make our personal and vocational lives even better than they are now. So which scenario do we believe? Is it the end of the world as we know it or the dawn of unprecedented human achievement and growth?

All of them, to one extent or another, are speculative. No one knows whether they will come to pass. But there is one event we *know* will come to pass: the Year 2000 Computer Crisis. This is one event that we can date with absolute precision—down to the exact *second* it will begin. That's a fact. What we don't know is exactly what *effect* it will have on our world. Trying to guess is speculation, and I will be the first to admit it.

**Based on the facts, the idea that the Year 2000 Computer Crisis will be a "nonevent" is simply *not* a viable scenario.**

I want to outline for you three possible scenarios. At the end of the chapter, I will give you my best guess, based on where we are now, as to where we will likely end up.

## The Nonscenario

Before I outline my three scenarios, I want to give you what I consider to be a nonscenario. Sally Katzen, who is head of Information Technology for the Office of Management and Budget (OMB) and who refers to herself as the nation's "virtual CIO,"[1] has stated before Congress that "we are confident that we will finish the work so that the year 2000 computer problem will be a nonevent."[2] In other words, there might be a few isolated computer problems here and there, but, by and large, government agencies, public utilities, businesses, and other entities will complete their Year 2000 conversion projects on time, and it will be a *smooth transition* into the next century. We will not experience any significant disruptions in our way of life, and we will all live happily ever after.

I have found only two others who publicly share Katzen's viewpoint,[3] and I have read literally thousands of articles on the Year 2000 Problem. With the exception of these, I have not come across anyone who thinks the Year 2000 Problem is pure hype or that all the computers will get fixed in time. Based on the facts we have seen in the first nine chapters, it is simply not a viable scenario; therefore, I have not included it as one of my official scenarios.

## Scenario 1: Brownout

The Brownout Scenario basically says that we will be 90 to 95 percent successful in converting our computer code and embedded chips. The few systems that don't make it will cause problems, to be sure. As a result, we can expect isolated system failures, particularly in smaller companies and less important federal, state, and local government agencies. These system failures will impact some other systems because of the domino effect, but for the most part they will be contained and damage will be minimal.

### *Primary Infrastructure*

What can we expect if this scenario comes to pass? Let's look at the primary infrastructure first. We can expect some persistent, recurring outages in the power grid. Even if our local electrical utility is compliant, it is going to be affected by the few that aren't. This will result in periodic interruption of service.

Several years ago, I had the misfortune of working in an office building next to a site where they were building a large mall. As part of the site preparation, they were doing a good deal of blasting in order to clear the land of boulders and other rock formations. Consequently, for a period of about three months, we lost the electricity in our building several times a week. Usually it would go out for only a few minutes. Since we had a battery-powered backup unit for our computer network, we could continue to work. But a few times the electricity went out for a few hours. And at least once, we lost it for more than a day. We had to power down the computer network and send everyone home. These are the kinds of outages I envision with the Brownout Scenario.

I also think we will see problems in the treatment and delivery of water. Part of this will be a result of a lack of electricity, but most of it will be the result of embedded chip systems failing. If this affects the quality of the water, we can expect the local authorities to warn the population. Some, of course, will either not hear the warning or not heed it. In any event, we will see a few isolated cases in which people get sick from contaminated water, but this will not be widespread. In those few cases in which a water utility is not able to pump water at all for more than a few days, we will see emergency delivery of water. Perhaps this will be done by the National Guard, the police, or even the local fire department. People may not be able to take as many showers as they would like, but no one will die of thirst.

There could be some annoying disruptions in transportation, especially for people who do much traveling by air. Not all the bugs will be worked out of the computers used to generate tickets. When you consider that there are scores of airlines and tens of thousands of travel agencies, it will be inevitable that some problems will arise. There will also be some confusion with flight plans and even some navigation problems, particularly for aircraft owners that, for one reason or another, neglected to upgrade their Global Positioning System (GPS) receivers. This assumes that the Federal Aviation Administration and the air traffic control systems are pretty much compliant. If they are not, we can expect to see some more serious—perhaps life-threatening—problems. We will also likely see a great deal of confusion in the shipping industry, particularly as it relates to trains. At this writing, Union Pacific is experiencing an extraordinary number of computer problems as a result of its merger with Southern Pacific. It has sent train cars to the wrong destination and even lost some cars altogether. This has resulted in delays and frustration for its customers. If this happens due to the Millennium Bug, we can expect a similar situation. If it continues for any length of time, it will result in major delays, and perhaps in higher prices as goods become more scarce.

Many of the Year 2000 problems will manifest themselves simultaneously, and phone lines will be jammed as callers attempt to report problems to the appropriate authorities. As a result, many, if not most, callers will receive a busy signal. If you've ever tried to call your electrical utility following a power outage, you know what I mean. This, of course, assumes that the phones are still working. The telecommunications system is a huge and complex web of interconnections. There will inevitably be problems that result in disruption of service for some. It could be a company phone system that shuts down because of an embedded chip system that can't process dates after December 31, 1999, or it could be a telephone switching system at the local baby Bell. Regardless, telecommunications will be interrupted until the system is repaired.

**Even if the Y2K Problem has a "small" impact, it could last for several weeks and be quite expensive.**

Some of these primary infrastructure entities—electrical, water, transportation, and telecommunications—will likely generate billing errors. No one will have his service terminated because he can't pay a six-figure water bill—the mistake will be obvious to all—but the water utility will be unable to collect revenues until it can generate accurate statements. Many of these errors will be comical to outsiders (expect, for example, Jay Leno and David Letterman to be making cracks about them), but they will result in enormous frustration and long hours for those trying to correct them—especially those in customer service. Nevertheless, after several grueling weeks, most of these issues will be resolved.

### *Secondary Infrastructure*

Because of the banking industry's dependency upon computers and the level of interconnectivity, it is unlikely that everything will roll over to the next century without a hitch. Many banks will be compliant, but they will not be able to protect themselves completely from corrupt data. Thus, there will be a number of banking errors on customer statements. Most of these, however, will be obvious and will eventually be corrected. In the meantime, banks will have to be forgiving toward their customers, giving them the benefit of the doubt until matters are resolved. Some people will panic at what they think will happen to their money on January 1, 2000, and will withdraw all of their cash sometime prior to that day. However, the FDIC will publicly reaffirm its commitment to insure depositors (perhaps in the form of Public Service Announcements), and, as a result, there will not be large-scale bank runs. Nonetheless, a few banks will not be able to solve their Y2K problems and will be shut down. Although these incidents will get media attention for a day or two, they will have no significant impact on the banking industry as a whole.

Despite Sally Katzen's assurances, not all federal government agencies will make it. The Internal Revenue Service (IRS) in particular will not come close. Attempting to incorporate changes to the tax code and ensure that its systems are Y2K–compliant will simply be more than the agency can do. This will become a government crisis during the first few months of the year 2000, resulting in a good deal of public debate. Eventually, Congress will either (1) pass a flat tax, because it will be easier to administrate without a fully computerized system, or (2) mandate that taxpayers pay the same amount they paid in 1999, promising to reconcile everything once the computers are fixed. Some taxpayers will consider taking advantage of the system and not pay anything at all, but the government will warn against this and put into place serious penalties for those who attempt it. The Social Security Administration will be the one bright spot on the federal landscape. Although it may not complete its state systems, it will be successful in renovating its computer systems, completing the project in the nick of time. As a result, government entitlement programs will continue without interruption, averting the social unrest that would have undoubtedly followed if large segments of society had not received their monthly stipends.

The U.S. military will experience a good number of Y2K-related failures in both its administrative and embedded chip systems. Despite what we've been told, there will be some noncompliant weapons systems that slip through the cracks, resulting in a few highly publicized accidents. Some of these may result in the loss of life. But for the most part, the military will keep its problems under wraps. You and I won't hear much about them, because their disclosure will threaten national security. Other projects will continue to take a back seat to the mission of achieving full Y2K compliance. Other law enforcement agencies, including the local police, will also experience problems. Most of the problems, however, will be fairly trivial (e.g., errors in issuing driver's licenses) and will not pose a threat to public security. Agencies will be able to cope with manual workarounds until the computers are fully compliant.

Health care providers will also experience problems. Most of these will manifest themselves in billing errors. And most will be obvious, but people will refuse to pay their bills until they are accurate, threatening the institutions' cash flow. There will also be significant problems for these institutions in trying to obtain Medicare, Medicaid, and health insurance reimbursements. Nevertheless, with a lot of hard work these systems will eventually be made compliant and the great majority of providers will weather the storm. Vendors and service providers will be forced to be patient (no pun intended) since everyone will be in the same boat, and they will have few alternatives. More troublesome, however, will be the failure of embedded chip systems in critical medical equipment. These systems are very difficult to test before the fact, and many hospitals won't know how big a problem they have until the date rolls over to January 1, 2000. Some sophisticated surgical procedures will be postponed until doctors can be certain that the medical equipment employed is safe. Other doctors will have to resort to more low-tech tools, but all in all, the health care industry will muddle through.

### *Bottom Line*

If this scenario comes to pass, I believe it will last at least two weeks. And it might last as long as three months before things return to "normal." That does not mean that every unrepaired system will be fixed by the end of this period, nor does it mean that there won't continue to be fallout from Year 2000 problems. What it does mean is that beyond this point, whether two weeks or three months, these problems will have no discernible impact on the majority of citizens.

All of this will be annoying, inconvenient, and frustrating for the public. But, as with past national and regional crises, it will also bring the citizenry together as they fight shoulder-to-shoulder against a common enemy. While there may be isolated riots and protests, these will be quickly quelled, and the public will remain confident of the future. Social stability will not be threatened. Nevertheless, the costs related to Y2K problems—including computer program renovations, hardware replacements, litigation, and lost productivity—will not be trivial and will have a significant negative economic impact, resulting in a severe recession.

## Scenario 2: Blackout

The Blackout Scenario basically says that we will not be successful in converting enough of our computer code and embedded systems to keep everything up and running. I don't know what the "magic percentage" is that we have to complete in order to avoid this scenario. But my guess is that even if we get 70 percent to 80 percent converted, the lights will still go out. Our world is simply too interdependent to keep this from happening. Whereas in the Brownout Scenario we saw *isolated* system failures, in the Blackout Scenario, we can expect to see *multiple* system failures. They will be all the more catastrophic because they will be *simultaneous*.

### *Primary Infrastructure*

In this scenario we can expect the power grid to collapse. It doesn't really take much for this to happen—a tree growing too close to a power line, a nuclear power plant being shut down, a solar flare—any number of things can cause it to happen. All of these can, of course, be fairly easily overcome by simply removing the cause. Unfortunately, the cause in this case is the Millennium Bug. And guess what? You can't work on the computers unless they are running. And if there is no electricity, they won't be running. Forget about backup electrical power systems. As we will know all too well by then, noncompliant computers can't be fixed overnight. It will likely take months, if they can be fixed at all.

Once you lose electricity, you lose almost everything else. If we are dependent upon computers, we are even *more dependent* upon electricity. It is the "breath of life" for virtually every inanimate object in our existence. Take a moment and look around the room where you are sitting. How many of the items you are looking at require electricity to run? I happen to be away from home, in a small efficiency apartment writing this chapter. From where I am sitting I can see:

- my laptop computer
- my computer's stereo speakers
- my tape backup system
- a laser printer
- the telephone
- a refrigerator
- a stove and oven
- a venting fan and light
- an electric can opener
- a microwave oven
- a coffeemaker
- a toaster
- a garbage disposal
- a dishwasher
- two overhead lights
- two lamps
- a clock radio
- a cassette tape recorder
- a television set
- a remote control
- a heating/air conditioning unit
- a fire alarm system

That's a total of twenty-two items. (Admittedly, two or three of these items are battery-powered, but this is still ultimately electrical. Once the batteries are dead, the device is, too.) How many of these items *could* I live without? Probably quite a few. How many would I *want* to live without? Not many. How about you?

Some isolated utilities that are not part of the national or regional power grid may be able to survive. But there won't be many when you consider that it will be the smaller electric utilities that are isolated from the grid, and it is these utilities that are, generally speaking, the least aware of Y2K issues. In any event, whether isolated or not, these utilities will eventually be brought back on line. It will be slow work, and it might require the complete rebuilding of our national infrastructure, but you can bet it will be a high priority—we are simply too dependent on electricity to go without it for long.

**Can you imagine what it would be like to live for four months without electricity, let alone three years?**

Because there will be no electricity for an extended period of time—perhaps months—other systems will fail, too. Even if they are Y2K–compliant. It won't matter. Consider water. Without electricity, water cannot be treated (purified) or pumped to residences, businesses, and factories. Some may be fortunate enough to have a private well or spring, but even then, they probably are dependent upon an electric pump to get the water into their home. Most of us have taken clean water for granted for so long that we have no idea what must be done to treat water before drinking it or what will happen if we don't. As a result, many people will get sick from drinking contaminated water.

Perhaps the worst part of not having any water is the problem it creates for the disposal of waste. I'm not talking here about garbage piling up on the street. (New Yorkers have proven that you can live with that.) I'm taking about the disposal of human excrement. I know it's not a pleasant subject, but we need to face it. Once again, we are completely dependent upon our modern conveniences. In this case, toilets and sophisticated sewage treatment facilities. Most of us never give the subject a second thought. But what happens if the toilets don't work and there is nowhere for the raw sewage to go? Not many of us have first-hand knowledge of a safe alternative. And if human excrement and other sewage is not properly disposed of, it will attract vermin and spread disease. As a result, in the Blackout Scenario, we can expect to see disease spreading rapidly through the population.

Transportation will eventually grind to a halt. Most of the larger systems—commercial airlines, railroads, trucking—are run by computers. And if there is no electricity, there will be no functioning computers. Some of these vehicles—particularly the smaller ones—could run without them, of course, but that assumes that they have access to fossil fuels. The problem here is that the petroleum plants will not be able to function without electricity. That leaves us with whatever fuel supplies we have in storage. Eventually, that will run out, even if you can get it out of a tank without an electric pump! Without a functioning transportation system, companies will not be able to distribute goods. Existing inventories will evaporate, and this includes food items. As a result, many, many people will be hungry. Gasoline and diesel will become extremely valuable commodities, assuming the value of "liquid gold." Those that have gas- or diesel-powered generators as well as those with gas-powered farming and gardening equipment will be willing to pay a high price.

Without electricity the telecommunications infrastructure will also come down. No phones. No television. No Internet. In short, no electronic communication. The majority of citizens will feel isolated and out of touch with what is happening outside their immediate community. The only ones that will be communicating extra-locally will be those with short-wave radios that run on solar batteries or some other alternative energy source. Perhaps eventually some old mechanical printing presses will be brought back into service. If so, then this may be a way for those that can gather news to share it with their neighbors and fellow citizens.

### *Secondary Infrastructure*

Like everything else, the banking industry is dependent upon electricity. No electricity, no computers. No computers, no banks. Period. Some have suggested that the banks could process transactions manually. Remember, Chase Manhattan, the largest bank in the United States, processes between $1 trillion and $2 trillion *a day*. So does the Fed. (In fact, in 1995 the Fed processed over twenty-seven million transactions totaling over $220 trillion.) How many bank clerks, complete with green visors and arm bands, do you think it would take to do this by hand? No doubt millions. And don't forget: if we truly don't have electricity, they will not even have the benefit of electronic calculators.

**The problems are so pervasive and interconnected that we cannot rule out the possibility of complete meltdown.**

Let's just assume, for the sake of argument, that the electricity stays on, but that the banking system is bitten hard by the Millennium Bug. So hard in fact, that simple transactions like check payments and debits cannot be processed accurately. How long can an electric utility operate if it can't pay its vendors, service providers, and employees? How long before employees walk off the job and the utility is forced to shut down? Banks can't survive without the electric utilities, and the electric utilities can't survive without the banks. It is a symbiotic relationship. If the banks are up, we will see full-scale bank runs—if not before the Year 2000, then certainly immediately after.

Without electricity, the power of federal, state, and local governments will be severely curtailed. And without banking, they, too, won't be able to pay their employees. How many government employees will stay on the job without getting paid—and for how long? Perhaps they will come up with a creative way to keep critical people at their posts (e.g., compensating them directly in some way without using the banks, or perhaps even forcing them). In any event, we can expect to see the president invoke the Emergency Powers Act. I'm not sure it will do him a lot of good, however, if he doesn't have electricity, computers, telecommunications, or banks. But if he does invoke it, and if he is able somehow to extend his arms across the nation, then I think we will see martial law. In essence, the military will be running things. And the IRS? Kiss it goodbye. Its back will finally be broken—at least for several years to come.

Without electricity and banking, the military will, of course, be in the same boat as the government. It will not be able to pay its soldiers—at least the vast majority of them—and some of these (if not most) will go AWOL unless they are coerced to stay. On the other hand, if the military is able to provide them with food and shelter, maybe they will stay on. They might not have many alternatives. In addition, because of the embedded chip systems problem, we can expect to see some weapons systems fail, resulting in injury or death to military personnel. Because the military will be in such disarray, we could be vulnerable to foreign invasion. I'm not particularly concerned about invasion from someone like Germany, Japan, Russia, or even an Arab state. What concerns me is an invasion from a low-tech country with a huge army. Say, for example, *China*. In addition to having the world's largest army, it also has a huge World War II–vintage navy. Although by today's standards it is outdated and not a threat, by Year 2000 standards, it might just be the most high-tech navy in the world.

The local police and other emergency personnel will be in the same boat as the military. If local municipalities are unable to pay their law enforcement and emergency preparedness personnel, they will eventually walk off the job. And we will be left to fend for ourselves against criminals, gangs, and the impact of accidents and calamities. Perhaps the National Guard will be sent in, but you have the same problem with them—who is going to pay them? My guess is that citizens will be forced to band together in small neighborhood militia groups. Unfortunately, many of them will be outgunned by the "bad guys." Over the last two decades, we have seen the systematic disarmament of the citizenry, and this is where we will pay the price for it.

Finally, few hospitals will be functioning. The quality of health care will resemble what is currently found in battlefield conditions.

Since they will not be able to get paid (except perhaps by some form of barter), the only doctors and nurses working will be those whose humanitarian spirit keeps them at it. The only medical equipment available will be what can be run without benefit of electricity. Sophisticated surgeries and other medical procedures will be a thing of the past. Triage will be the operative principal, and only those who need emergency treatment will be accommodated. Health care will return to what it was one hundred years ago.

### *Bottom Line*

If this scenario comes to pass, I believe it will last four months to three years. Regardless, it will seem like forever. Can you imagine what it would be like to live for four months without electricity, let alone three years? Our society will quickly resemble that of a third-world country.

I do think the electricity will eventually come back. And once it does, the focus will turn to restoring other lost infrastructures. Banking will be a high priority, since it provides the "monetary lubricant" that makes everything else work. Nevertheless, this will be a protracted process with many starts and stops. Chaos will be the norm—at least for a while.

Initially, people will be frustrated and angry. Caught unprepared, many will have no way to provide for their basic needs. There will be widespread looting, rioting, and vandalism. Some inner cities will go up in flames. Others will resemble bombed out war zones. Because of this, the frustration and anger will soon turn to fear and panic. People will be afraid to venture far from home, knowing that there will be little to protect them from the attacks of robbers and thugs, and even of desperate people who can justify certain crimes for the sake of feeding their families. The economy will be in a massive depression. Everyone will be focused on survival rather than productivity.

## Scenario 3: Meltdown

I am not going to spend a lot of time on the Meltdown Scenario. Frankly, it's depressing enough just getting through the Blackout

Scenario. The only real difference between Scenarios 2 and 3 is the impact of failed systems and the degree of disruption it will cause.

Imagine, for example, what would happen if there were so much chaos that electric utilities couldn't be brought back on line for years rather than months. Think what would happen if the Nuclear Regulatory Commission allowed some nuclear reactors to stay open, believing they were Year 2000–compliant. And then imagine what would happen, if, unknown to the commission at the time, the Millennium Bug were still lurking in some mission-critical embedded system. And what if that system were *so* critical that it causes a meltdown? Don't think it can't happen. Just remember Three-Mile Island and Chernobyl.

In the Blackout Scenario, I predicted widespread *hunger* as a result of the shipping and transportation industry's inability to distribute food. In this scenario it is even worse; it is *starvation.* Our country and most others do not have a significant, on-hand supply of food. And since most of the food production is done by a handful (relatively speaking) of food producers, it wouldn't take much to disrupt the supply. And further, if you can't get the food to the people who need it, it really doesn't matter how much you have. This is the lesson we have learned again and again in attempting to send food and medical supplies to famine-struck and war-torn areas of the world.

In this scenario the banks would simply be shut down. U.S. currency—and that of most other developed nations—will be worthless. The economy will be reduced to barter and some hard money (e.g., gold and silver). There will be little use for the federal government. Without electricity, telecommunications, and banking, the long arm of Washington will have zero effect on most local situations. No one will think twice about what the feds think; they will be a nonissue.

In addition to no government, there will be no federal troops. This is perhaps the scariest of all. It will make us extremely vulnerable to foreign invasion. The police will be totally out of commission, too, though local areas might appoint sheriffs. I could see possible civil war conditions in many areas between local militias and organized gangs. These may even be racial in nature. For a time, things will once again resemble the "wild, wild west." Don't forget that these conditions were exactly what we had in parts of this country as recently as 150 years ago.

Again, the health care situation will be similar to what I described in the Blackout Scenario. The only difference is that medicines will eventually run out and it will be more and more difficult to keep disease and pestilence in check. In fact, I would expect some diseases we thought we had licked making a comeback. If this scenario comes to pass, the public will live in a state of terror. In the words of Roberto Vacca, we will be living in a "new dark age"[4] and all that that will mean: war, famine, and pestilence.

## So What's It Going to Be?

I am not a pessimist by nature, let alone a prophet of doom. I prefer to focus on the positive. Surely our "good ol' American ingenuity" will solve this problem. If we can put a man on the moon, we ought to be able to squash the Millennium Bug. But this is one area in which all the positive thinking in the world isn't going to fix the problem. We are simply out of time. From my perspective, it all comes down to one question: *How bad is it really going to be?*

The three scenarios I have outlined above are summarized in Table 9.1. These aren't the only three possibilities, of course. It would be easy, for example, to imagine a scenario that is worse than my first one but not quite as bad as my second. The same could be said of the second and third. My only purpose in outlining the scenarios I have is to stimulate your thinking and help you see the importance of preparing *now* while you still have time.

## What Do the Computer Experts Think?

One place where mainframe programmers hang out to talk about the Year 2000 Problem is an Internet newsgroup called "Comp.Software.Year-2000." In July 1997 Phil Edwards, a

**Table 9.1**

| Description | | Scenario 1: Brownout |
|---|---|---|
| Impact of Y2K overall | | Isolated system failures, particularly in smaller companies and agencies |
| Length of time before things return to "normal" | | Two weeks to three months |
| Primary Infrastructure | Impact of Y2K on the Power Grid | • Some persistent, recurring local outages<br>• Billing problems |
| | Impact of Y2K on Water | • Some problems with treatment and pumps, resulting in some unsafe water and flow problems<br>• Billing problems |
| | Impact of Y2K on Transportation | • Ticketing problems<br>• Some confusion with flight plans and navigation<br>• Some lost railroad cars and delays in delivery of goods<br>• Higher prices for everything, including gasoline |
| | Impact of Y2K on Telecommunications | • Lots of busy signals (unable to authorize credit card purchases)<br>• Periodic, interrupted service<br>• Some billing problems, particularly from local carriers |

**Possible Y2K Scenarios**

| Scenario 2: Blackout | Scenario 3: Meltdown |
|---|---|
| Multiple system failures and social upheaval | Multiple system failures and complete breakdown of society |
| Four months to three years | Four to ten years |
| • Power grid is completely out for an extended period<br>• Some isolated utilities are still able to function<br>• Eventually, systems are brought back on line, one at a time | • Two or more nuclear meltdowns<br>• Utilities cannot be brought back on line because there is so much disruption elsewhere |
| • Because there is no electricity, water cannot be treated or pumped<br>• Some people get sick drinking from alternative sources<br>• Disease begins to spread from untreated sewage | • Same as Scenario 2 |
| • All planes are grounded<br>• Majority of other vehicles stop running as petroleum products are used up<br>• Cannot deliver basic food items; supermarkets are empty; people are hungry<br>• Gasoline has the value of "liquid gold" | • Very few vehicles in operation<br>• No extra-local distribution of goods<br>• All types of vehicles are rusting away<br>• People are starving in some places |
| • No phones<br>• Internet is completely down<br>• Short-wave radio use by individuals with ability to generate power | • Same as Scenario 2 |

**Table 9.1 (con't.)**

| Description | | Scenario 1: Brownout |
|---|---|---|
| Secondary Infrastructure | Impact of Y2K on Banking | • Bank errors<br>• Some withdrawls by individuals, but not a widespread problem<br>• FDIC reaffirms commitment to bank deposits |
| | Impact of Y2K on Government | • Some agencies don't make it<br>• President and Congress reassure people; encourage cooperation<br>• IRS doesn't have its systems working; Congress enacts a flat tax |
| | Impact of Y2K on the Military | • Still functioning<br>• Experiencing some problems, but keeping them under wraps for the sake of national security |
| | Impact of Y2K on Police | • Still functioning<br>• Some administrative problems |
| | Impact of Y2K on Health Care | • Smaller hospitals have billing problems<br>• Some medical devices malfunction<br>• Litigation |
| | Impact of Y2K on Public Mood | Frustration |
| | Impact of Y2K on Social Stability | Isolated riots and protests |
| | Impact of Y2K on Economy | Recession |

**Possible Y2K Scenarios**

| Scenario 2: Blackout | Scenario 3: Meltdown |
|---|---|
| • Banks runs<br>• Temporary government shutdown of banks ("cooling off" period)<br>• Some banks never re-open | • Banks shut down (no electricity)<br>• Currency is worthless (people use it for kindling)<br>• Total hard money and barter economy |
| • President invokes Emergency Powers Act<br>• Martial law<br>• IRS is a nonissue | • No federal government to speak of<br>• Federal anarchy |
| • Major problems<br>• Soldiers going AWOL<br>• Accidents with some weapons systems<br>• Highly vulnerable to foreign invasion | • Local militias; no federal troops<br>• Widespread problems with gangs |
| • Can't get paid<br>• Many quit<br>• National Guard is sent in to maintain order | • No police, some sheriffs<br>• The "Wild West" returns |
| • Few hospitals functional<br>• Medical equipment won't work (no electricity)<br>• Difficult to perform surgery<br>• Health care is about what it was 100 years ago | • No hospitals to speak of<br>• Medicines are hard to come by<br>• Anyone with medical training is highly esteemed<br>• Rampant disease |
| Fear and Panic | Terror |
| Widespread rioting and looting | Civil war between gangs and militias |
| Depression | Nonexistent |

programmer himself, surveyed an international group of thirty-eight computer experts and Year 2000 researchers. He asked them to cast their vote on how they thought the Y2K crisis would affect the civilized world. Edwards defined the scale as follows:

> 5 = probable collapse of economy, start hoarding now (this correlates to my Blackout Scenario)
>
> 3 = bump in the road, eighty-hour weeks for all 1999–2000 (this correlates to my Brownout Scenario)
>
> 1 = it ain't gonna happen (this correlates to my Nonscenario Scenario)

Voting on a scale of 1 to 5, experts used the Delphi Technique and the Internet to state their opinion on the issue. The thirty-eight respondents had a total of 669.5 years of experience, or an average of 17.6 years each. The average score was 3.96.[5]

## Conclusion

What do I think will happen? Like the computer experts referenced above, I think we will end up somewhere between the Brownout and the Blackout scenarios. It really all comes down to whether the power grid and the banking system make it. Lose either one of these, and we will find ourselves in some version of the Blackout Scenario. If the grid and the banks stay down long enough, we could end up in the Meltdown Scenario.

But it really doesn't matter what I think. The real question is *what do you think?* You've seen most of the evidence. (Believe me, there is plenty more, but you probably know more than you want to know now.) The fact is, the point of absolute certainty will never come.

Already, government agencies and companies are moving into spin-control mode. They cannot afford to tell us the truth—they don't want to create panic. More than anything else, they need to maintain our confidence. As a result, you are going to have to make a decision about what to do *without* having as much honest information as you would like. And the longer you postpone making a decision, the more you will pay for your procrastination. It could get very expensive. *Very expensive*, indeed.

# Chapter Ten

## Where the Rubber Meets the Road

*Practical Considerations in Preparing for the Year 2000 Crisis*

**Self-preservation, nature's first great law**
**All the creatures, except man, doth awe.**

—Andrew Marvell (1621–1678)

Years ago, when our children were small, a good friend advised my wife and me to take up camping. He explained that it was a good way to build family togetherness. Because his family was a perfect model for what he was advocating, we bought his theory "hook, line, and sinker." So we packed up the family and headed, not for the woods, but for the local discount sporting goods store.

When we arrived, we entered a warehouse *full* of sporting goods. There were several different departments, including a complete, thoroughly furnished camping department. It had everything from tents to high-tech compasses. It even sold self-inflating, double-strength air mattresses. For a "gadget guy" like me, it was heaven.

Two hours and three shopping carts later we checked out. We had spent almost $1,000. Even now that's a lot of money, but at the time it was an *incredible* amount of money, especially as a percentage of our annual income. Nevertheless, we found it easy to justify. "It's an investment in our family," I mumbled to my wife, as I reluctantly signed the credit card receipt. "Yeah," she sighed, "and since we bought the best stuff, it will probably last a lifetime." In those days, we were optimistic—and naive—about everything.

We went home and immediately began to get ready to depart on our adventure. Gail went to the store to buy food. The girls packed their clothes, books, and dolls. And I packed the equipment and supplies. By the time we were ready to leave for the campgrounds, we barely had room to squeeze ourselves into our overloaded van. It didn't look as if we were going camping—it looked as if we were moving!

**With the Y2K Crisis, you need to plan *thoroughly* for every contingency.**

We drove to a beautiful, secluded spot about two hours from our home. We got everything set up, including the tent and table awning, without a problem. The girls staked out their sleeping spots in our brand new, super-deluxe, six-man tent. I gathered some wood and built a fire. Gail soon began making dinner. We were enjoying our first-ever campout dinner. It was glorious.

After a little singing around the campfire, we went to bed. The fresh air and the melodic chirping of the crickets quickly put us to sleep. Everything was perfect—until about 3:30 AM. At that time, a loud clap of thunder yanked us from our slumber. My wife and I both sat straight up, our hearts pounding. Amazingly, the children slept on. Then we heard the rain begin to fall in torrents.

We looked at each other, and both knew what we had to do. Without a word, we slipped on our flip-flops and bolted out of the tent. We hastily began tying the flaps down on the tent windows. When we were finished, we dove back into the tent, sopping wet. We then prayed that our flimsy canvas shelter wouldn't leak—or be blown away. After what seemed like an eternity, the darkness gave way to light and the rain subsided.

Since all the wood was wet, we were forced to eat a cold breakfast. Because we had invested *so much money* in our camping gear, I wasn't about to throw in the towel. We were going to stay and experience the family togetherness my friend had promised us—even if it killed us!

After breakfast, I herded everyone into the van and we headed for town. If we were going to brave the elements, we had to have the proper equipment. What we needed—and what we had forgotten—was rain gear. After spending an additional $100 and two hours shopping, we had what we needed: an immense tarp to put over the tent (just in case) and rain ponchos for everyone. Nothing could stop us now. We were prepared. Let the rains come. We were ready.

I don't think we saw another drop the rest of the week.

In most situations, failure to plan simply results in an inconvenience. But with the Y2K Crisis, there will be no running out to the store for forgotten necessities. The stores will likely be closed—at least for a time—and your neighbors will probably be in worse shape than you are. You will have to make do with what you have; therefore, you need to plan *thoroughly* for every contingency.

## A Baker's Dozen

There are at least *thirteen specific areas* you need to consider in preparing for the Y2K Crisis. I refer to these as my "Baker's Dozen of Y2K Preparations." As you read this list, you might be easily overwhelmed. Don't be. Taking *some* action is better than none. Start small and add to your preparations as time, energy, and resources permit.

With the exception of the first couple of items, these are not in order of priority.

*1. Secure hard copies of important documents.* I used to tell my secretary, "If that document is *really* important, someone, somewhere has a copy of it." With the Y2K Crisis looming on the horizon, this axiom is obsolete. Once the crisis hits, unless you have a hard copy of some document, you may never have a chance to get another one. And without an official hard copy, you may not be able to prove some things you need to prove—things like your age, citizenship, marital status, property owned, debts owed and paid, and so on.

If you don't have them already, secure copies of at least the following documents:

- birth certificates for each member of your family
- marriage licenses or certificates
- baptismal, confirmation, ordination, and other religious records
- social security cards
- deeds, titles, and other proofs of ownership
- mortgages and other loan agreements
- loan statements showing exactly what you owe (just retain the monthly statements)
- credit card statements
- tax returns (if you owe money to the Internal Revenue Service [IRS], make sure you retain any statements you receive showing how much you owe)

One important document you need to secure is a Personal Earnings and Benefit Estimate Statement (PEBES) from the Social Security Administration (SSA). Call their national toll-free number and ask for a copy of SSA-7004 or, easier yet, fill out a copy on the SSA's Web site at <www.ssa.gov>. (You can also get this form from some insurance agents or your local SSA office.) Complete the form and mail it in. You should receive your statement in the mail in about six weeks. You will want to repeat this process every few months in order to keep it current.

Once you collect these documents, you might want to think of a place other than a safety deposit box to store them. If the bank closes, you don't want to have to worry about how you are going to get your documents.

*2. Build an emergency preparedness library.* Your best weapon against uncertainty is knowledge. If the computers go down, and if they are down as long as I think they will be, you are going to have to learn to function in a low-tech world. There are many things our forebears knew and took for granted that we don't. For example, do you know how to:

- Dress a wound, set a broken bone, cure an infection, or treat yourself or others for food poisoning?

- Secure an alternative source of water should your tap water suddenly dry up? Or purify water so that you don't make yourself or your family sick when you drink it?

- Distinguish edible plants from those that are deadly?

- Deliver a baby, pull a tooth, or set a broken bone?

- Dress a deer, butcher a cow or pig, clean a fish, or pluck a chicken?

- Dispose of human waste (when the toilets aren't working) in a way that keeps disease from rapidly spreading?

If you answered no to any of these questions, you need to educate yourself. The list above is only the beginning. Fortunately, this information exists; it just isn't readily available. I have listed additional resources in Appendix A. There you will find a list of Web sites, computer forums, books, and vendors.

*3. Evaluate your current location.* Even in good times, large cities are not always the best place to live. When the infrastructure breaks down, they can be absolutely horrible—and often dangerous. They might well be the worst places to live when the Y2K Crisis hits.

Try this mental exercise. Imagine what it would be like to live in your current neighborhood *without* electricity, water, or the benefit of police protection. Would you survive? For how long? How would you heat your home? (Don't forget the Y2K Crisis will begin in the dead of winter.) Where will you get water? How will you protect yourself?

Or think about this: how vulnerable is your neighborhood to looters? Don't make the mistake of thinking that looting is just an urban phenomenon. What happens when the inner cities have all been looted? Where will the looters go next? Would your subdivision, apartment complex, or neighborhood be an attractive target? How long will it take for them to get to you? What will you do when they come?

**Don't be overwhelmed: There are a number of simple steps you can take to prepare yourself.**

If you've been thinking about moving to a smaller city, a town, or even the country, this might be a good time to act. Even if the Y2K Crisis never materializes, you might still be glad you did. Living in a small town is often cheaper, safer, and less stressful than living in a city. And, with a little planning and creativity, you can probably still commute to your current job or negotiate a work-at-home arrangement with your employer.

What should you look for in your target location? I would suggest the following:

- *A small population.* Ideally, I'd pick a city of not more than twenty-five thousand residents, preferably less than ten thousand.

- *A volunteer fire department.* At the very least, look for a partially volunteer fire department. I want to live in a place where people still have a sense of civic responsibility and *esprit de corps* and know how to pitch in and help their neighbors in a crisis.

- *Slack zoning laws.* If I want to dig a well, I don't want to be stopped by bureaucrats. If I want to plant a garden or raise chickens, I don't want to be in violation of city ordinances or my subdivision covenants.

- *An armed citizenry.* I know guns are controversial,

and I'm not going to defend them here. But gangs, thugs, and looters prey on the weak. As a general rule, they avoid homeowners with guns.

- *Low crime rates.* I don't know about you, but I want to live in a place where my nearest neighbors are God-fearing, moral, and decent. You know the kind of place—where people keep their word and treat other people as they want to be treated. Where there are absolutely no gangs or organized criminals. Do such places still exist? You bet. Just take a drive into the country and visit one of the thousands of small towns that are scattered across the landscape. By virtue of frequency and volume the media would have you believe that urban life is the norm. Don't believe it; it's not. It's just that it makes for more interesting subject matter when it comes to producing television shows and the evening news.

Find some way to live in a safe place. If you need to move, do so. If you can set up a vacation retreat, that might be an option. If you absolutely can't move, don't despair. Many people will find themselves in this situation. Simply "dig in" and make the best of it. Here are five things you can do to your existing home to make it more safe and livable in a crisis, regardless of where you live:

- Get to know your neighbors. People who know each other can band together for the common defense and assist one another in providing for basic needs. You will be safer in a group than on your own.

- Install dead-bolts on your doors and make sure *all* your windows have *working* locks. (It probably goes without saying, but an electrical security system will do you no good if the electricity is out.)

- Learn to defend yourself in a way that is congruent with your personal values. This does not necessarily mean you have to buy a gun if you are not comfortable doing so. There are other alternatives.

- Consider purchasing a gas or diesel generator for emergency power. You will also need an adequate supply of fuel. Solar energy may also be an option.

- Modify your fireplace (if you have one) to make it more efficient. Most fireplaces are designed as a decoration, not a source of heat. There are many devices that can be installed; just make sure you don't use one that depends on electricity. If you don't have a fireplace, consider installing a wood-burning stove.

*4. Determine your self-defense philosophy.* Most of us have never had to consider what we would be willing to do, if pressed, to defend ourselves or our family members. We take rapid-response law enforcement for granted. *Help is only a 911 call away*, we think. In the past fifteen or so years, we have been systematically conditioned to believe that gun ownership—or worse, gun use—is politically incorrect or even morally wrong.

You need to think seriously through what you would do if you or a loved one were attacked. Would you be willing to hurt someone—perhaps seriously—to stop him from hurting you, your spouse, or your children? Would you be willing to shoot him? Even kill, if necessary? What does the law say in your state? What are your rights? What are your obligations? How do these apply to different situations? The time to ask these questions is *not* when you discover that you have an intruder in your house. You must be clear about these issues *before* you encounter the threat and be willing to live with the consequences of your decisions.

If you opt for gun ownership, you need to take a class in basic gun use. Many state and local governments provide these classes for free, or for a nominal fee, as part of the gun registration or "concealed carry permit" process. Some even require it. There are few things more dangerous than a frightened and untrained person with a gun. Training gives you confidence and will minimize your chances of hurting yourself or others—unless that is your intention. A good class will cover the basics of loading, shooting, and cleaning a gun. It will also teach you important safety procedures.

**Time is not on your side. You must get started now.**

If you are going to purchase a gun (or guns), make sure you get one that is appropriate for your size and goals. Practice using it, so you know how to reload it under pressure and how to shoot it accurately. You also want to know what kind of recoil and noise level to expect. Both of these can be frightening the first few times you fire the weapon. If other family members will be armed, then make sure they get the necessary training as well. You might even want to make this a family activity.

I remember reading a story about a trailer park that was unscathed during the Miami riots. A couple of the residents owned .22 rifles, which, as you may know, are not very effective weapons against humans. They are primarily used for target practice or hunting small game. Nevertheless, when the looting began, these guys grabbed their guns, a couple of folding chairs, and headed for the park entrance. They sat in their chairs, gun stocks on their knees, their guns pointed to the sky. All day long they saw looters running by. Some had their arms full of stolen merchandise; others were looking for something to steal. Regardless, all of them kept their distance. The two men didn't utter a single threat or fire a shot all day. In this situation, just owning a gun and publicly displaying it was a deterrent to would-be attackers.

*5. Find an alternative source of water.* If there's one thing we take for granted in civilized society, it is clean water. For most of us, it is as close as the nearest faucet. Perhaps the only time we consider the water supply is when we venture out of the country. If you've ever had the misfortunate of drinking contaminated water (e.g., "Montezuma's Revenge"), then you know first-hand how incredibly debilitating the experience can be. Few things can incapacitate a person faster than ingesting bad water.

How much water do you need? The average person uses a whopping *fifty-four gallons a day*. Table 10.1 breaks out how this is used.[1]

**Table 10.1:**
**Typical Water Use Per Person Per Day**

| | |
|---|---|
| Shower | 25 Gallons |
| Toilet Flush (Four flushes @ 5 gallons each) | 20 Gallons |
| Hand washing (Twice @ 2 gallons each time) | 4 Gallons |
| Brushing Teeth (Twice @ 2 gallons each time) | 4 Gallons |
| Drinking and Cooking | 1 Gallon |
| **Total** | **54 Gallons** |

The above amount does not include water used in dish washing (another twenty gallons) or lawn and garden care. Drinking is not optional, but perhaps the other items are—at least in the short term. Nevertheless, you should plan on having available a *minimum* of one gallon per day per person. (You need two quarts a day for just drinking—more in hot weather.) That's a lot of water, I know, but it is absolutely essential to survival. You might want to have more water available to share with friends and neighbors that didn't plan as well as they should have.

If the local city water department cannot provide your home with safe, reliable water on demand after the crisis hits, you have six options:

- *Purchase the water once the crisis hits.* This is the "day-late-and-a-dollar-short" strategy. If you follow it, you will be buying water at exorbitant prices from merchants who have it in stock. At best, even if you have a form of currency they will still accept, this is a short-term option. Most of the water will be gone in less than a day.

- *Depend on the local authorities to distribute water.* In a crisis, they usually do this by truck. Depending on the routing and the circumstances, you may have to wait a few days, a few weeks, or perhaps even more. I don't like being dependent on anyone other than God. I especially don't like being dependent on the government. If you don't plan, you will be in this situation, and I think you will be putting your family at a high level of risk, not to mention outright discomfort.

- *Use water already stored in your house.* At any one time, you have more water in your house than you think. For example, I have a seventy-five–gallon water heater. With my family of seven, we need a minimum of seven gallons a day. So, my water heater will give me a ten-day supply. Toilet storage tanks contain another five gallons each. (Notice I didn't say toilet "bowls.") With three toilets I have a little more than two days' supply. (The water in toilet tanks is usually perfectly clean; however, you will not be able to drink it if you have put any chemical freshener in it.) If you fill up your bathtubs on the eve of the crisis, you will get another fifteen gallons per tub.[2] If you turn off your water main, before the water stops flowing from the city, you will also trap a lot of water in your pipes and keep it from being inadvertently siphoned back into the municipal supply. That could give you another ten to twenty gallons. Depending on the size of your family and the size of your house, you may have enough water for fifteen to thirty days, assuming that all you do is drink it.

- *Store additional water.* Unfortunately, the crisis could easily—in fact, probably will—last more than a month. So you'll need even more water. Storing water is one possibility. If you store water in large containers, make sure they are sufficiently anchored so they cannot fall. Water is *very* heavy. You and your children could be badly hurt from a falling container. Plastic containers should be your first choice. They won't break, and they are easy to find and transport. Two-liter plastic soft-drink bottles work best. When you've emptied the original contents, rinse the bottle out, refill it with water, add a few drops of Clorox, and store it in a dark place. If the water in the bottles is likely to freeze, leave a little room at the top, so the frozen water can expand without rupturing the container. Please note: do not use plastic milk cartons. Many of these containers are bio-degradable and will split open or deteriorate over time. As an alternative to soft-drink bottles, you can buy larger containers made especially for storing water.

- *Secure an alternative source of clean water.* Ideally, it's best to have your own well. This would make you completely self-reliant for water. A well won't cost you as much as you think, but you will need to get the necessary permits. Unfortunately, you will likely be prohibited from drilling a well if you live in a subdivision or the suburbs. If you do have a well, don't depend on an electrical pump; buy a simple handpump. Well water won't do you any good if you can't get to it. Other sources of clean water include springs, creeks, and some ponds. It is a good idea, however, to have the water tested well before the crisis hits, to make sure it is safe.

- *Purify whatever water you can find.* Even if you don't have a well or if you run out of stored water (which is inevitable no matter how much you store), it is likely that you can still find some source of water; you just need to make it safe to drink. Fortunately, this is a fairly simple process. The best method for sterilizing water is to boil it. In order to kill bacteria and viruses you need to bring water to a *full boil* for at least fifteen minutes. You need to boil it for an additional five minutes for every one thousand feet you are above sea level. But boiling alone might not kill everything. As an added precaution, use iodine compounds specifically made for water purification. They are available at most sporting goods or camping stores.

These recommendations only scratch the surface of this important topic. Water is essential. Consider your options and carefully plan your strategy.

*6. Stockpile food and common household goods.* As self-sufficiency expert Duncan Long says, "purchasing food when it is plentiful and storing it for an emergency is *not* hoarding (despite what some government workers and TV commentators might have you believe). Storing food during a time of plenty is *stockpiling.* Hoarding will be done after a disaster when those who didn't prepare strip grocery shelves and squirrel away the food for their own use."[3] Since grocery stores turn over their inventory three times a week, and since they can be completely emptied in a few hours during a crisis, you need to plan ahead and store the food you think you will need. There are several things to consider as you begin storing food:

- *Know how much you need.* Plan on a minimum of 2,500 calories per day per person. If you are going to be doing strenuous work, you will need more than that. In addition to food, you may also want to store vitamins and food supplements. These can assist you in *preventing* sickness and promoting good health.

- *Remember that food has a finite life.* Canned foods have the shortest shelf-life. While they may be edible for up to two years, they begin losing their nutritional value after six months. Canned food, however, is easy to store and fairly inexpensive. If you opt for this method, organize the cans so that you eat the oldest food first. Pasta products such as dried spaghetti, noodles, macaroni, etc., have shelf lives of nearly two years and provide maximum food value for the least cost. Foods that are freeze-dried or dehydrated can often be stored for several years. This is particularly true of unprocessed grains and dried beans. If these are protected from vermin and stored in nitrogen-filled containers, they can last several decades. Food supply companies can help evaluate your options.

- *You may not have time to do elaborate food preparation in a crisis.* One easy-to-use food system developed by the U.S. military is MREs (Meals, Ready to Eat). These come precooked in plastic bags. They are edible right out of the box. They are palatable at room temperature, but they are even more so if they are heated up. MREs will last anywhere from four years to more than ten years, depending on how they are stored.

- *Don't forget the condiments.* Store the basic condiments (salt, pepper, sugar, honey, etc.), seasonings, and nonessentials (coffee, tea, cocoa, etc.). They'll make your food less spartan and are also good barter items.

- *Store enough to share with others.* You are going to need the support of your friends and neighbors, and they are not likely to be too helpful if you are eating well and they are going hungry.

You will also need some means of cooking or warming your food. Some type of camp stove would probably be a good investment.

In addition to basic food items, you may want to stockpile some of the following household items:

- Toilet paper
- Paper towels
- Feminine hygiene products
- Toothpaste / toothbrushes / floss
- Soaps and cleansers
- Shampoo / conditioner
- Matches / lighters
- Candles / kerosene lamps

*7. Purchase adequate clothing.* Because the Y2K Crisis will start in the middle of the winter, make sure you have adequate clothing for every member of your family. If the electrical grid goes down, so will your heater.

The best way to stay warm is by layering your clothing. Long underwear and extra socks, as well as mittens, gloves, stocking caps, sweatshirts, sweaters, and jackets are all a good idea. Double your supply of underwear; since you will be rationing water, you won't be washing clothes too often. Also invest in a good, heavy sleeping bag for every member of your family.

*8. Develop an alternative source of heat and energy.* If you don't have a fireplace, you might consider putting in a wood-burning stove, which can be used to heat your home as well as cook your food. Wood-burning stoves are generally far more efficient than fireplaces, because the heat doesn't escape through the chimney. If you already have a fireplace, consider converting it to a wood-burning stove. Many companies offer these units and they combine the best of aesthetics (you can actually view the flames) and efficiency. Whether you use a fireplace or a stove, you will also need to store plenty of fuel. Remember: it takes considerably more wood actually to heat a room than it does to "decorate" one.

After you've solved your heating problems, plan for an alternative source of lighting. Whenever there is a crisis of any sort—even something as simple as a big thunderstorm—the first thing to get hit is the electrical grid. If this happens at night things can get *really* dark, especially when all the lights are out, including street and security lights.

The first thing you need to secure is several flashlights with *plenty* of batteries. Store the flashlights in strategic places around your home. Your master bedroom and the kitchen are good places to begin.

In addition to flashlights, you may want to purchase some "light sticks" (also known as "snapsticks"). These create a cold chemical light that is nonflammable. They have a very long shelf life and can be activated by simply bending the plastic body of the stick. They are also waterproof. Once activated, however, they cannot be turned off. They burn for approximately twelve hours.

You might then want to consider candles. They are relatively safe and inexpensive. Special "emergency" candles burn for up to fifty hours each and sell for around $3 apiece. Candles also make excellent barter items and gifts for neighbors. Stock several boxes.

Consider stocking some gasoline or diesel fuel. Gasoline has a shelf life of only about a year. You can extend this with off-the-shelf additives to double its life. Diesel lasts far longer, but few cars or tools use it.

*9. Prepare an emergency medical kit.* At a bare minimum buy a good first aid kit. This will get you started with the basics: aspirin, bandages, iodine, antibacterial salve, and so on. But a first aid kit is *only a start*. You will need extra rubbing alcohol, hydrogen peroxide, cortisone, pain relievers (e.g., Tylenol, Ibuprofen, Aleve, etc.), anti-acids, allergy medicines, cough syrup, and cold remedies. Don't forget any prescription drugs, including disposable contacts. (If you wear glasses, invest in a second pair.)

Whenever possible, buy medicines that have a long storage life and do not require refrigeration. If you have any questions, check with your pharmacist.

**Perhaps you can't do everything, but you can do *something*. And some preparation is better than none.**

In addition to securing the basic implements and medicines, you need knowledge and training. Many community colleges and service organizations like the Red Cross offer basic first aid classes. Once you've got that under your belt, you might want to sign up for a full-blown EMT (emergency medical training) course. This will enable you to treat more serious injuries, including heart attacks, gunshot wounds, serious bone breaks and bleeding, and other complications. You might also want to add some basic medical how-to books to your emergency preparedness library. I have listed one in Table 10.2.

***10. Determine how you will dispose of waste.*** This is not a pleasant subject to discuss, but it is essential that you deal with it. Remember, if the electricity goes out, the water and sewage systems soon follow. And few things can spread disease faster, attracting flies, cockroaches, rats, and other vermin, than improper disposal of human waste. The good news is that all you really need is a shovel and a little know-how.

If you don't have running water, don't use the toilets. Tape them shut with duct tape so that no one in your family—especially the children—forgets that the toilets are "broken." You have only two real options:

- At night, when you may not want to leave the house, or during the first days of the crisis, you can use a jar, a bucket, or a chemical toilet. The latter are readily available wherever camping supplies are sold. The chemicals help reduce the odor. But you will need to make sure you have an adequate supply of the chemical additive. If you opt for buckets, have two—one for urine and one for excrement. This will simplify the disposal process. In the excrement bucket, use a garbage bag as a plastic liner to make disposal easier. When it fills up, simply tie it off and bury it.

- Bucket and chemical toilets are not a permanent solution. If the crisis lasts longer than a week or two, you will need to build a more permanent latrine or "outhouse." The basics are pretty simple. Dig a deep hole, then build a wooden platform over the top. Insert one or two "bottomless" buckets. You can even affix a toilet bowl cover on top if you want to get fancy. You can cover the latrine with a small shed or perhaps even locate it behind some tall bushes. Regardless, make sure surface water doesn't run into the latrine during storms. This could cause it to overflow. Also, you should take care to keep buckets and other openings sealed when not in use so that flies and other insects can't reach the waste and spread disease.

In addition to human waste, you'll need to dispose of garbage and spoiled food. Garbage can be stored in garbage bags—just make sure they are tightly sealed. Do not, however, use these to store spoiled food. If you do, they will attract animals that will claw and bite the bags open. Separate organic items from the trash and add them to your compost pile.

*11. Secure an alternative form of currency.* Hope for the best, but plan for the worst. I know it is almost inconceivable, but what if the government-issued currency fails? In an age of "fiat" money like we have now, money has value only as long as people *believe* the government will stand behind it. It has no *intrinsic* value of its own. If people lose faith in the government, then the value of government-issued money can plummet overnight. Digital cash—the kind that is stored in your checking account or credit card—will be completely worthless if the computers go down and no one can get to it.

In an extended emergency, the first form of currency is "barter." People begin trading with one another for the goods and services they need. Eventually, a few items become the predominant medium of exchange. In the past, these have included cigarettes, ammunition, and even toilet paper. You might want to stock some of these items, just for this purpose. I would suggest stockpiling:

- Ammunition, especially .22 caliber
- Toilet paper
- "Bic" lighters
- Coffee and tea
- Sugar

Sooner or later, hard money, particularly silver, gold, and possibly platinum will become the preferred method of purchasing goods. Such money is valuable (intrinsically so), portable, and durable.

There are two kinds of gold and silver coins: (1) junk coins, meaning coins that have been in circulation and are worn, and (2) numismatic coins that have a collectors value above and beyond the value of the metal contained in them. For most barter purposes (as opposed to investment purposes), junk coins are probably the best. One of the best sources of junk silver is pre-1965 U.S. dimes, quarters, and half dollars. (After 1965, the U.S. government began diluting the value of the coins by adding other, less-expensive metals to the mix.) If you have the money to invest in gold or platinum, make sure you carefully consider where and how you can safely store it.

You don't have to be rich to begin purchasing silver and gold. You can get started for as little as $100. Simply find a dealer who will help you construct a plan that fits your current budget. (I list one such dealer in Table 10.2.)

*12. Develop an alternative communications system.* If the electricity is out, how will you get news? A battery-operated radio is a start, though radio stations will fade off the air once their back-up generators fail (this will happen after a few weeks). Once the radio stations are down, you'll have to depend on short-wave radio. These can be purchased for as little as $200. (They're also a good form of entertainment before the crisis hits.)

Another alternative is a CB radio. These were very popular in the 1970s, before the availability of cellular phones. You can pick them up *very* inexpensively—usually less than $50. They have a range of approximately one mile.

*13. Acquire a basic selection of hand tools.* If the electrical grid goes down, you will want to have a good selection of hand tools to make repairs. For working with wood, you'll want a variety of saws, hand-operated drills, chisels, rasps, planes, hammers, and screwdrivers. For all-around maintenance, you will also need a good hacksaw, wrenches, pipe-cutters, pliers, and a crowbar. Don't forget basic gardening supplies. Shovels, weed-diggers, hoes, clippers, shears, and perhaps even an old push mower could prove helpful. Some basic sewing supplies are also a good idea.

Don't forget a supply of nails, screws, and staples. Duct tape, rope, wire, and adhesives are important, too. You will also want to make sure that you have recently sharpened all blades, including saws, hatchets, shovels, and axes. You will need these for cutting wood if your stockpile runs out.

Tools will not be very helpful if you don't know how to use them. Fortunately, there are many good how-to books available. You can check many of these out at the local library, or alternatively, you can purchase them at a store like Home Depot and add them to your Emergency Preparedness Library.

## Your Number One Enemy

If you are like most people, when you think of everything that needs to done between now and January 1, 2000, you probably feel overwhelmed. The problem is that that emotion, left unchecked, can turn into paralysis, and paralysis can quickly turn into *procrastination*—and *that's* your number one enemy.

Time is not on your side. You must get started now. Preparing for the Year 2000 Crisis is like tackling any other large project. You must take it one step at a time and do a little bit every day. If you do that, you will be prepared, and you won't be caught by surprise when the Millennium Bug bites. Here are a few principles to consider as you begin your preparation:

1. *Act or be acted upon.* You don't have to be a victim. You have been forewarned, and you have been given some resources to begin making preparations. Like the Nike advertisement says, "Just do it!"

2. *Don't let the best be the enemy of the good.* Perfectionism will only result in procrastination. Perhaps you can't do everything, but you can do *something*. And some preparation is better than no preparation. Get started!

3. *The sooner you start the less you will spend.* As more and more people realize that a crisis of some proportion is inevitable, the more they will be scrambling to prepare. And because more and more dollars will be chasing fewer and fewer supplies, prices will begin rising. The longer you wait to prepare, the more expensive it is going to be. Start now!

Here's a list of ten things you can do today:

**Table 10.2:**
**Ten Things You Can Do Today to Begin Preparing for the Year 2000 Crisis**

- *Make a list of friends and form a study group.* It will be easier to prepare if you do it with a small group.

- *Place a "want" ad to sell some assets you no longer need.* At the very least, schedule a garage sale. This will help you generate some cash that you can reinvest in supplies.

- *Make a list of all the important documents you need* (see p. 186). Start by either calling the SSA or visiting their Web site.

- *Start storing water.* Go to the store and buy ten two-liter bottles of your favorite soft drink. When they are empty, rinse them out, refill with water, add a few drops of Clorox, and store them in your basement or garage. Try to add to your supply weekly.

- *Develop a food storage plan.* Visit Walton Feed's Web site at <www.waltonfeed.com> and download a copy of their food storage catalog. Alternatively, you can call (800) 269-8563 and request a free copy.

- *Buy a camp stove to use for emergency cooking.* If you already have one, make sure you have plenty of fuel.

- *Consider moving to a safer area.* Schedule a time to discuss this with your spouse or roommate. You may not be able to do so, but it's at least worth considering your options.

- *Get some basic emergency medical knowledge.* Order a copy of *Where There Is No Doctor*, an excellent resource for nonprofessionals. At this writing, Amazon.com sells it for $17.00.

- *Get to know neighbors you've never met.* Take them a plate of cookies or just stop by and get acquainted. A solid relationship with your neighbors is perhaps the best form of self-defense.

- *Secure an alternative form of currency.* I suggest you call Franklin Sanders, a silver and gold coin dealer, at (901) 853-6136. Ask about his "Monthly Acquisition Plan" (MAP). This program allows you to begin acquiring coins for as little as $100 per month.

# Epilogue

## The Myth of Continuity

### *Preparing for the Inevitable*

**A prudent man sees danger and takes refuge, but the simple keep going and suffer for it.**

—Proverbs 23:3

In previous generations, emergency preparedness was a way of life. No one was seduced by the "myth of continuity"; everyone assumed that life would be periodically interrupted by crises in one form or another. But many of us—particularly those of us who are baby-boomers—have never really had to face a widespread social crisis. War, famine, and pestilence are outside the realm of our first-hand experience. We get up expecting that today will be pretty much like yesterday, and tomorrow will be pretty much like today.

In the past, people expected their lives to be periodically disrupted, and they planned accordingly. When I was growing up in rural Nebraska, for example, many folks had a storm shelter and an extensive food pantry. The "cellar" (as we all called it) was protection against summer tornadoes, and the pantry was protection against winter blizzards. No one questioned the wisdom of preparing for emergencies. The opposite would have been true; a lack of preparation would have been seen as foolishness. We would often go years without a tornado or a blizzard. But that did not make my parents or grandparents any less vigilant.

Insurance is based on a similar notion. Every year I spend thousands of dollars on various insurance premiums: life insurance, disability insurance, car insurance, fire insurance for my home, and—last but certainly not least—health insurance. I bet you do, too. Because I have five children my health insurance is ridiculously high. (In fact, my insurance premiums are higher than the mortgage payments were on our first house!)

**Preparing for Y2K is like taking out an insurance policy: Hope for the best, but plan for the worst.**

I don't know about you, but I never get to the end of the year and say to my wife, "Gee, honey, we paid out over $6,000 in health insurance premiums this year, and we didn't have a single major medical claim. What a waste! I think we should cancel our policy." No, I would be happy if we *never* had to use it. Why? Because I operate by this principle: *hope for the best, but plan for the worst!* Y2K is no different.

In the last chapter I suggested that you begin preparing for the fallout of the Year 2000 Problem. In essence, this preparation is a kind of "insurance policy"—a Y2K insurance policy. If you don't end up needing it, so much the better. All you will have wasted is some time and a little money. But unlike every other insurance policy you buy, this one has two unique characteristics. First, you have a high probability of actually using it, and second, you know exactly when you are going to need it.

Thus, you have a choice. Either you can ignore the Year 2000 Problem and go on with life as though you had never read this book, or you can begin now taking steps to prepare for what may be the worst disaster our world has experienced in centuries. If you choose the former, you may end up a victim. If you choose the latter, you may ensure that you and your loved ones survive this crisis in one piece. It's up to you.

# Appendix A

## Where to Go from Here

### *Additional Resources to Explore on Your Own*

If you want to do further research on your own, or if you simply want to stay current on the Year 2000 Problem, I would encourage you to visit any or all of the following Internet Web sites:

*Dr. Ed Yardeni's Y2K Reporter*
<http://www.yardeni.com/cyber.html>. This site has some good links and also some interesting commentary.

*Gary North's Y2K Links and Forums*
<http://www.garynorth.com>. This is *the* place to begin. The site is not fancy—no beautiful graphics or frames—but efficient. Dr. North has rendered an invaluable service to the public by making these links and his commentary available. You won't always agree with his conclusions, but you will *always* be stimulated by them.

*Mother of All Year 2000 (Y2K) Link Centers*
<http://pw2.netcom.com/~helliott/00.htm>. This is really a directory of other Y2K sites. It is designed primarily for Information Technology professionals, but it also has some useful information for laypeople.

*The Cassandra Project*

<http://millennia-bcs.com/CASSIE.HTM>. This site is dedicated to promoting public awareness, monitoring state and local Y2K activities, and providing contingency planning. It contains sample letters that you can use in writing to your local utilities and financial institutions.

*Westergaard Year 2000*

<http://www.y2ktimebomb.com>. This site provides a daily commentary on Y2K-related news. In its own words, it provides "strategic analysis of the y2k problem."

*Year 2000 Information Center*

<http://www.year2000.com>. This is Peter de Jager's Web site. He is one of the early Y2K prophets and has spoken widely on the subject, especially to computer information industry professionals. His site attempts to catalog and provide links for every Y2K-related story available on the Web. Often, this amounts to several listings per day.

# Appendix B

## The Top Ten Myths About the Year 2000 Problem

### *Bad Information, Misguided Beliefs, and False Hopes*

1. Someone will come up with a "silver bullet" to solve the whole problem (see pp. 12–13).

2. The Year 2000 Problem affects only mainframe computers (see pp. 22–31).

3. Mainframes aren't used that much anymore (see pp. 20–22).

4. Most companies are on schedule to finish their Y2K projects by the end of 1998. That will give them a full year for testing (see p. 13).

5. This is just a routine maintenance problem. Information Systems departments are routinely engaged in these kinds of projects (see p. 35).

6. If your computer system is compliant, you don't have anything to worry about (see pp. 42–52).

7. The federal government has a comprehensive plan in place to make sure everyone is compliant by the year 2000 (see pp. 106–113).

8. We have until January 1, 2000, to fix the problem (see pp. 34–39).

9. If the computers go down, we can revert to a manual system (see p. 77, p. 120).

10. If the problem is not fixed, it will affect institutions, but it will have little impact on me personally (see pp. 159–181).

# Appendix C

## Prepared Testimony of Jeff Jinnett Before the Senate

### *President, LeBoeuf Computing Technologies*

*"Oversight Hearing on Financial Institutions and the Year 2000 Problem," Before the Senate Banking, Housing, and Urban Affairs Committee, Subcommittee on Financial Services and Technology, 10 July 1997*

Mr. Chairman, distinguished Members of the Subcommittee:

My name is Jeff Jinnett and I am President of LeBoeuf Computing Technologies, L.L.C., a business subsidiary of the law firm of LeBoeuf, Lamb, Greene & MacRae, L.L.P., of which law firm I was formerly a Partner and now serve as Of Counsel. I appreciate the opportunity to testify before this Subcommittee and wish to note that the testimony I give today represents my personal views and does not necessarily represent the views of either LeBoeuf Computing Technologies, L.L.C. or its parent law firm. Consistent with the expressed scope of this hearing, my testimony will be devoted to assessing (a) the magnitude of the Year 2000 computer problem and its impact on the financial services industry and U.S. consumers, (b) business risks associated with the Year 2000 computer problem, (c) the adequacy of risk management and remediation efforts currently being undertaken, and (d) possible government roles and regulations in connection with the remediation process. I ask that a copy of my written statement be included in the record.

## I. Magnitude of the Year 2000 Computer Problem

### *A. Overview of Problem*

The Year 2000 computer problem, variously known as the "Century Date Change," "Millennium Bug" or "Y2K" problem, arises because most business application software programs written over the past few decades use only two digit date fields to specify the year, rather than four digit date fields. Therefore, on January 1, 2000, unless the software is corrected, most computers with date-sensitive programs will recognize the year as "00" and may assume that the year is 1900 rather than 2000. This could either force the computer to shut down (a hard crash) or lead to incorrect calculations (a soft crash). An example of a hard crash is an application software program which refuses to accept a settlement date after December 31, 1999. Examples of soft crashes caused by the Year 2000 problem are (a) incorrect calculation of maturity dates on debt instruments that mature after December 31, 1999, (b) incorrect calculation of a four year loan from 1996 to 2000 as a minus 96 year loan, and (c) incorrect calculations in risk management, hedging and derivative software models.

It is generally understood that programmers in the past used two digits rather than four digits in order to save then-expensive memory during processing and believed that the software they designed would have been replaced before the turn of the century. Unfortunately, many of the software programs ("legacy systems") they designed are still in use. Further, the Year 2000 computer problem can exist not only in software, but also in mainframe computers, midrange computers and personal computers (specifically with respect to BIOS chips) and in embedded microprocessors in non-computer equipment (e.g., "microcontrollers" operating equipment such as security systems, HVAC, elevators and telephone equipment). Although a recent study indicates that on a cost-benefit analysis, more money was saved by reducing the need for processing memory over the past decades than will be spent on Y2K corrective work, we must now "pay the piper."

The initial Gartner Group estimate that the total cost of correcting the Y2K problem worldwide would total $300 billion to $600 billion was originally thought excessive by some. For example, J.P. Morgan conducted an independent analysis and estimated the total corrective cost for the Y2K problem worldwide to be in the range of $200 billion. Recently, however, J.P. Morgan reevaluated their $200 billion estimate and advised that the Gartner Group estimate might not be as "outrageously high" as originally thought. Recent announcements by various entities of their individual estimated Y2K corrective costs (e.g., Chase Manhattan Bank at approximately $250 million) indicate that Y2K corrective work will indeed be costly. The costs for Y2K correction for U.S. commercial banks has been estimated by one consulting group to be $7.2 billion. The estimated cost of Y2K correction for the U.S. securities industry has been reported to be $4 billion. None of the above estimates takes into account the added potential cost to the financial services industry of productivity losses resulting from computer system shutdowns due to the Year 2000 problem. One study has estimated that U.S. securities firms each typically suffer 6.9 on-line system failures per year, which collectively resulted in $3.4 billion in productivity losses in 1992.

### B. Problem Areas Outside of an Entity's Control

There is no technological silver bullet for the Year 2000 computer problem. The reason for this is that although "silver bullet" technologies may be developed to automate and speed up corrective work on certain software languages, there may be as many as 500 different software languages in current use and automated corrective tools will not be developed for all of these languages. For many languages, correction will depend solely on use of programmers trained in the particular software language. Further, inventory and corrective work represents less than half of the typical Y2K corrective plan, with unit and system testing possibly comprising up to 55% of the total effort. Finally, with respect to replacing noncompliant embedded microcontrollers in non-computer equipment, financial institutions must first locate the defective microcontroller, identify the responsible manufacturer and obtain a compliant microcontroller to replace the defective microcontroller.

To illustrate the magnitude of the embedded microcontroller problem, it has been estimated that over 2 billion microcontrollers were sold in 1993 alone. As an example of how a noncompliant microcontroller might seriously cause an item of non-computer equipment to malfunction, consider an item of medical equipment in a hospital emergency room which measures the flow of blood or plasma into a patient. The microcontroller in this hypothetical medical equipment keeps track of when the equipment was last calibrated and automatically shuts the equipment down as unsafe if it is not calibrated on schedule. If the microcontroller is not Year 2000 compliant, on January 1, 2000 it might compare "00" to the date of last calibration (say, June 1, 1999, or "99") and miscalculate that 99 years had passed since the last calibration, shutting down the equipment.

In addition, even if an entity were to succeed in its Y2K corrective effort, it still might suffer a system failure due to the failure of one of its business partners to become Year 2000 compliant—a business dependency risk. For example, the failure of a national clearinghouse for the settlement of securities trades, such as the National Securities Clearing Co. (NSCC), the Depository Trust Company (DTC), the Government Securities Clearing Corp (GSCC) or the MBS Clearing Corporation (MBS), would have a serious negative impact on their associated financial customers. The failure of a value-added-network (VAN) handling electronic data interchange (EDI) transactions for numerous financial institutions and customers would have a similar negative effect. Above all third party dependency risks, the financial services industry is totally dependent on maintaining access to power and telephone service in order to function normally. Some Year 2000 experts are concerned that Year 2000 compliancy efforts and status with respect to power, telephone and other critical infrastructures may vary significantly from country to country outside the U.S. and from state to state within the U.S.

### *C. Structural Impact on the Financial Services Industry*

Since financial institutions frequently deal with date-sensitive calculations, such as interest calculations, they obviously are heavily impacted by the Year 2000 computer problem. In addition, since these calculations are often forward-looking, such as with the calculation of a mortgage payment schedule, financial institutions have found that portions of their computer systems have already encountered Year 2000 problems. Indeed, one large investment company encountered this problem in the 1980's with forward-looking calculations on zero coupon bonds which matured on or after the year 2000. The occurrence of the Year 2000 impact on a program or system is known as the "Event Horizon," which can occur earlier than January 1, 2000 for many applications.

Aside from the obvious system disruptions, the Year 2000 computer problem may also cause, or accelerate, certain structural changes in the financial services industry. First, since financial institutions may not have sufficient software programming and other personnel to carry out a full-scale correction of impacted computer systems, financial institutions may decide to outsource portions of their operations which do not represent core competencies (e.g., credit card processing to a vendor such as First Data Resources or trust account processing to a vendor such as SEI). In addition, rather than incur Y2K corrective costs for a subsidiary which is not viewed as critical, a financial institution may instead sell off the noncompliant subsidiary. Accordingly, some mergers and acquisitions activity during the next three years may be due to the Year 2000 problem. In addition, since an increasing portion of information technology budgets during the next three years will be devoted to Y2K work, a decreasing portion of investment may be devoted to developing new technologies, such as electronic commerce software for banking over the Internet. Finally, for multinational companies doing business in Europe, the need to handle the proposed single European currency (the "euro") between 1999 and 2002 may tend to exacerbate the difficulties arising out of the Year 2000 problem.

## II. Associated Business Risks

### *A. Risks to the Financial Services Industry*

The following business risks may negatively impact the financial services industry as a result of the Year 2000 computer problem: (a) loss of faith by the investing public in the financial services sector and by depositors in the security of their banks, (b) a rise in security problems due to computer "hackers" taking advantage of Y2K disruptions, (c) an increase in bad debt problems within bank loan portfolios, (d) an increase in litigation involving financial institutions due to the failure of third parties, and (e) the possibility that some losses may not be covered by existing business interruption, Directors' and Officers' (D&O) liability and other insurance policies.

***1. Loss of Faith by Investors and Depositors.*** Unfortunately, the tone of many Year 2000 articles in the public press is long on melodrama and "doomsday" predictions, most of which are unlikely to occur with the severity imagined. Accordingly, even if almost all of the U.S. financial institutions become fully Year 2000 compliant, a highly publicized computer system failure of one institution, together with the resulting litigation, may prompt stock market analysts and investors to "short" the stocks of other companies in the affected business sector. One site on the Internet, "http://www.y2kinvestor.com", is devoted to gathering information for investors concerned about the impact of the Year 2000 problem on their stock portfolios. If a bank is involved in a highly publicized systems failure, depositors may become concerned about their ability to access their funds if a "run" on their bank ultimately occurs. "Doomsday" articles alleging that Federal government agencies and/or state agencies are unlikely to become Year 2000 compliant in time may add "fuel to the flames". A recent survey of 40 CEO's and CFO's of Fortune 500 companies conducted privately by Yankelovich Partners, Inc., a recognized market research firm, confirmed that the executives were fully confident that their companies would successfully become Year 2000 compliant. A significant percentage of the executives, however, were concerned that stockholders might sell off their companies' stock due to unsupported fears over the Year 2000 problem.

*2. Breaches of System Security.* It is possible that financial institutions will have to turn to numerous third party vendors for help in undertaking Year 2000 corrective work and site testing. The employees and independent contractors brought in by these vendors may be given extensive access to the institution's computer systems and gain considerable knowledge as to the firewall layouts and other security designs utilized by the institutions. In addition, computer hackers may attempt to take advantage of general system disruptions caused by the Year 2000 computer problem to gain unauthorized access to the institutions' systems. Both of these developments may increase the likelihood that breaches in financial institutions' security systems may occur. The Federal government recognition that computer system security is a critical concern is evidenced by the introduction of H.R. 1903 ("The Computer Security Enhancement Act of 1997").

*3. Increase in Bad Debt Losses in Loan Portfolios.* Although major corporations appear, for the most part, to be fully funding their Year 2000 corrective plans, some smaller entities may not have sufficient funding to undertake a full Year 2000 corrective plan.

This situation may have been unintentionally exacerbated further due to a July 18, 1996 consensus reached by the Emerging Issues Task Force (EITF) of the Financial Accounting Standards Board (FASB) to the effect that companies must expense their Year 2000 corrective work as incurred. This decision appears reasonable from a securities disclosure point of view, since to rule otherwise would result in companies listing their multimillion dollar Y2K corrective work as assets on their financial statements, misleading potential investors that a new asset had been created. However, some smaller companies may not be able to take the "hit" to their bottom line in one or two years and may spread out their corrective work through 1999. This may result in the companies having insufficient time in which to test their corrective work, since it is generally advisable to leave at least one year for testing. These companies may experience an above average number of system failures due to a poorly planned Year 2000 corrective plan and may ultimately produce bad debt losses for their bank lenders. Of course, banks will be reviewing their loan portfolios in the next two years in order to determine if adequate allowances have been made for possible loan defaults due to the Year 2000 computer problem.

*4. Litigation Risk.* In testimony before the U.S. House of Representatives Science Committee on March 20, 1997, Ann Coffou, a Managing Director of the Giga Information Group, predicted that litigation arising out of the Year 2000 computer problem could near or exceed $1 trillion. Year 2000 litigation could be based on numerous legal theories. Contrary to recent press reports, I personally do not wish to speculate as to the total amount of potential Y2K litigation. Since there has been no substantial litigation reported as having been filed to date and since the ultimate amount of litigation filed will depend on how much necessary corrective work is not completed on time, any prediction as to the total amount of litigation which will arise is pure speculation. The Year 2000 problem is not solely a technical problem, but is also a business and legal problem of the highest order, requiring the involvement of each company's Chief Information Officer, Internal Auditor, Chief Financial Officer, General Counsel, Chief Executive Officer and Board of Directors. Use of proper risk management techniques can substantially reduce the likelihood of a company becoming involved in Year 2000 litigation.

*5. Losses May Be Uninsured.* Financial institutions should face the possibility that some losses which they may incur due to the Year 2000 computer problem may ultimately not be covered by their existing insurance policies. For example, insurers may decline to cover business interruption losses under the institution's property and casualty policy on the grounds that a loss due to the Year 2000 computer problem is not an insurable "fortuitous event". Further, the issue of what Year 2000 losses are, or in the future will be, covered under standard Directors and Officers (D & O) liability policies is in a state of flux. Several insurance underwriters are in the process of sending their D & O insureds questionnaires concerning their Year 2000 problems and corrective plans in order to raise awareness. If the insurers determine that they have serious exposure with respect to a particular insured in a D & O portfolio, the insurer might also decide to change the terms of the policy at the time of renewal or even decline to renew the policy. This could pose a significant problem for a financial institution which needs to maintain D & O coverage in order to attract and retain qualified independent directors. Such independent directors may be anxious about their potential personal liability if the institution were to experience a Year 2000 system failure, attracting a shareholder derivative suit alleging inadequate securities law disclosures in annual reports filed with the U. S. Securities and Exchange Commission. Accordingly, prospective new independent directors may require assurances prior to joining the board of directors that the company's D & O policy will cover the directors for possible Y2K shareholder derivative suits.

### *B. Risks to Consumers*

U.S. consumers may be faced with the following risks arising out of the disruption of normal operations of financial institutions, among others: (a) loss of transaction records, disruption of wire transfers, miscalculation of transactions impacting savings, checking and brokerage accounts, and miscalculation of interest with respect to mortgages, bonds and other instruments, (b) inability to access bank funds when needed, which could be especially critical if welfare and other public assistance benefits are delivered electronically, (c) increase in unemployment due to failures of small businesses unable to become Year 2000 compliant in time, (d) diminution of value of stock market holdings due to a Year 2000 computer problem "bear market", and (e) disputes with the U.S. Internal Revenue Service over underpayment of taxes on tax filings using incorrect calculations received from noncompliant third party financial institutions. In addition, to the extent there are bank failures due to the Year 2000 computer problem, U. S. taxpayers would ultimately "foot the bill" for any Federal bail-out efforts, as occurred in connection with the savings and loan crisis. In this regard, it should be noted that if a bank were to fail, it may be technically difficult for another bank to quickly take over the failed bank's transaction processing due to computer system memory and other capacity limitations and difficulties arising due to use of incompatible account formats.

## III. Risk Management Efforts Currently Being Undertaken

### *A. Efforts by the Financial Services Industry*

It has been estimated that U.S. commercial banks will spend $19 billion on information technology in 1997. Further, global spending by commercial banks on risk management has been estimated to grow to be $4.2 billion by 1999. This commitment of the financial services industry to risk management is evidenced in the efforts of the Securities Industry Association (SIA) Data Management Division (DMD) Year 2000 Committee, the National Securities Clearing Co. (NSCC)/Securities Industry Automation Corp. (SIAC) and the American Bankers Association (ABA)/Bank Marketing Association (BMA) to raise Y2K awareness within the financial services industry. These efforts can be seen in the SIA's Financial Services Industry Scorecard questionnaire, which has been sent by the SIA to the CEO's of all of its members (and also to 1000 banks and 1500 institutional firms), in the awareness materials on the SIA-DMD Year 2000 Subcommittee Internet site, in the ABA/BMA Year 2000 FYI Research Kit # 58 ("Year 2000 and Your Computer System"), and in the various Year 2000 conferences sponsored by various financial industry organizations. The SIA will also provide critical assistance in the implementation of "street-wide" testing of the SIA members' systems after completion of their Y2K corrective plans.

Other organizations have adopted a mandate/penalty approach. For example, the VISA credit card organization has adopted a monetary penalty program whereby VISA members which cannot certify that their point of sale (POS) devices and processing pathways can handle credit cards bearing expiration dates of 2000 and beyond will be subject to fines.

One Year 2000 expert has estimated that as of March, 1997, only 40% of U.S. banks had begun an earnest assessment of their Year 2000 impact. It appears that some financial institutions are now recognizing that they are late in commencing their Year 2000 corrective work and may not have sufficient personnel and other resources to be able to correct 100% of their computer systems by January 1, 2000. Accordingly, instead of correcting all systems using a full four digit date field expansion, some systems will be corrected using a logic fix, such as a 100 year window. In addition, institutions are prioritizing their corrective work so that mission-critical systems will be fixed first. For example, one approach for a U.S. bank would be to first correct programs which deal with customers, the Federal Reserve Bank, accruals and financial applications. Programs that generate purely internal reports could be assigned a lower priority.

These efforts at "triage" conform to the recommendations of many Year 2000 experts.

Although the financial services industry appears to be leading some other industries in the Y2K corrective effort, it should be recognized that financial services entities, such as stock brokerage firms, often have a higher percentage of their computer systems which qualify as "mission-critical" than do manufacturing firms and entities in other industries. This is reflected in the fact that the financial services industry spends an average of 12% of its annual budget on information technology resources, with the computer industry and banking industry each spending 10% of their annual budgets on IT resources. The next highest expenditure is by the utilities industry at 7%.

### *B. Assistance from the Insurance Industry*

In order to assist insureds to cover the likely business interruption insurance "gap", the insurance industry has produced two new forms of Year 2000 insurance. J & H Marsh & McLennan is currently marketing a $200 million risk transfer insurance product to cover business interruption losses, D & O claims and liability to third parties. Significantly, the policy also covers risks of loss suffered by an insured due to the failure of scheduled third parties to become Year 2000 compliant. In addition, the policy offers an optional coverage which would cover the expense of an insured having to run scheduled back office functions such as payroll and benefits at a predesignated data processing service bureau running its own Year 2000 compliant software. The second policy being offered in the marketplace is a $100 million finite risk policy offered by AIG through J.H. Minet, which has coverage similar to the J & H Marsh & McLennan policy, but excludes the back office processing coverage and carries premiums at approximately 60-80% of the purchased limit of the policy.

With respect to qualifying audits, the J & H Marsh & McLennan product, 2000 Secure, requires an initial audit and quarterly monitoring audits after issuance of the insurance. The audit company performing the audits, 2000 Secure Audit Company, L.L.C., is a joint venture of LeBoeuf Computing Technologies, L.L.C. and Ascent Logic Corporation. Each insured is required to license Year 2000Plus risk management software developed by Ascent Logic Corporation in order to assist the insured in mapping out its internal and external business dependencies. Project management software is also used in conjunction with the Ascent Logic Corporation software to produce reports on the insured's progress in implementing its Year 2000 corrective plan. One non-insurance benefit to a company which qualifies for such Year 2000 insurance is that the insured can use the fact of its being subject to ongoing monitoring audits to help reassure industry analysts, shareholders, regulators, auditors and business partners that the insured is likely to become Year 2000 compliant in time.

### *C. Assistance from the Accounting Industry*

A new set of auditing standards, entitled "Control Objectives for Information Technology (CobiT) has been developed under the auspices of the International Systems Audit and Control Association (ISACA), Unisys, Coopers & Lybrand and other sponsors, to assist independent public accountants in the audit of information technology systems. The new standards cover auditor's independence, technical competence, work performance and reporting and should prove useful in assisting management, regulators and auditors by providing generally accepted IT security and control practices to benchmark an entity's existing and planned IT environment. In addition, the AICPA is considering identifying information technology as a fourth practice area for accountants in addition to the existing practice areas of audit, accounting and tax services.

### *D. Assistance from the Technical Community*

The Institute of Electrical and Electronics Engineers-Computer Society (IEEE-CS) announced its intention at the International Symposium on the Year 2000 held at the National Institute of Standards and Technology (NIST) on June 10, 1997, to produce a Year 2000 test method specification within the next six months. This specification would build on the "Test Assertions For Date and Time Functions" document produced by Gary Fisher of NIST.

### *E. Assistance from the Federal Government*

A number of activities merit favorable comment with respect to the role of the Federal government in raising awareness in the financial services industry over the Year 2000 problem. First, the Chairman should be commended for his February 27, 1997 letters, together with Senator D'Amato (R-NY), to the FDIC, the Federal Reserve System, the Office of Thrift Supervision, the National Credit Union Administration, the Office of the Comptroller of the Currency and the Securities and Exchange Commission, making inquiries as to their plans for ensuring Year 2000 compliance in the institutions they regulate. Also noteworthy is the excellent Securities and Exchange Commission "Report to the Congress on the Readiness of The United States Securities Industry and Public Companies to Meet The Information Processing Challenges of The Year 2000", produced in June, 1997 in response to a request from Representative Dingell (D-MI). The Year 2000 Interagency Committee of the Federal CIO Council should also be commended for its work in coordinating Federal Year 2000 awareness and remediation efforts. The latest positive development is the announcement of funding by the Federal CIO Council for a multi-agency database on Y2K vendor compliance, to be maintained by the General Services Administration on its Internet site. The present hearing by this Subcommittee and the hearings which have taken place in the U.S. House of Representatives before the Science Committee and the Government Reform and Oversight Committee also have played a large role in heightening awareness of the complexity of the Year 2000 computer problem.

In addition to the above efforts by Congress, various Executive Branch organizations have the potential to play a significant role in raising Year 2000 awareness. The first is the President's Commission on Critical Infrastructure Protection, which was created with the mandate to identify threats (including the Year 2000 computer problem) to critical national infrastructures (telecommunications, electrical power systems and banking and finance, among others) and advise the President on legislative options and policies to protect the critical infrastructures. Further, the U.S. General Services Administration's Access America plan includes as part of its program action items that the Federal CIO Council, the Intergovernmental Enterprise Panel (IEP) and the National Association of State Information Resource Executives (NASIRE) coordinate to prepare an intergovernmental action plan to assist both Federal and state agencies to become Year 2000 compliant. Finally, the Internet "Year 2000 Information Directory" Web site managed by the CIO Council Subcommittee on the Year 2000 and the U.S. General Services Administration, Office of Governmentwide Policy (MKS) has proven extremely useful in making widely available on an expedited basis critical Federal Year 2000 materials. Of course, more can be done by the Federal government in this regard and recommendations as to possible additional actions are set forth below.

## IV. Possible Governmental Roles and Regulations

I recommend the following be considered as possible additional actions which could be taken by this Subcommittee, other Congressional Committees and other individual members of Congress: (1) enact Senate Bill 22 ("Commission on the Year 2000 Computer Problem Act") into law, (2) consider mandating participation by financial institutions in the SIA "street-wide" testing plan, with appropriate regulatory oversight and penalties for noncompliance, (3) consider enacting a cap on potential Year 2000 litigation damages, under appropriate circumstances, in order to encourage more open disclosure of Year 2000 problems and remediation technologies and product upgrades, (4) examine and reevaluate default rules in statutes, regulations and in case law which place the burden of discovering fraud and transaction errors in banking and other financial records on U.S. consumers, and (5) reexamine existing control mechanisms relating to stock exchange trading volatility and "run on the bank" scenarios in light of potential public loss of faith in financial institutions due to "doomsday" articles in the public press and over-publicized Year 2000 failures.

### *A. Senate Bill 22 ("Commission on The Year 2000 Computer Problem Act")*

I recommend that Members of this Subcommittee endorse Senate Bill 22, which was introduced by Senator Moynihan (D-NY), has been co-sponsored by Senators Hollings (D-SC), Dorgan (D-ND), Lieberman (D-CT) and Inouye (D-HI) and has been referred to the Committee on Governmental Affairs. I have authored an extensive article discussing the importance of the issues raised by S. 22 and the valuable contribution the Commission could make to raising awareness as the complexity of the Year 2000 problem and to developing risk management and audit methodologies for the benefit of the Federal government, state governments and the private sector. I recommend the article to interested Senators.

### *B. Street-Wide Year 2000 Testing Mandates*

The SIA is currently developing plans for conducting "street-wide" testing beginning in February, 1999 and finishing in October, 1999 in order to confirm that the SIA members' computer systems have in fact been made Year 2000 compliant. If any SIA member refuses to participate in street-wide testing or fails such testing, the names of such SIA members should be disclosed so that appropriate protective measures may be taken by the impacted member's transaction partners. In order to avoid exposing the SIA and individual SIA members to legal actions, I recommend that the appropriate Federal regulatory agency mandate participation in the SIA "street-wide" testing and mandate disclosure to the agency and all SIA members of the results of the testing.

### *C. Cap on Year 2000 Litigation Damages*

Financial institutions currently face a problem with respect to embedded microcontrollers in non-computer equipment, since they are totally dependent on the equipment manufacturers to identify the location of the microcontrollers, to advise whether the microcontrollers are date-sensitive and will cause the associated equipment to malfunction on or after January 1, 2000, and to provide Year 2000 compliant microcontrollers. In some instances the manufacturers may decide not to expend the money necessary to produce Year 2000 compliant microcontrollers for outdated equipment. In order to motivate these manufacturers to devote the time and money necessary to locate noncompliant microcontrollers in all equipment currently in use in the economy, Congress could enact legislation capping the manufacturer's potential liability for Year 2000 product liability litigation arising out of the anticipated equipment malfunctions due to the Year 2000 problem, provided the manufacturers actually supply the needed Year 2000 compliant microcontrollers. Precedent for this legislation can be found in the swine flu vaccine legislation and the Price-Anderson provisions of the U.S. Atomic Energy Act. Caps on Year 2000 litigation liability could be extended to other types of entities (third party hardware and software vendors, financial institutions) as deemed appropriate by Congress. The concept of a cap on Y2K litigation damages was recently cited by Representative Constance Morella (R-MD) in her presentation at the NIST International Symposium on the Year 2000, where she noted that "[s]ome have suggested that the only method to open up an effective discourse among industry and speed up some action is to statutorily limit or cap private sector legal liability".

### *D. Default Rules Affecting Consumers*

Under certain circumstances, applicable statutes, regulations and/or case law place the burden on U.S. consumers to detect errors in their financial transaction records or bear the consequences of those errors. If the Year 2000 problem results in more widespread errors in financial transaction records than is currently anticipated, a more extensive consumer disclosure system may be necessary in order to protect unsuspecting consumers, who may not fully realize their exposure to loss with respect to inaccurate bank accounts and other financial records.

### *E. Stock Exchange/Bank Volatility Controls*

The major stock exchanges have adopted and maintain various "collar" and "circuit breaker" controls on trading and program trading in order to reduce excessive volatility in market trading. Given the current flood of "doomsday" articles on the Year 2000 problem and the likelihood that at least some highly publicized systems failures will eventually occur, with resulting litigation, this Subcommittee may wish to reexamine the current exchange trading controls to determine if they are sufficient to maintain an orderly market in the face of an irrational wave of stock selling due to overpublicized Year 2000 worries. A similar review of current banking controls may be appropriate in the unlikely event that a bank suffers a Year 2000 system failure and some depositors become "spooked" and start a "run on the bank". Since the Federal Deposit Insurance Corporation (FDIC) insures deposits up to $100,000, the potential "run" on a bank would more likely be caused by large institutional investors.

## Conclusion

I hope that my testimony has evidenced my personal belief that the Year 2000 computer problem is neither overblown hype on the one hand, nor the end of the world as we know it on the other hand. The Year 2000 computer problem represents the most significant information technology challenge the U.S. economy has yet faced, but the challenge is not purely a technical one. The Year 2000 computer problem is at its core not a technical problem with a solely technological solution, meriting delegation only to the chief information officer and technical staff. Instead, the Year 2000 computer problem is a business and legal problem which merits the attention of each affected company's top management and board of directors. There is no technological "silver bullet" for the Year 2000 computer problem. There is a "silver bullet" solution to the Year 2000 computer problem, however, and it is called project management. Further, an essential element of each company's project management approach to solving its Year 2000 computer problem has to be risk management. With proper project management and risk management, the Year 2000 computer problem can be brought under control. Finally, I believe that government can play a significant role in the Y2K arena, not just in remediating its own Y2K problem so that essential governmental services can continue to be provided, but also in providing needed oversight and guidance to the critical financial services industry in the course of its remediation efforts, both for the benefit of the financial services industry and for the protection of U.S. consumers.

Mr. Chairman and distinguished Members of the Subcommittee, that concludes my testimony and I would be pleased to address any questions you may have.

# Appendix D

## Prepared Testimony of Dr. Edward Yardeni Before the Senate

### *Chief Economist, Deutsche Morgan Grenfell*

*"Hearing on Mandating Year-2000 Disclosures for Publicly-Traded Companies," Before the Senate Banking, Housing, and Urban Affairs Committee, Subcommittee on Financial Services and Technology, 4 November 1997*

Mr. Chairman, Distinguished Members of the Subcommittee:

My name is Ed Yardeni. I am the Chief Economist of Deutsche Morgan Grenfell, a global investment banking firm. I appreciate the opportunity to testify before this Subcommittee on the issue of mandating Year 2000 disclosure by publicly traded companies. The title of my prepared testimony today is, *The Year 2000 Problem: We Need Answers.* Of course, all the opinions I express today are my own and may or may not be shared by my company. I am here as a concerned citizen, not as an official spokesman of my company or industry.

The Year 2000 Problem (Y2K) is a very serious threat to the US economy. Indeed, I believe that it is inevitable that it could disrupt the entire global economy in several ways. If the disruptions are significant and widespread, then a global recession is possible. The depth and duration of such a downturn is hard to predict at this time. To do so requires answers from government and business leaders around the world to many questions about the problem.

They must publicly provide much more information, so that we can determine the economic risks ahead and prepare for any foreseeable and plausible worst-case scenarios if we fail to fix the problem properly in time. With regard to the specific topic of this hearing today, I believe that all businesses, both incorporated and unincorporated, should be required by a new law to publicly reveal their cumulative and current quarter outlays on fixing Y2K. They should also be required to reveal their best- and worst-case projections of such outlays. Most importantly, all business establishments should be required to post a "Y2K Progress Report" of their current and projected progress. This report should be very detailed, including:

1. a schedule of companywide progress, showing the projected and realized dates of the standard five stages of remediation: Awareness, Assessment, Renovation, Validation, and Implementation;

2. individual schedules of progress on all mission-critical activities, or at least a summary of how many mission-critical activities exist and what percentage of them are at each of the five stages listed above;

3. specific lists of business activities that are expected to be impaired or terminated, either temporarily or permanently, as business triage decisions are made between now and January 1, 2000;

4. a discussion of progress and risks related to outside vendors and customers who might not be Y2K compliant in time, including suppliers of electricity and telecommunications services;

5. a discussion of Y2K-related legal issues, including

budgets for anticipated litigation expenses and liability outlays;

6. and, finally, a discussion of contingency plans in the event that Y2K compliance is not achieved on a companywide or a line-of-business basis.

I recognize that the current regulatory system does require each individual corporation to report Y2K outlays and risks that are likely materially to affect the corporation's financial condition. The current requirements for reporting Y2K issues are the same as those required for any other event that might have a material impact on a corporation's balance sheet and income statement. However, Y2K is a unique business risk that requires unique disclosure requirements. It is a systematic risk that will affect all businesses, all vendors, and all customers all of us. It will affect even those who long ago anticipated the problem and expect to be completely ready for the year 2000.

In other words, it is a risk to the well-being of our entire local, national, and global community. We must protect not only the interests of investors, but also the general public. As I discuss below and in the attached appendix to my testimony, there will be Y2K problems that are bound to disrupt all our lives. We need all the information available to prepare for this problem as a community. Our system of self-interested capitalism is not designed to handle a systemwide indeed global risk to our collective well-being. Individual business management must protect the interests of their own entities. For competitive reasons, they are likely to reveal as little as possible about material risks to their business. In this case, the public's need to know all the Y2K risks must prevail over the legitimate, but parochial interests of business managers.

I am not a lawyer. I am an economist. My proposal might raise legal issues, possibly even issues of constitutionality. I am not advocating any change in our supervised and regulated free-market system of capitalism. I am advocating a leveling of the disclosure playing field. If all companies are required to disclose their Y2K activities and risk, then none will be at a competitive disadvantage if it provides full Y2K disclosure, as it is under the current disclosure system.

As an economist, I need more information to assess the risks to our national economy and global financial markets from Y2K. The current disclosure system simply will not provide our policy makers with the information they need as soon as possible to anticipate and to prepare for plausible worst-case scenarios. Conceivably, such information may show that the economic risks and the risks to our well-being are quite small and temporary. I hope so, but I doubt this will be the case. If we don't get more information soon, then we risk more problems and greater hardship.

It is not too late to reduce the risk of Y2K failures by giving this problem a top priority. My proposal would focus public pressure on management who are not appropriately addressing the problem. One objection is that too much information especially as much as I am asking for might panic the public. Perhaps, if we all panic a bit now, we can minimize the disruptions two years from now. Besides, I have talked to reporters who are working on Y2K stories. The public may be relatively uninformed and unconcerned about Y2K now, but they are bound to become increasingly anxious as the millennium date approaches.

This Subcommittee is responsible for banking issues, as well as disclosure issues. Bank loan officers must assess the risk of earnings losses and even business failure of their borrowers who fail to be Y2K compliant. My proposal would establish a national standard Y2K reporting system that would level the playing field for our bankers. It would force them all to use more or less the same checklist for assuring Y2K compliance. Of course, my proposal might increase the macroeconomic risk of a Y2K "credit crunch," as bankers refuse to lend to companies that are not likely to meet the Y2K deadline. Again, it is better that we increase this risk for business borrowers now, than later, so that they will take Y2K more seriously as a threat to their survival. Those that won't survive may come to this conclusion sooner and seek Y2K-compliant acquirers while there is still enough time to integrate them into compliant computer systems.

I have spent the past six months collecting as much information as possible on Y2K. Based on what I know so far, I believe there is a 40% risk of a worldwide recession that will last at least 12 months starting in January 2000, and it could be as severe as the 1973-74 global recession. That severe downturn was caused by the OPEC oil crisis, which is a useful analogy for thinking about the potential economic consequences of Y2K. Just as oil is a vital resource for our global economy, so is information. If the supply of information is disrupted, many economic activities will be impaired, if not entirely halted.

The Y2K problem is both trivial and overwhelming at the same time. Unless fixed, most computers, including many PCs, will produce nonsensical results or crash because "00" in the widely used two-digit year field will be recognized as 1900 rather than 2000. Obviously, there are simple solutions to this. The two-digit fields can be found and replaced with four-digit ones. The software programs can be "windowed" to recognize incoming years in a range, say, between 0 and 40 as being in the 21st century. New software programs can be written to replace "legacy" programs that may be too difficult to fix.

The problem is time. All the money in the world will not stop January 1, 2000, from arriving at the rate of 3,600 seconds per hour. There is not enough time to fix and test all the systems, with billions of lines of software code around the world, that need to be fixed. Many businesses, governments, and organizations have become aware of the Year 2000 Problem only recently and may simply run out of time.

Testing is much more time-consuming than repairing noncompliant code. This might not be a problem for some stand-alone systems. However, the majority of software programs are part of a bigger corporate, industrial, national, and even global network. They often depend on input information generated by other programs. They must all remain compatible as they are fixed.

In other words, the sum total of all interdependent computer systems must all be compliant. The network is the computer. A problem in one system could trigger a Domino Effect, which poses a great risk to all who fail to test whether their local compliant system is compatible with their global network. The networks that must function perfectly at the risk of partial and even total failure include:

1. electrical power systems,
2. telecommunications,
3. transportation,
4. manufacturing,
5. retail and wholesale distribution,
6. finance and banking,
7. government services and administration (including taxation),
8. military defense, and
9. international trade.

In other words, the Y2K virus has infected all the vital organs of our global body. It must be removed from all of them. A failure in any one system could corrupt other systems. Most obvious would be a serious disruption in the supply of electricity. The Year 2000 Problem will be a non-event only if the global network is fixed

100%. Undoubtedly, much will be fixed in time. But there is no doubt that some significant fraction will not be ready in time. Indeed, most so-called embedded microchip systems will be stress tested for the first time under real world conditions starting at midnight on New Year's Eve 2000. There are billions of these minicomputers embedded in appliances, elevators, security systems, processing and manufacturing plants, medical devices, and numerous other vital applications. Most are probably not date-sensitive. But many are and could seriously disrupt vital economic activities and create serious safety hazards.

Of course, those of us who earn our living on Wall Street have known about Y2K for at least two years. Investors have sharply bid up the prices of several Y2K companies that offer various tools and solutions for fixing the problem. However, none has a "silver-bullet" solution that can fix Y2K over a weekend. They can help to find and repair code that is not Y2K compliant. But every change requires time-consuming testing of each system. Each change has the potential of creating a new bug in the repaired program, which then requires another round of "debugging" and testing. There is simply no silver bullet for this process.

I am amazed by the lack of concern about Y2K by our political and business leaders, journalists, and the general public. The widespread mantra I hear over and over again is "Bill Gates will fix it." The official position of Microsoft is that this is a problem that everyone must fix on his own. It is too big and overwhelming for even Microsoft.

The lack of concern may also reflect the fact that we have become very dependent on technology in a very short period of time the last 20 years. We depend on it, but very few of us understand how it works and its limitations. We marvel at the achievements of technology. But it doesn't always work as expected and as promised. Anyone who owns a PC has experienced the frustration of unexpected crashes. Most PCs work fine as long as we don't add any new programs. As soon as we do so, other programs sometimes misbehave. None of us would be happy if our PC was 95% functional. So why are we so complacent about a global computer network that might be 95% Y2K compliant in a best-case scenario and maybe only 50% compliant in a worst-case scenario?

Software programming is far less disciplined and rigorous than most of us realize. Two different programmers can and do write completely different programs that will perform exactly the same task. Programming is more of an art than a science. One of the biggest Y2K headaches is that few programmers take the time or are even asked to document the logic of their programs. Also, the original source code for many older programs is lost. The source code was translated into "machine language," i.e., the binary combinations of zeros and ones that computers understand, by so-called "compiler" programs. Reverse compiling is possible, but many of the original compiler programs are also lost.

On Wall Street we have focused our research efforts on how to make money on Y2K. I think it is time for all of us to focus more on the disruptions that may occur because the problem will not be completely fixed in time. There are plausible worst-case disruption scenarios that would undoubtedly cause a global recession, possibly one of the longest and deepest on record. With so much at risk, we must do more to prepare for possible troubles. To do so, we need answers; we need more Y2K disclosure from our business community. Then we can prepare for the worst, and thereby realistically hope for the best.

# Appendix E

## Prepared Testimony of David Iacino Before the Senate

### *Senior Manager, Bank of Boston, N.A.*

*"Oversight Hearing on Financial Institutions and the Year 2000 Problem," Before the Senate Banking, Housing, and Urban Affairs Committee, Subcommittee on Financial Services and Technology, 10 July 1997*

Mr. Chairman and members of the Subcommittee, my name is David Iacino and I am the Senior Manager of the Millennium Project at BankBoston. I am pleased to have this opportunity to present my views on the magnitude of the Year 2000 problem, the associated business risks, and the adequacy of remediation and risk management efforts being undertaken by the financial services industry.

Let me first tell you a little about who we are. We are a large New England based Superregional Bank holding company with $65 billion in assets, ranked number 15 in the United States with 475 branches and 275 offices located in 24 countries. We offer a complete range of financial products and services both domestically and internationally.

The Year 2000 computer problem is pervasive and is global in scope. It affects not only the financial services industry, but all industries. Each business is itself both a customer and a supplier in the food chain of international commerce. Each industry is simultaneously competing for available human resources to complete its remediation processes against a fixed deadline in order to mitigate its Year 2000 risks. The millennium challenge is a significant project management challenge that requires institutionally focused attention as well as addressing dependencies on its suppliers that are facing the very same challenge. These are the parameters that make the millennium challenge unique.

Financial institutions are extremely dependent on one another as well as common service providers for the interchange of electronic commerce. The national payment system is dependent upon automation to clear checks principally through the Federal Reserve System. The Automated Clearing Houses represent the primary means of processing pre-authorized payments enabling automated payroll deposits to the consumer's Bank of choice in addition to processing standing orders for repetitive payments such as insurance premiums, automobile payments, and investments. The retail consumer is dependent on the use of credit and debit card conveniences offered internationally through suppliers such as VISA, MASTERCARD, and AMERICAN EXPRESS which have extensive electronic networks linking a transaction from its point of sale to the consumer's financial institution. The Corporate customer, heavily dependent on Electronic Data Interchange (EDI), Wire Transfers, and Letters of Credit, uses the nation's financial institutions as their financial intermediaries. The increasing globalization of the business enterprise radiates these dependencies beyond our borders to include financial institutions worldwide. It should be clear from these examples that there are significant risks associated with such tightly woven interdependencies.

Like all financial institutions, BankBoston is heavily dependent on computer technology in the conduct of our business. We have major Data Centers in New England, London, Brazil, Argentina, and Singapore with large scale data communications networks linking these Centers to our branches, remote offices, customers, and service providers like the Federal Reserve. Additionally, we participate in multiple delivery networks for ATM processing, point of sale services, information exchange, and other forms of electronic commerce. This dependence on technology was the prime motivation for BankBoston to begin its Millennium Project in the Spring of 1995. The initial assessment of our systems inventory revealed that roughly fifty percent of our software is supplied to us by external Vendors, and that this Vendor supplied software is usually customized to meet the unique needs of our institution. This heavy reliance on external Vendor software, which is common within the financial services industry, represents the single biggest risk in being able to meet the millennium challenge since the timely delivery of this millennium compliant software is outside of each bank's control. However, even managing these types of software risks that are germane to individual institutions will help ensure millennium compliance only within their own spheres of influence.

The Year 2000 problem is also very real. At BankBoston, we have identified and corrected millennium related logic errors within our systems that have already been through the remediation process. For example, we found that:

- we would not have been able to mature our customers' Certificates of Deposits in the year 2000 and beyond;

- our Negotiable Collateral system would have lost expiration dates and review dates on collateral used to secure loans in the event of loan default;

- the system processing a daily volume of $800 million of Controlled Disbursements for our corporate customers would have been inoperable for ten days while the problem was corrected in January, 2000 resulting in massive overdrafts to the Bank, and;

- our Precious Metals business would have been inoperable for up to two weeks while systems changes

> were being made to correct erroneous date processing. And keep in mind that had these situations not been identified in advance, our ability to respond to all of them simultaneously in the Year 2000 may have been hampered by the availability of computer resources and the pressures brought on by the demands of our customer base.

As I mentioned earlier, BankBoston had begun its millennium preparedness in early 1995. As such, I feel comfortable that we will be able to complete our internal preparedness given the project organization and processes that we currently have in place. It has taken us two years to structure the very rigorous program that we have in place today. Our inventory of technology applications is under constant review and newly acquired or developed applications are being scrutinized for their millennium compliance, both contractually and in their acceptance testing, in order not to propagate the millennium problem.

We have developed an extensive Communications and Awareness program within the Bank to sensitize every facet of the business to review the risks of the millennium challenge to their business. This is a mandatory program for every financial institution. We have also instituted a very rigorous Vendor and Contracts Management program to track the millennium readiness and delivery of the vendor supplied applications which account for more than half of our application inventory. We have developed comprehensive remediation and certification processes to carefully examine and test all of our systems to assure accurate operability in the year 2000 and beyond. We have developed sound Project Administration practices to track costs, maintain accurate inventory, and manage issues. We have put in place and continually monitor the Technical Support infrastructure required to conduct remediation and certification concurrently with the day to day systems demands of our business. And we have developed an elaborate

Planning and Scheduling program that integrates our resource requirements planning, Vendor software availability, and triage program founded on an already existing Disaster Recovery Plan that orders our most critical applications for renovation before those of lesser importance. Complementing the systemic preparations being undertaken within BankBoston, we have a corporate-wide millennium risk management program underway where the potential impacts of the Year 2000 challenge are being addressed as risk related business issues and opportunities to gain competitive advantage. Headed by our Director of Risk Management Assessment, this program is reviewing the potential risks associated with each major line of business:

*Credit.* Credit policy is being reviewed to account for the potential risk that the borrower's ability to repay outstanding debt may be affected by the impact of the year 2000 on the borrower. Increased allowances for potential loan losses are accordingly being evaluated. Existing loans requiring customer unqualified financial statements are being watched in the event that the customer's own millennium preparation expense may erode comfortable profit margins. Loan participations and syndications require the cooperation of all participants in the evaluation of millennium related risk.

*Finance.* Regulatory requirements concerning SEC 10K and 10Q millennium disclosures are being reviewed as are FASB's treatment of accounting and tax implications of millennium related expenses.

*Third Party Suppliers.* Critical outsourcing arrangements such as loan portfolio servicing are being reviewed to ensure uninterrupted revenue streams. The risks associated with potential disruption of critical point solutions that augment the bank's business functions (such as news services, stock quotations, et al) are also under review.

*Joint Ventures.* The millennium preparedness of all joint ventures in which BankBoston is a participant is being investigated to protect the value of our investment.

*Legal Issues.* BankBoston is taking aggressive steps to conduct the appropriate due diligence associated with its preparedness for the millennium. These include supplier contract review of indemnification and warrantee provisions, board level project review, and escalation of critical business related issues.

*Mergers and Acquisitions.* BankBoston has just completed a merger with BayBanks. This merger involved extensive best of breed product integration into the surviving systems that serve the combined entity. This fifteen month effort required extensive systems renovation which consumed the attention of systems personnel involved with the merger. In future M&A activities, the valuation of any acquired software will have to be significantly discounted unless it is already millennium compliant. There simply isn't enough time remaining to affect product integration concurrent with providing for millennium readiness.

*Insurance.* It is imperative for all businesses to review Director and Officer liability insurance in addition to business interruption insurance policies currently in place or under renewal. Given the estimated certainty of forthcoming lawsuits surrounding predicted business failures, BankBoston has begun such reviews.

*Marketing.* The millennium prepared financial institution will enjoy a competitive advantage over other Banks' inaction. Cross selling of additional products and services to a nervous customer base will provide an opportunity for additional fee income to the millennium compliant bank. Communicating millennium strategy to the retail and corporate customer is becoming more of a sensitive issue as our customers' awareness of the millennium issue increases.

I bring the BankBoston model to your attention, not only because I am proud of what we have accomplished, but to underscore to you the fact that it has taken us two years to experience and overcome some of the project management complexities associated with the Year 2000 challenge. Knowing that all financial institutions must address the very same issues that we have faced with much less time remaining, I am concerned with the general preparedness of the rest of the financial services industry. In my discussions with other banks, customers, and service suppliers, I feel that unless comparable programs to BankBoston's are put in place within the next few months, the effect will adversely impact even those that are adequately prepared.

On a positive note, a cohesiveness is developing in the Banking industry to address the millennium challenge. The Bank Administration Institute (BAI), a US banking industry association representing about 80% of the nation's banking assets, has been quite proactive in bringing together its membership and service providers to address common issues. The Canadian Banker's Association has undertaken similar activities, and the two groups have cross-pollinated to address common Banking related millennium issues across North America.

The majority of the critical work, however, lies ahead. As I mentioned earlier, there is an enormous interdependency among all financial institutions on the viability of the payments system. All must be prepared for the millennium. All common financial services providers must be prepared. All systems and application vendors must be prepared. All suppliers and customers must be prepared. And then we must all test the interdependencies we share well before the year 2000 to ensure stability of the system not only domestically, but also globally.

The Federal Financial Institutions Examination Council (FFIEC), has been proactive in delivering the urgency of the millennium challenge to the industry and appears poised to step up its examinations. In many cases, especially to smaller institutions that do not have the resources to manage such large scale projects against an immutable deadline, the Regulatory bodies represented by the FFIEC will be required to offer assistance. As each financial institution must mitigate risk through rigorous contingency planning, our Regulators must develop contingency plans to assure stability of the Banking system. We have a collective fiduciary responsibility to our customers and must continue to relax the roles of the Regulator and the Regulated by working together to ensure the safety and soundness of this nation's banking system.

This concludes my testimony. Thank you.

# Notes

## Chapter 1: Penny Wise and Pound Foolish

1. Levy and Hafner, "The Day the World Shuts Down" 53–54.
2. Leon Kappelman and Phil Scott, "What Management Needs to Know About the Year 2000 Computer Date Problem," *Com.Links Magazine*, 1996. Available from <http://www.comlinks.com/mag/kapsco1.htm> (28 October 1997); INTERNET.
3. "The Impact of the Year 2000 Date Change Situation on PC Users," Prepared Testimony of Harris N. Miller, President, The Information Technology Association of America, Before the Joint Committee Hearing of the House Science Committee, Technology Subcommittee, and House Government Reform and Oversight Committee, Government Management, Information, and Technology Subcommittee, United States House of Representatives, 10 September 1997. Available from <http://www.house.gov/science/harris_miller.htm> (28 October 1997); INTERNET.
4. This list is based on one that appeared in Mike Elgan, "It's the End of the World As We Know It," *Windows Magazine*, October 1996. Available from <http://www.winmag.com/library/1996/1096/10a02.htm> (28 October 1997); INTERNET.
5. To test this for yourself, use your spreadsheet to divide a number by "0." On most systems, including *Excel 97*, you will generate an error.
6. It could also be that, in subtracting the first number from the second, the computer thinks you have been talking on the telephone for a *negative* 53 million minutes. In this case, you might actually get a credit

from your long distance carrier for $5 million. If so, you won't have to pay your phone bill for many, many years! Should this happen to enough customers—and it will unless the problem is successfully repaired—it could break the phone company. While this probably won't happen, the calculations are going to yield unexpected results, and leave a tidal wave of billing and customer service problems.

7. This is the current term that is used to refer to computers that have been repaired and do not experience any problems in processing dates in the next century.
8. Not only do the programs have to be Year 2000–compliant, but the data validation routines must be as well.
9. "Getting Federal Computers Ready for 2000," Report of the U.S. Office of Management and Budget, 6 February 1997, 1 (electronic edition). Available from <http://infosphere.safb.af.mil/~jwid/fadl/world/crsrpt.htm> (28 October 1997); INTERNET.
10. Levy and Hafner, "The Day," 54.
11. Ibid.
12. Ibid., 56.
13. Ibid.
14. Ibid.
15. Ibid.
16. Mike Feinsilber, "Head of Congressional Panel Warns of Year 2000 Bug," *New York Times CyberTimes*, 11 June 1997. Available from <www.nytimes.com/library/cyber/week/061197millennium.html> (28 October 1997); INTERNET.
17. Levy and Hafner, "The Day," 54.
18. For this list I am indebted to Capers Jones, "The Global Economic Impact of the Year 2000 Software Problem," Revision 5.2, 23 January 1997, 7–8. Available from <www.spr.com/index.htm> (28 October 1997); INTERNET. This white paper is widely quoted by the media, consultants, and government officials.
19. Levy and Hafner, "The Day," 58.
20. Patrick Thibodeau, "Year 2000 Legal Issues, Staffing Are Top Worries of State CIOs," *ComputerWorld*, 13 October 1997, 1 (electronic edition). Available from <http://cwlive.cw.com:8080/home/print9497.nsf/All/SL40nasire163AA> (28 October 1997); INTERNET.
21. Levy and Hafner, "The Day," 54.
22. "Oversight Hearing on Financial Institutions and the Year 2000

Problem," Prepared Testimony of Jeff Jinnett, president, LeBoeuf Computing Technologies, Before the Senate Banking, Housing, and Urban Affairs Committee, Subcommittee on Financial Services and Technology, 10 July 1997. Available from <http://www.senate.gov/~banking/97_07hrg/071097/witness/jnnett.htm> (28 October 1997); INTERNET.

23. "The Year 2000 Challenge," Congressional Research Service of the Library of Congress, 4. Quoted in Gary North, "11-Page Government Summary of the Y2K Problem," *Gary North's Y2K Links and Forums*, 27 May 1997. Available from <http://www.garynorth.com/y2k/Detail.CFM?Links__ID=142> (31 October 1997); INTERNET.
24. "Fortune 500 Companies Have Not Yet Begun Code Repairs," *Reuters*, 9 April 1997. Quoted in Gary North, "Fortune 500 Companies Have Not Yet Begun Code Repairs," *Gary North's Y2K Links and Forums*, 9 April 1997. Available from <http://www.garynorth.com/y2k/Detail.CFM?Links__ID=111> (31 October 1997); INTERNET.
25. "Oversight Hearing on Financial Institutions and the Year 2000 Problem," Prepared Testimony of Larry Martin, President of Data Dimensions, Before the Senate Banking, Housing, and Urban Affairs Committee, Subcommittee on Financial Services and Technology, 10 July 1997. Available from <http://www.senate.gov/~banking/97_07hrg/071097/witness/martin.htm> (28 October 1997); INTERNET.
26. William Ulrich, "A Serious State of Delusion—Most Executives Who Say Their Companies Are on Track," *InformationWeek*, Issue: 629: 5 May 1997. Available from <http://www.techweb.com/se/directlink.cgi?%20IWK19970505S0087> (28 October 1997); INTERNET.
27. This story actually combines two separate encounters with two separate friends. I have combined the accounts and changed some of the facts in order to protect them.
28. Jones, "The Global Economic Impact," 10.
29. "Chaos," The Standish Group, 1995, 2 (electronic edition). Available from <http://www.standishgroup.com/chaos.html> (28 October 1997); INTERNET.
30. Peter G.W. Keen, "Year 2000: Give Up, Move On—Now," *ComputerWorld*, 16 June 1997. Available from <http://www2.computerworld.com/home/print9497.nsf/All/SL0616pk> (28 October 1997); INTERNET.

## Chapter 2: Bigger Than Big

1. Levy and Hafner, "The Day," 53.
2. Keen, "Year 2000."
3. Testimony of Bruce H. Hall, Research Director, Applications Development Methods and Management, Before the Subcommittee on Technology and the Subcommittee on Government Management, Information, and Technology, 20 March 1997. Available from <http://www.house.gov/science/hall_3-20.html> (28 October 1997); INTERNET.
4. Julia Vowler, "Half of All New PCs Fail 2000 BIOS Test," *ComputerWeekly*, 22 May 1997. Available from <http://www.computerweekly.co.uk/news/22_5_97/08643218486/A.html> (28 October 1997); INTERNET.
5. Ibid.
6. Mike Elgan, "It's the End of the World."
7. Douglas Hayward, "Beware Millennium Claims, Experts Warn," *TechWire*, 29 May 1997. Available from <http://www.techweb.com/wire/news/may/0529y2K.html> (28 October 1997); INTERNET.
8. The Gartner Group, "Beyond IT Systems, The Year 2000 Touches Everything," an excerpt from *The Year 2000 Crisis: An Enormous Challenge That Must Be Addressed*, 12 March 1997, 1 (electronic edition). Available from <http://www.advantage.com/atvhome/wsj/ggdoc2.htm> (27 June 1997); INTERNET.
9. This list is based on "Year 2000: Embedded Systems and Computer Problems in Your Organization," The Computer Information Centre (CompInfo), 6 August 1997, 2–3 (electronic edition). Available from <http://www.compinfo.co.uk/Y2K/examples.htm> (7 September 1997); INTERNET.
10. Most PCs contain embedded systems *in addition* to their CPU or central processing unit.
11. The Gartner Group, 1.
12. Julia Vowler, "The Heart of Embedded Systems," *ComputerWeekly*, 8 May 1997, 1 (electronic edition). Available from <http://www.computerweekly.co.uk/news/8_5_97/08598503239/H1.html> (27 June 1997); INTERNET.
13. The Gartner Group, 1.
14. "IEE Throws Lifeline to Users Embedded in Chip Quagmire," *ComputerWeekly*, 2 October 1997, 1 (electronic edition). Available from <http://www.computerweekly.co.uk/news/2_10_97/08598503239/C30.html> (3 October 1997); INTERNET.
15. "Embedded Chips Pose Threat to Staff Safety," *ComputerWeekly*,

25 September 1997, 1 (electronic edition). Available from <http://www.computerweekly.co.uk/news/25_9_97/08598503239/B2.html> (20 October 1997); INTERNET.

16. "IEE Throws Lifeline," 1.
17. "Year 2000 Embedded Systems: Why We Should Be Worried," *Computer-Weekly*, 5 August 1997, 1 (electronic edition). Available from <http://www.computerweekly.co.uk/news/8_5_97/08598503239/H1why.html> (27 June 1997); INTERNET.
18. Cited in Jones, "The Global Economic Impact," 17.
19. Ibid., 21.
20. Ibid., 20.
21. Ibid., 21. The author cites Algol, APL, BASIC, CHILL, CMS2, CORAL, Forth, Lisp, Modula, MUMPS, PASCAL, Prolog, Ratfor, and RPG.
22. Ibid., 21. The author cites ITT's ESPL/1 and IBM's PLS.
23. "Oversight Hearing on Financial Institutions," Jinnett.
24. Jones, "The Global Economic Impact," 21–22.
25. Ibid., 21.
26. Warren S. Reid and Steven Brower, "Beyond Awareness: Ten Management and Legal Pitfalls Regarding the Year 2000 Computer Problem That You May Not Have Considered, Yet!" *Year2000*, 22 June 1997. Available from <http://www.year2000.com/archive/beyond.html> (28 October 1997); INTERNET.
27. "Millennium Rollover: The Year 2000 Problem," National Institute of Standards and Technology," n.d. Available from <http://www.nist.gov/itl/lab/2000.txt> (28 October 1997); INTERNET.
28. Testimony of Bruce H. Hall.
29. "The Impact of the Year 2000 Date Change," Miller.
30. William D. Rabin and Terrence P. Tierney, "The Year 2000 Problem: It's Worse Than We Thought," J.P. Morgan Securities, Inc. Industry Analysis, 15 May 1997. Available from <http://www.jpmorgan.com/MarketDataInd/Research/Y2Kupdate/Y2K.HTM> (28 October 1997); INTERNET.
31. Elgan.
32. This is sometimes called a program's Time Horizon to Failure, or "THF."
33. "Millennium Bug for 1999?" *CNNfn*, 17 June 1997. Available from <http://cnnfn.com/digitaljam/9706/17/timebomb/index.htm> (28 October 1997); INTERNET.

34. Reid and Brower, "Beyond Awareness."
35. Bruce Caldwell, "Testing Time? Try Rent-a-Mainframe—Sabre and Comdisco Offer Rentals for Application Testing," *InformationWeek*, 5 May 1997.
36. Caldwell.
37. Levy and Hafner, "The Day," 57.
38. Rabin and Tierney, "The Year 2000 Problem."
39. "The World in 1998," *The Economist*, December 1997, special edition, 121.
40. Ibid.
41. Rabin and Tierney, "The Year 2000 Problem."
42. Ibid.
43. Ibid.
44. Rajiv Chandrasekaran, "'Year 2000' Is No Cheap Date," *Washington Post*, 11 September 1997, A13.
45. Reid and Brower, "Beyond Awareness."
46. Rabin and Tierney, "The Year 2000 Problem."
47. Ibid.
48. Testimony of Bruce H. Hall.
49. Ibid.
50. See Rabin and Tierney, "The Year 2000 Problem." They said, "We find it more and more difficult to remain optimistic given the current status of the problem."
51. Gary North, "Category: Compliance," *Gary North's Y2K Links*, n.d. Available from <http://www.garynorth.com/y2k/Results.CFM?Links__Category=Compliance> (28 October 1997); INTERNET.

## Chapter 3: One Bad Apple Spoils the Whole Bunch

1. The Gartner Group, "The Domino Effect of Hidden Year 2000 Problems," *Research Notes, Key Issue Analysis*, 13 March 1997, 1. Available from <http://www.atvantage.com/atvhome/wsj/00035912.htm> (27 June 1997); INTERNET.
2. Tim Wilson, "Year 2000 Countdown—Protect Your Net!" *Communications Week*, 5 May 1997. Available from <http://www.techweb.com/se/directlink.cgi?CWK19970505S0040> (29 October 1997); INTERNET.
3. C. Lawrence Meador and Leland G. Freeman, "Year 2000: The Domino Effect," *Datamation*, January 1997, 2. Available from

<http://www.datamation.com/PlugIn/issues/1997/jan/01depend.html> (29 October 1997); INTERNET.

4. "GM, Workers to End Strike," Associated Press, 22 March 1996. Available from <http://www.spub.ksu.edu/issues/v100/sp/n120/AP-strike.html> (29 October 1997); INTERNET.
5. "Tentative Pact May End GM Walkout," *Los Angeles Times*, 26 July 1997. Available from <http://www.latimes.com/HOME/NEWS/LIFE/AUTO/AUTONEWS/t000066368.html> (29 October 1997); INTERNET.
6. "Idaho Transmission Line Caused July 2 Western Power Outage," *Wall Street Journal*, 21 July 1996. Available from <http://interactive.wsj.com> (29 October 1997); INTERNET.
7. "Power Grid Failure Tuesday Affected 1.5 Million in U.S. West," *Wall Street Journal*, 3 July 1997. Available from <http://www.wsj.com> (29 October 1997); INTERNET.
8. Ibid.
9. See Dirk Johnson, "U.P.S. Walkout: For Small Businesses, Big Problems," *New York Times*, 9 August 1997. Available from <http://search.nytimes.com/search/daily/bin/fastweb?getdoc+site+site+11778+3++%28U.P.S.%29%20OR%20%28Walkout%29%20OR%20%28%29> (29 October 1997); INTERNET.
10. Leon Kappelman and Phil Scott, "What Management Needs to Know About the Year 2000 Computer Date Problem," *ComLinks.com Magazine*, 2 February 1997. Available from <http://www.comlinks.com/mag/kapsco1.htm> (29 October 1997); INTERNET. Professor Kappleman is co-chairman of the Year 2000 Working Group of the Society for Information Management (SIM).
11. Ibid.
12. "The Year 2000 Problem," A SSA White Paper Presented to FIRMPOC Members, July 1995. Available from <http://www.itpolicy.gsa.gov/mks/yr2000/y203swp1.htm> (29 October 1997); INTERNET.
13. Actually, the federal government will probably do what it has always done when it can't cover its hot checks: print more money!
14. BankBoston is a shining example of one organization that started early and has worked aggressively to make its computers compliant.
15. Prepared Testimony of David Iacino, Senior Manager, Bank of Boston, Before the Subcommittee on Financial Services and Technology of the

Senate Banking, Housing, and Urban Affairs Committee, 10 July 1997. Available from <http://www.senate.gov/~banking/97_07hrg/071097/witness/iacino.htm> (29 October 1997); INTERNET.

16. Ed Yourdon, "The Personal Consequences of Year 2000," *The Yourdon Report*, June 1997. Available from <http://www.cutter.com/ads/tyr0697.htm> (29 October 1997); INTERNET.
17. Quoted in Gary North, "Farming: Heavily Dependent on Computers," *Gary North's Y2K Links and Forums*, 5 August 1997. Available from <http://www.garynorth.com/y2k/Detail.CFM?Links__ID=327> (31 October 1997); INTERNET.
18. Geri Guidetti <arkinst@concentric.net>, "Non-hybrid Gardening Forum," *Gary North's Y2K Links and Forums*, 8 August 1997. Available from <http://www.garynorth.com> (29 October 1997); INTERNET.
19. Wilson, "Year 2000 Countdown."
20. Ibid.
21. Ibid.
22. Neil Randall, "Welcome to the Millennium," *PC Magazine*, 23 September 1997. Available from <http://www8.zdnet.com/pcmag/iu/toolkit/y2k-pctech-1.htm> (29 October 1997); INTERNET.
23. As quoted in Wilson, "Year 2000 Countdown."

## Chapter 4: When the Bottom Falls Out

1. This list is adapted from "Year 2000 and Operating Nuclear Power Plants," U.S. Nuclear Regulatory Commission, Appendix B of SECY-97-213, 24 September 1997, 1 (electronic edition). Available from <http://www.nrc.gov/NRC/Y2K/S97213B.html> (29 October 1997); INTERNET.
2. John Kappenman, Lawrence J. Zanetti, and William A. Radasky, "Geomagnetic Storms Can Threaten Electric Power Gird," *Earth in Space*, March 1997, 9:7, 3 (electronic edition). Available from <http://www.agu.org/sci_soc/eiskappenman.html>; INTERNET.
3. Stephen Bowman, *When the Eagle Screams: America's Vulnerability to Terrorism* (New York: Carol Publishing, 1994), 125.
4. Rick Cowles, "Transmission and Distribution," *Utilities and the Year 2000*, n.d., 1 (electronic edition). Available from <http://www.accsyst.com/writers/tnd.htm> (29 October 1997); INTERNET.
5. Rick Cowles, "Embedded Logic and Controls," *Utilities and the Year 2000*,

n.d., 1 (electronic edition). Available from <http://www.accsyst.com/writers/embedded.htm> (29 October 1997); INTERNET.

6. David Foster, "Blackouts on the Western Grid: Are More Dark Days Ahead?" *Source News and Reports*, 15 August 1996, 11 (electronic edition). Available from <http://sddt.com/files/librarywire/96wireheadlines/08_96/DN96_08_15/DN96_08_15_fc.html> (13 September 1997); INTERNET.
7. Levy and Hafner, "The Day," 54.
8. Bowman, *When the Eagle Screams*, 125.
9. Rick Cowles, "Nuclear," *Utilities and the Year 2000*, n.d., 1 (electronic edition). Available from <http://www.accsyst.com/writers/nuclear.htm> (29 October 1997); INTERNET.
10. Ibid., 1.
11. Ibid., 2.
12. Ibid., 3.
13. Ibid., 2.
14. Kappenman, et al., "Geomagnetic Storms," 1.
15. J. Madeline Nash, "Cosmic Storms Coming," *Time*, 9 September 1996, 1 (electronic edition). Available from <http://www.pathfinder.com/@@DxyHWQUAVCHr79f8/time/magazine/domestic/1996/960909/space.html> (29 October 1997); INTERNET.
16. Ibid., 2.
17. Kappenman, et al., "Geomagnetic Storms," 1.
18. Nash, "Cosmic Storms," 2.
19. Kappenman, et al., "Geomagnetic Storms," 3.
20. Kim Girard and Robert L. Scheier, "Telcos Lag On Year 2000, Analysts Warn," *ComputerWorld*, 11 November 1996, 2 (electronic edition). Available from <http://www.computerworld.com/search/AT-html/9611/961111SL46200.html> (29 October 1997); INTERNET.
21. Ibid., 1.
22. Ibid.
23. As quoted in Mary E. Thyfault, "Call Center Crisis?—Outdated PBXs Called Vulnerable to Date-Field Problems," *InformationWeek*, 2 June 1997, 1 (electronic edition). Available from <http://www.techweb.com/se/directlink.cgi?IWK19970602S0065> (29 June 1997); INTERNET.
24. Ibid., 2–3
25. Ibid., 2.
26. Girard and Scheier, "Telcos Lag," 1.

27. Brad Bass, "Feds Tackle Telecom Date Problems," *Federal Computer Week*, 29 September 1997. Available from <http://www.fcw.com/pubs/fcw/1997/0929/fcw-newdate-9-29-1997.html> (3 October 1997).
28. Megan Jones, "Budget for Millennium Bug Blows Out," *The Age (Melbourne)*, 30 September 1997, 1 (electronic edition). Available from <http://www.the age.com.au/daily/970930/bus/bus4.html> (30 June 1997); INTERNET.
29. A posting by Karl Feilder, a PC specialist, on Peter deJager's discussion forum, 3 October 1997.
30. Letter from David Harrington of Britain's Telecommunications Managers Association to Dr. Pekka Tarjanne, secretary general of the International Telecommunications Union in Geneva, Switzerland, 10 July 1997, 1 (electronic edition). Available from <http://www.tma.org.uk/industry/millennium/itutmalet.htm> (29 June 1997); INTERNET.
31. This information is paraphrased from a Web site maintained by the Metropolitan Government of Nashville and Davidson County, Department of Water and Sewerage Services. Available from <http://www.nashville.org/ws/drinking_h2o.html> (12 October 1997); INTERNET.
32. Juli-Ann Gasper, Ph.D., Barry B. Schweig, Ph.D., and Michael E. Echols, Ph.D., *North Platte, Nebraska: A Case Study of the Year 2000 Computer Problem* (Omaha, NE: Creighton University, College of Business Administration, 1997), 16. Available from <http://genteel.creighton.edu/y2k.htm#Case Study> (20 October 1997); INTERNET.

## Chapter 5: Hot Checks and Cold Bankers

1. Mike Phillips <75557.232@compuserve.com>, "Y2K and Banks," A Message to Susan Heller on CompuServe's Year2000 Forum, 24 September 1997. Used by permission.
2. This list is based on the Prepared Testimony of Jeff Jinnett, president LeBoeuf Computing Technologies, Before the Oversight Hearing on Financial Institutions and the Year 2000 Problem, Held by the Senate Subcommittee on Financial Services and Technology, 10 July 1997, 3–5 (electronic edition). Available from <http://www.senate.gov/~banking/97_07hrg/071097/witness/jnnett.html> (29 October 1997); INTERNET.
3. Ibid., 4.
4. Remarks by William J. McDonough, President of the Federal Reserve

Bank of New York, "The Year 2000 Challenges," Before the Annual Membership Meeting of the Institute of International Finance, Hong Kong, 21 September 1997, 2 (electronic edition). Available from <http://www.ny.frb.org/pihome/news/speeches/sp970921.html> (2 October 1997); INTERNET.

5. Prepared Testimony of Jeff Jinnett, 4.
6. Wilson, "Year 2000 Countdown."
7. Prepared Testimony of Jeff Jinnett, 5.
8. Again, this list is based, in part, on Prepared Testimony of Jeff Jinnett, 5–6.
9. Prepared Testimony of Edward W. Kelley, Governor of the Federal Reserve Board, Before the Subcommittee on Financial Services and Technology of the Committee on Banking, Housing, and Urban Affairs, U.S. Senate, 30 July 1997, 4 (electronic edition). Available from <http://www.bog.frb.fed.us/BOARDDOCS/TESTIMONY/19970730.htm> (17 October 1997); INTERNET.
10. Ibid., 1.
11. Gary North, "The Federal Reserve: Way Behind," *Gary North's Y2K Links and Forums*, 5 August 1997. Available from <http://www.garynorth.com/banking> (18 October 1997); INTERNET.
12. Prepared Testimony of Edward W. Kelley, 4–5.
13. Ibid., 1.
14. Ibid.
15. Aaron Pressman, "Federal Reserve Computers May Be Unprepared for 2000," *ZDNet* (a Reuters story), 15 April 1997, 2 (electronic edition). Available from <http://www5.zdnet.com/zdnn/content/reut/0415/reut001.html> (23 October 1997); INTERNET.
16. Posted on the Federal Reserve Bank of New York's Web site in an article entitled, "Fedpoint 43: FedWire," October 1996. Available from <http://www.ny.frb.org/pihome/fedpoint/fed43.html> (27 October 1997); INTERNET.
17. Prepared Testimony of Edward W. Kelley, 2.
18. Pressman, "Federal Reserve Computers," 1.
19. Ibid., 2.
20. Prepared Testimony of Edward W. Kelley, 2.
21. Ibid., 6.
22. Ibid., 6.

23. Letter from Richard Spillenkothen, director of the Board of Governors of the Federal Reserve System, Regarding "Year 2000 Supervision Program," to the Officer in Charge of Supervision at Each Federal Reserve Bank, 6 May 1997 [SR 97-16 (SPE)], 6 (electronic edition). Available from <http://www.bog.frb.fed.us/boarddocs/SRLETTERS/1997/SR9716.HTM> (15 October 1997); INTERNET.
24. Prepared Testimony of David Iacino, 1–2.
25. Prepared Testimony of Jeff Jinnett, 6.
26. Ibid., 2.
27. Ibid.
28. Prepared Testimony of David Iacino, 1.
29. "'What We Found Was Terrifying' Says BankBoston's Chief Technology Officer," *The Economist*, 10 March 1997, as reported on the Westergaard Year 2000 Web site. Available from <http://www.y2ktimebomb.com/banking/bnkcost9711.htm> (10 October 1997); INTERNET.
30. Ibid.
31. Ibid.
32. Ibid.
33. Patrick L. Porter and Deborah Radcliff, "At Chase, the Task Amounts to 200 Million Lines of Code," *Software* Magazine, March 1997, 1 (electronic edition). Available from <http://www.sentrytech.com/sm037fla.htm> (12 October 1997); INTERNET.
34. Ibid., 1.
35. Ibid., 2.
36. Ibid.
37. Ibid., 3.
38. Ibid.
39. "Banks Embark on Preparation for Year 2000," *Northwestern Financial Review*, 7 June 1997, 1 (electronic edition). Available from <http://www.206.10.119.100/nfr/news25.htm> (25 September 1997); INTERNET.
40. Ibid.
41. Bruce Caldwell, "Banks Lag in Preparing for Year 2000—Many Small Banks Just Raising Awareness of the Problem; Big Banks Doing Better," *InformationWeek*, 15 September 1997, 1 (electronic edition). Available from <http://www.techweb.com/se/directlink.cgi?IWK19970915S0073> (15 September 1997); INTERNET.
42. Lon Wagner, "Credit Cards Offer a Visible Sign of the Year 2000

Problem," *The Virginian-Pilot*, 1 May 1997, 1 (electronic edition). Available from <http://www.pilotonline.com/business/bz0501car.html> (2 October 1997); INTERNET.

43. Ibid., 2.
44. Wylie Wong, "Credit Card Outfits Say Year 2000 Solution Is Near," *ComputerWorld*, 19 August 1997, 1 (electronic edition). Available from <http://www.cwlive.cw.com:8080/home/online9697.nsf/All/070819credit> (3 October 1997); INTERNET.
45. Wagner, "Credit Cards," 1.
46. Ibid.
47. Letter from Cory Hamasaki, a well-known Y2K programmer, to Gary North, 22 August 1997. Available from <http://www.garynorth.com> (10 September 1997); INTERNET.
48. Prepared Testimony of Larry Martin, President of Data Dimensions, Before the Subcommittee on Financial Services and Technology of the Banking, Housing, and Urban Affairs Committee, U.S. Senate, 10 July 1997, 2 (electronic edition). Available from <http://www.senate.gov/~banking/97_07hrg/071097/witness/martin.htm> (10 August 1997); INTERNET.
49. Allan E. Alter, "Your Other Millennium Problem," *ComputerWorld*, 26 May 1997, 1 (electronic edition). Available from <http://www.computerworld.com/search/AT-html/9705/970526SL0526euro.html> (12 August 1997); INTERNET.
50. "Early Euro Roll-out Risks Havoc," *ComputerWeekly*, 19 June 1997, 1 (electronic edition). Available from <http://www.computerweekly.co.uk/news/19_6_97/08592369439/B1.htm> (12 August 1997); INTERNET.
51. United Press International article, 22 July 1997, as quoted by Gary North, *Gary North's Y2K Links*, 28 July 1997, 1 (electronic edition). Available from <http://www.garynorth.com> (15 August 1997); INTERNET.
52. David Poppe, "Year 2000 Problem Looms for Latin Tech," *Miami Herald*, 7 October 1997, 1 (electronic edition). Available from <http://www.herald.com/business/docs/038047.htm> (23 October 1997); INTERNET.
53. Nick Edwards, "Millennium Bug Threatens Financial Chaos," *The Netly News*, 6 October 1997. Available from <http://cgi.pathfinder.com/@@KLW0SwYAoS2pR*W1/netly/latest/RB/1997Oct06/259.html> (31 October 1997); INTERNET.

## Chapter 6: The Tax Man Cometh—*Not!*

1. Jacob M. Schlesinger, "Senate Hearings to Focus on Alleged Taxpayer Abuse," *Wall Street Journal*, 22 September 1997, 1 (electronic edition). Available <from http://www.wsj.com> (3 October 1997); INTERNET.
2. Ibid., 3.
3. Jacob M. Schlesinger, "Senate Opens Hearings into Alleged IRS Abuses," *Wall Street Journal*, 23 September 1997, 2 (electronic edition). Available from <http://www.wsj.com> (4 October 1997); INTERNET.
4. Jacob M. Schlesinger, "Hearings Focus on IRS Abuses, But Reforms Remain Uncertain," *Wall Street Journal*, 25 September 1997, 1 (electronic edition). Available from <http://www.wsj.com> (4 October 1997); INTERNET.
5. Tom Herman, "IRS Staffers Tell Senate Panel of Wrongdoing by Fellow Aides," *Wall Street Journal*, 25 September 1997, 1 (electronic edition). Available from <http://www.wsj.com> (4 October 1997); INTERNET.
6. Robert Molter, Chairman of the Defense Department's Year 2000 Working Group and Member of the Interagency Year 2000 Committee. Quoted in Andrew C. Braunberg, "Defusing the Millennium Time Bomb," *Signal Magazine*, June 1996, 3 (electronic edition). Available from <http://www.us.net/signal/Archive/June96/defusing-june.html> (22 June 1997); INTERNET.
7. Bob Violino and Bruce Caldwell, "And Now for the Bad News," *TechWeb*, 21 April 1997, 1. Available from <http://www.techweb.com/iw/627/27iuyr4.htm> (29 October 1997); INTERNET.
8. John Moore, "Mainframe Readiness Falls Behind Schedule," *Federal Computer Week*, 26 August 1996, 1 (electronic edition). Available from <http://160.147.68.21/army-Y2K/articles/agency2.htm> (14 September 1997); INTERNET.
9. U.S. Senate. January 21, 1997. *Commission on the Year 2000 Computer Problem Act*, 105th Cong., 1st sess., S.22. 2.6.A.
10. Bob Starzynski and Tim Deady, "Government Agencies Stalling on Year 2000," *Washington Business Journal*, 2 June 1997, 1 (electronic edition). Available from <http://www.amcity.com/washington/stories/060297/story2.html> (29 October 1997); INTERNET.
11. David Braun, "Feds Face Y2K Disaster, GAO Warns," *TechWire*, 7 July 1997, 1 (electronic edition). Available from <http://www.techweb.com/wire/news/jul/0710year2000.html> (8 August 1997); INTERNET.

12. Ibid., 3.
13. Ibid., 2.
14. Ibid.
15. Moore, "Mainframe Readiness," 1.
16. "Government Said to Move Too Slowly on Year 2000 Computer Problem," *Washington Post*, 10 July 1997, 1 (electronic edition). Available from <http://washingtonpost.com/wp-srv/Wplate/1997-07/10/087L-071097-idx.html> (3 August 1997; INTERNET.
17. Thibodeau, "Year 2000 Legal Issues," 1.
18. Starzynski and Deady, "Government Agencies," 2.
19. James F. Hinchman, Acting Comptroller General of the United States, "High Risk Series: Information Management and Technology," *Special General Accounting Office (GAO) Report*, February 15, 1997. Available from <http://www.gao.gov/highrisk/hr97009.txt> (12 August 1997); INTERNET.
20. Braun, "Feds Face Y2K Disaster," 4.
21. Ibid.
22. David Braun, "U.S. Agencies in Trouble on Year 2000 Glitch," *Tech Wire*, 15 September 1997, 1 (electronic edition). Available from <http://www.techweb.com/se/directlink.cgi?WIR1997091508> (18 September 1997); INTERNET.
23. "Remarks by President Clinton at the White House Millennium Event, n.d., 4 (electronic edition). Available from <http://www.whitehouse.gov/Initiatives/Millennium/announcement.html> (28 October 1997); INTERNET.
24. David Braun, "Grading Uncle Sam for Year 2000 Progress," *TechWire*, 16 September 1997, 1 (electronic edition). Available from <http://www.techweb.com/wire/news/1997/09/0917y2kside.html> (29 October 1997); INTERNET.
25. Ibid. For some reason, this was an A-minus in the text of the article but an A in the table.
26. David Braun, "Year 2000: Countdown to Federal Meltdown," *TechWire*, 16 September 1997, 2 (electronic edition). Available from <http://www.techweb.com/wire/news/1997/09/0917y2k.html> (18 October 1997); INTERNET.
27. Andrew J. Glass, "Government May Be Late in Fixing Millennium Bug," *Cox News Service*, 12 December 1997. Available from <http://www.hotcoco.com/news/nation/stories/dan27094.htm> (15 December 1997); INTERNET.

28. Elana Varon, "Agencies, Industry Differ on Cost of Necessary Upgrades," *Federal Computer Week*, 6 February 1997, 1 (electronic edition). Available from <http://www.fcw.com/pubs/fcw/1997/0203/flash2000.htm> (29 October 1997); INTERNET.
29. Peter Lewis, "U.S. Drops Count on Computer Fix," *Seattle Times*, 18 September 1997, 2 (electronic edition). Available from <http://www.seattletimes.com/extra/browse/html97/year_091897.html> (29 October 1997); INTERNET.
30. This information is taken from an Internet newsgroup posting from Mr. Chris Murphy of the Social Security Administration. Quoted in Gary North, "No Date Standard = Chaos in the Year 2000," *Gary North's Y2K Links*, 13 January 1997, 1–2 (electronic edition). Available from <http://www.garynorth.com/Y2K/Detail.CFM?Links_ID=13> (29 October 1997); INTERNET.
31. Ibid.
32. Prepared Testimony of George Muñoz, Assistant Secretary of the Treasury for Management/Chief Financial Officer Before the House Subcommittee on Government Management, Information, and Technology, 16 April 1996, 5 (electronic edition). Available from <http://www.ustreas.gov/treasury/t01munoz.html> (29 October 1997); INTERNET.
33. Ibid., 2.
34. Ibid., 4.
35. Ibid., 5.
36. Bill Orr, "Uncle Sam Goes Digital," *U.S. Banker*, July 1997, 1 (electronic edition). Available from <http://www.banking.com/aba/tech_0797.htm> (29 October 1997); INTERNET.
37. Elana Varon, "IRS Seeks $258M More for Year 2000 Solution," *Federal Computer Week*, 23 June 1997, 1 (electronic edition). Available from <http://www.fcw.com/pubs/fcw/1997/0623/fcw-newbudget-6-23-97.htm> (29 October 1997); INTERNET.
38. Sharon Machlis, "IRS Y2K Woes Cost More," *ComputerWorld*, 15 September 1997, 1 (electronic edition). Available from <http://cwlive.cw.com:8080/home/print9497.nsf/All/SL37irs15ABE> (29 October 1997); INTERNET.
39. This posting appeared in the comp.software.year-2000 newsgroup. I have deleted the author's name.
40. "U.S. Social Security Administration: Building Awareness," *CIO*

*Magazine*, 15 September 1996, 1 (electronic edition). Available from <http://www.cio.com/forums/091596_socsec.html> (29 October 1997); INTERNET.

41. Ibid.
42. "The Year 2000 Problem," An SSA white paper.
43. "U.S. Social Security Administration," 1.
44. Rajiv Chandrasekaran, "Social Security Gets Year 2000 Warning: More Work Needed on Glitch, GAO Says," *Washington Post*, 5 November 1997, A-19. Available from <http://www.washington.com/wo-srv/Wplate/1997-11/05/1121-110597-idx.html> (20 November 1997); INTERNET.
45. Joel C. Willemssen, General Accounting Office, "Medicare Transaction System: Success Depends Upon Correcting Critical Managerial and Technical Weaknesses," 16 May 1997, 16 (electronic edition). Available from <http://www.gao.gov/new.items/ai97078.pdf> (20 June 1997); INTERNET. Note: you will need the Adobe Acrobat software to read this report.
46. Ibid., 2.
47. Ibid.
48. Robert Pear, "Modernization for Medicare Grinds to Halt," *New York Times*, 16 September 1997. Available from <http://search.nytimes.com/search/daily/bin/fastweb?getdoc+site+site+17812+0++%28MTS%29%20OR%20%28GTE%29%20OR%20%28%29> (29 October 1997); INTERNET.
49. Ibid.
50. This assumes 250 work days in a year.
51. Jones, "The Global Economic Impact," 35–36.
52. The figure is, in fact, even higher; it is actually $76,317,772,400.
53. Bob Violino, "50 States of Alert," *InformationWeek*, 24 March 1997, 1 (electronic edition). Available from <http://www.techweb.com/se/directlink.cgi?IWK19970324S0054> (29 October 1997); INTERNET.
54. Ibid.
55. John Wagner, "Two-Digit Computer Chaos Looming," *News & Observer* (Raleigh, NC), 6 April 1997, 2 (electronic edition). Available from <http://www.nando.net/newsroom/nao/nc/040697/nc01_9346.html> (29 October 1997); INTERNET.
56. Violino, "50 States," 2.
57. Bruce Caldwell, "Two More States Claim Year 2000 Compliance,"

*InformationWeek*, 7 July 1997, 1 (electronic edition). Available from <http://www.techweb.com/se/directlink/.cgi?IWK19970707S0039> (8 August 1997); INTERNET.

58. Cory Johnson, "Angst in D.C.," *theStreet.com*, 22 February 1997, 1–2 (electronic edition). Available from <http://www.thestreet.com/premium/companies/topstories/18411_2111997.html> (29 October 1997); INTERNET. You have to register to get access to this Web site.

## Chapter 7: Dropping Our Guard

1. *Microsoft Encarta 98 Encyclopedia*, s.v. "Air Warfare."
2. Dennis J. Reimer, General, United States Army, Chief of Staff, and Togo D. West, Jr., Secretary of the Army to the Department of the Army, internal memorandum, 31 March 1997, 1. Available from <http://www.year2000.com/archive/army.html> (14 October 1997); INTERNET.
3. Reimer and West, 1.
4. Prepared Testimony of the Honorable Emmett Paige, Jr., Assistant Secretary of Defense, Before the Subcommittee on Government Management, Information, and Technology of the Committee on Government Reform and Oversight, U.S. House of Representatives, 16 April 1996, 1 (electronic edition). Available from <http://www.army.mil/army-Y2K/osd)Y2K/c3itest.htm> (22 June 1997); INTERNET.
5. Ibid.
6. Tony Valetta, speech delivered at "The Millennium Crisis: Time Is Running Out for Federal Agencies," a seminar co-sponsored by Information Technology Association of America and Government Computer News, 31 January 1996. Available from <http://www.army.mil/army-y2k.osd_y2k/valletta> (16 October 1997); INTERNET.
7. *Microsoft Encarta 98 Encyclopedia*, s.v. "Global Positioning System."
8. "Test and Evaluation Year-2000 Team Report" to the Test and Evaluation Board of Operating Directors, Department of Defense, 10 July 1996, 1 (electronic edition). Available from <http://www.infowar.com/CIVIL_DE/sectone.htm> (22 June 1997); INTERNET.
9. Jack K. Horner <jkh@lanl.gov>, "Risks Associated with the Year 2000 Problem," 27 March 1997, <http://catless.ncl.ac.uk/Risks/18.96.html#subj9.1> (18 October 1997). This was originally a private message to Rick Light <rxl@lanl.gov>.

10. Ibid.
11. Prepared Testimony of the Honorable Emmett Paige, Jr., 2.
12. As quoted in Gary North, "Category: Military," *Gary North's Links and Forums*, <http://www.garynorth.com/Y2K/Results.CFM?Links_Category=Military> (18 October 1997); INTERNET.
13. Braunberg, "Defusing the Millennium Time Bomb."
14. Ibid.
15. "Test and Evaluation," 1.
16. David Braun, "Year 2000: Countdown to Federal Meltdown," *TechWire*, 16 September 1997, 2 (electronic edition). Available from <http://www.techweb.com/wire/news/1997/09/0917y2k.html> (18 October 1997); INTERNET.
17. "The Millennium Crisis," 1.
18. When the MITRE corporation was hired by the DoD to do a six-week study of the problem, they could not find an inventory of military information systems. They were also unsuccessful in determining the total lines of code contained in defense systems. See Braunberg, "Defusing the Millennium Time Bomb," 4.
19. Prepared Testimony of the Honorable Emmett Paige, Jr., 2.
20. Braunberg, "Defusing the Millennium Time Bomb," 2.
21. Prepared Testimony of the Honorable Emmett Paige, Jr., 3.
22. David Eddy, "Triage for Year 2000 Efforts," *ComLinks.Com*, n.d. Available from <http://www.comlinks.com/mag/detria.htm> (4 October 1997); INTERNET.
23. Braun, "Year 2000," 1.
24. Ibid., 3.
25. Bob Violino, "Year 2000: Getting Down to the Wire," *InformationWeek*, 10 February 1997, 2 (electronic edition). Available from <http://www.techweb.com/se/directlink.cgi?IWK19970210S0017> (4 October 1997); INTERNET.
26. Reimer and West, 1.
27. "GCN Web Digest," *Government Computer News*, 15 September 1997. Available from <http://www.gcn.com/breakingnews/gcnnews.htm> (18 September 1997); INTERNET.
28. U.S. Office of Management and Budget, *Progress on Year 2000 Conversion*, Rept., 15 August 1997, 9 (electronic edition). Available from <http://www.cio.fed.gov/y2krp897.htm> (10 October 1997); INTERNET.

29. Sharon Machlis, "GAO Blasts DoD's Year 2000 Method," *Computer-World*, 18 August 1997. Available from <http://cwlive.cw.com:8080/home/print9497.nsf/All/SL33dod> (13 September 1997); INTERNET.
30. Bob Cohen, "ITAA Year 2000 Outlook," *ComLinks.com*, 5 September 1997. Available from <http://www.comlinks.com/news/itaa233.htm> (13 September 1997); INTERNET.
31. "DoD's Year 2000 Vulnerabilities," *Science News*, 13 September 1997, quoted in Gary North, "90,000 Items Missing," *Gary North's Y2K Links and Forums*, 18 September 1997. Available from <http://www.garynorth.com/Y2K/detail_.cfm/446> (18 September 1997); INTERNET.
32. Braun, "Year 2000," 1.
33. Sharon Machlis, "GAO Sounds Y2K Alarm on Army Procedures," *ComputerWorld*, 1 October 1997, 1 (electronic edition). Available from <http://cwlive.cw.com:8080/home/online9697.nsf/All/971001gao1893A> (4 October 1997); INTERNET.
34. *Progress on Year 2000 Conversion*, 6.
35. Glass, "Government May Be Late."
36. Ibid., Appendix 4.
37. James Kim, "One-man Army Fights His City's Year 2000 Hitch," *USA Today*, 2 September 1997, Web edition. Available from <http://usatoday.com/life/cyber/tech/cta367.htm> (18 October 1997); INTERNET.
38. Gasper, et al., *North Platte, Nebraska*, 16.
39. PITO (Police Information Technology Organization) and Mentis Management Consultants, Ltd., *Year 2000 Compliance: A Guide for the Police*, May 1997 Version 4.2. Available from <http://www. homeoffice.gov.uk/Y2K.htm> (4 October 1997); INTERNET.
40. See, for example, Giles Turnbull, "Doctors in the Dock if Y2K Bug Kills Their Patients," *PA* (Australia) *News Centre*, 11 August 1997, 1 (electronic edition). Available from <http://www.pa.press.net/tech/year110897.html> (10 October 1997); INTERNET. Also see Giles Turnbull, "Hospital Patients Could Sue Over Microship Malfunction," *PA* (Australia) *News Centre*, 8 October 1997, 1 (electronic edition). Available from <http://www.pa.press.net/tech/year081097.html> (10 October 1997); INTERNET.
41. Giles, "Hospital Patients," 1.
42. "Patient Care at Risk from Millennium Bug," *ComputerWeekly*, 8 May

1997, 1 (electronic edition). Available from <http://www.computerweekly.co.uk/news/8_5_97/08598503239/B3.html> (10 October 1997); INTERNET.

43. A press release summarizing the results of this survey is available from Gordon & Glickson's Web site at <http://www.ggtech.com/hospital.htm> (10 October 1997); INTERNET. It is entitled, "National Survey Reveals Hospital Computers are Unprepared for the Next Century." See also Clare Haney, "Hospitals Show Low Resistance to Year 2000 Threat," *TechWire*, 26 February 1997. Available from <http://www.techweb.com/se/directlink.cgi?WIR1997 022614> (10 October 1997); INTERNET.

## Chapter 8: See You in Court

1. Ilaina Jonas, "Market's Computer Already Hates Year 2000; Owners Sue," *Detroit Free Press*, 7 August 1997. Available from <http://www.freep.com/browsing/tech/qcredit7.htm> (30 October 1997); INTERNET.
2. National Center for State Courts: Research Department, (757) 253–2000.
3. Kevin Maney, "Lawyers Circle Over 2000 Time Bomb," *USA Today*, 1 December 1997. Available from <http://www.usatoday.com/life/cyber/tech/ctb716.htm> (17 December 1997); INTERNET.
4. Written Statement of Vito C. Peraino Before the Subcommittee on Technology and the Subcommittee on Government Management, Information, and Technology, U.S. House of Representatives, 20 March 1997. Available from <http://www.house.gov/science/peraino_3-20.html> (29 October 1997); INTERNET.
5. Jones, "The Global Economic Impact," 40.
6. Maney, "Lawyers Circle."
7. Jon Newberry, "Beat the Clock," *ABANet*, June 1997. Available from <http://www.abanet.org/journal/jun97/06FYEAR.html> (30 October 1997); INTERNET.
8. Written Statement of Vito C. Peraino.
9. This list is based on Jones's, "The Global Economic Impact." However, items seven and eight are my own.
10. Written Statement of Vito C. Peraino.
11. "Solve Your Year 2000 Problem Now or Risk Being Sued," *The Year 2000*

*Information Network*, n.d., Available from <http://web.idirect.com/~mbsprog/y2ksue.html> (30 October 1997); INTERNET.

12. Ibid.
13. Ronald J. Palenski, "Sidebar: Liability Issues in Year 2000 Compliance," *Infosecurity News*, June 1997. Available from <http://www.infosecnews.com/articles/9706/arti01b.html> (31 October 1997); INTERNET.
14. Written Statement of Vito C. Peraino.
15. Jeff Jinnett, "Legal Issues Concerning the Year 2000 'Millennium Bug,'" *Year 2000 Legal Issues*, 21 August 1996. Available from <http://www.year2000.com/archive/legalissues.html> (30 October 1997); INTERNET.
16. Ibid.
17. Written Statement of Vito C. Peraino.
18. Paraphrased from Jinnett, "Legal Issues."
19. Erich Luening, "Lawsuits Focus on Y2K Upgrades," *C/Net*, 4 December 1997. Available from <http://www.news.com/News/Item/0,4,17023,00.html> (17 December 1997); INTERNET.
20. Jinnett, "Legal Issues."
21. "Solve Your Year 2000 Problem."
22. Written Statement of Vito C. Peraino.
23. Ibid.
24. Jon Newberry, "Beat the Clock."
25. Julia King, "Lawsuits Galore," *ComputerWorld*, 20 October 1997. Available from <http://http://www2.computerworld.com/home/cwlaunch.nsf/launch?ReadForm&/home/print9497.nsf/$defaultview/79984CCFC249A38085256536005l2288> (17 December 1997); INTERNET.

### Chapter 9: Seeing Through a Glass Darkly

1. Bob Violino, "Year 2000—Getting Down to the Wire," *InformationWeek*, 10 February 1997, 1 (electronic edition). Available from <http://www.techweb.com/se/directlink.cgi?IWK19970210S0017> (24 October 1997); INTERNET.
2. Prepared Testimony of Sally Katzen, Administrator, Office of Information and Regulatory Affairs, Office of Management and Budget, Before the Subcommittee on Technology of the Committee on Science and the Subcommittee on Government Management, Information, and

Technology of the Committee on Government Reform and Oversight, U.S. House of Representatives, 10 July 1997, 3 (electronic edition). Available from <http://www.comlinks.com/gov/kat710.htm> (24 October 1997); INTERNET.

3. For example, see Sam Vincent Meddis, "Hyping the 'Millennium Bomb,'" *USA Today*, 3 June 1997, Web site edition. Available from <http://167.8.29.8/plweb-cgi/idoc.pl?2911+unix+_free_user_+cgi. usatoday.com.80+USATODAY_ONLINE+ USATODAY_ONLINE+ NEWS+NEWS++y2k> (24 October 1997); INTERNET. Also, see Robert L. Scheier, "IS Chief: Year 2000 a Fraud," *ComputerWorld*, 7 July 1997, 1 (electronic edition). Available from <http://www.cwlive.cw.com: 8088/home/print9497.nsf/All/SL27starr> (16 October 1997); INTERNET.
4. See Roberto Vacco, *The Coming Dark Age*, (New York, Doubleday, 1973). This book is currently out of print. I obtained a copy through the interlibrary loan program of my local library.
5. From a press release from Cory Hamasaki, Comp.Software.Year-2000, 24 July 1997. Available from <http://www.garynorth.com/y2k/ Detail.CFM?Links__ID=321> (24 October 1997); INTERNET.

## Chapter 10: Where the Rubber Meets the Road

1. This material is taken from a Web site maintained by the Metropolitan Government of Nashville and Davidson County, Department of Water and Sewerage Services. Available from <http://www.nashville.org/ws/ drinking_h2o.html>; INTERNET.
2. Ibid.
3. Duncan Long, *Survival 2000* (Phoenix, AZ: Wave Publications, 1995), 56.

# Acknowledgments

As an author, sending a manuscript off to the publisher is perhaps the most satisfying of all experiences. After months of research and writing, and long hours and late nights staring at the computer screen, the ball is finally in someone else's court. However, I am profoundly aware of the contributions others have made to this project. Without their encouragement, hard work, and support, this book would have never been written. Therefore I would like to acknowledge and thank the following people.

First, my wife Gail, who has been my constant source of joy for almost twenty years. She has always been my biggest cheerleader, telling me, "C'mon, you can do it!" when I wasn't at all sure that I could. She didn't complain *once* during the entire writing process, although she had to pull double-duty on many occasions.

My five daughters—Megan, Mindy, Mary, Madeline, and Marissa—who constantly shower me with affection and remind me of life's most important priorities. They willingly gave up their daddy for days at a time, faithfully praying that I would finish the book, so I could get back to more important things like long walks and talks, and reading story books.

My agent and dear friend David Dunham, of Wolgemuth & Hyatt. He was the one who first gave me the idea for this book and nagged me about it until I finally gave him a finished book proposal.

He did everything you would expect an agent to do—and a whole lot more! He also read through the final draft, offering invaluable suggestions and catching typos.

My business partner and longtime friend, Robert Wolgemuth. We've worked as a team now for over fifteen years. We've been through thick and thin (mostly thin, I think) and have grown together through one adventure after another. In ways too numerous to mention, he has been a role model for me and constant source of encouragement. Without his enthusiastic support, I would have not been able to take time away from our business to work on this project.

Jack Parsons, my research assistant, who spent countless hours on the Internet, locating and printing scores of articles on the Year 2000 Computer Problem. His mainframe programming background and experience were also an invaluable asset in helping me analyze and interpret the data.

Karen Anderson, the editor who assisted me with the manuscript before I sent it to Regnery Publishing. Not only did she do an excellent job helping me say what I intended to say, she also made sure I wrote the book in a way that reached the widest possible audience.

Harry Crocker III, my editor at Regnery who challenged me at every turn and insisted that I not get bogged down in dull and boring details. He kept me on track and helped with the flow of content in innumerable ways.

Also, those who read the first draft of the manuscript and offered suggestions: Bob Allen, Bill Baumgartner, Karl Bruce, Sid and Jeanne Bruce, David Farris, George Grant, Robert and Jacque Hyatt, Paul and Nicole Johnson, Dave Koechel, John Peterson, Franklin Sanders, Mike Tant, and Bruce Tippery. Their suggestions and encouragement were invaluable.

Finally, Dr. Gary North, whose Web site literally made this book possible. He collected hundreds, if not thousands, of articles related to the Year 2000 Problem, which made my own research immeasurably easier. If by some miracle the problem is fixed in time and we somehow manage to avoid the meltdown of our society, it will be due in large part to the foresight of this watchman who sounded the trumpet when others were silent and spread the word on the Internet.

# Index